The Policy Driven Data Center with ACI Architecture, Concepts, and Methodology

Lucien Avramov, CCIE No. 19945

Maurizio Portolani

Cisco Press

800 East 96th Street

Indianapolis, IN 46240

The Policy Driven Data Center with ACI: Architecture, Concepts, and Methodology

Lucien Avramov and Maurizio Portolani

Copyright © 2015 Cisco Systems, Inc.

Cisco Press logo is a trademark of Cisco Systems, Inc.

Published by:
Cisco Press
800 East 96th Street
Indianapolis, IN 46240 USA

Printed in the United States of America

Fifth Printing: July 2015

Library of Congress Control Number: 2014955987

ISBN-13: 978-1-58714-490-5

ISBN-10: 1-58714-490-5

Warning and Disclaimer

This book is designed to provide information about Cisco ACI. Every effort has been made to make this book as complete and as accurate as possible, but no warranty or fitness is implied.

The information is provided on an "as is" basis. The authors, Cisco Press, and Cisco Systems, Inc. shall have neither liability nor responsibility to any person or entity with respect to any loss or damages arising from the information contained in this book or from the use of the discs or programs that may accompany it.

The opinions expressed in this book belong to the author and are not necessarily those of Cisco Systems, Inc.

Feedback Information

At Cisco Press, our goal is to create in-depth technical books of the highest quality and value. Each book is crafted with care and precision, undergoing rigorous development that involves the unique expertise of members from the professional technical community.

Readers' feedback is a natural continuation of this process. If you have any comments regarding how we could improve the quality of this book, or otherwise alter it to better suit your needs, you can contact us through email at feedback@ciscopress.com. Please make sure to include the book title and ISBN in your message.

We greatly appreciate your assistance.

Trademark Acknowledgments

All terms mentioned in this book that are known to be trademarks or service marks have been appropriately capitalized. Cisco Press or Cisco Systems, Inc. cannot attest to the accuracy of this information. Use of a term in this book should not be regarded as affecting the validity of any trademark or service mark.

Publisher: Paul Boger

Associate Publisher: Dave Dusthimer

Business Operation Manager, Cisco Press: Jan Cornelssen

Executive Editor: Brett Bartow

Managing Editor: Sandra Schroeder

Development Editor: Marianne Bartow

Project Editor: Mandie Frank

Copy Editor: Bill McManus

Technical Editors: Tom Edsall, Mike Cohen, Krishna Doddapaneni

Editorial Assistant: Vanessa Evans

Designer: Mark Shirar

Composition: Bumpy Design

Indexer: Cheryl Lenser

Proofreader: Debbie Williams

Americas Headquarters	Asia Pacific Headquarters	Europe Headquarters
Cisco Systems, Inc.	Cisco Systems (USA) Pte. Ltd.	Cisco Systems International BV
San Jose, CA	Singapore	Amsterdam, The Netherlands

Cisco has more than 200 offices worldwide. Addresses, phone numbers, and fax numbers are listed on the Cisco Website at **www.cisco.com/go/offices.**

CCDE, CCENT, Cisco Eos, Cisco HealthPresence, the Cisco logo, Cisco Lumin, Cisco Nexus, Cisco StadiumVision, Cisco TelePresence, Cisco WebEx, DCE, and Welcome to the Human Network are trademarks; Changing the Way We Work, Live, Play, and Learn and Cisco Store are service marks; and Access Registrar, Aironet, AsyncOS, Bringing the Meeting To You, Catalyst, CCDA, CCDP, CCIE, CCIP, CCNA, CCNP, CCSP, CCVP, Cisco, the Cisco Certified Internetwork Expert logo, Cisco IOS, Cisco Press, Cisco Systems, Cisco Systems Capital, the Cisco Systems logo, Cisco Unity, Collaboration Without Limitation, EtherFast, EtherSwitch, Event Center, Fast Step, Follow Me Browsing, FormShare, GigaDrive, HomeLink, Internet Quotient, IOS, iPhone, iQuick Study, IronPort, the IronPort logo, LightStream, Linksys, MediaTone, MeetingPlace, MeetingPlace Chime Sound, MGX, Networkers, Networking Academy, Network Registrar, PCNow, PIX, PowerPanels, ProConnect, ScriptShare, SenderBase, SMARTnet, Spectrum Expert, StackWise, The Fastest Way to Increase Your Internet Quotient, TransPath, WebEx, and the WebEx logo are registered trademarks of Cisco Systems, Inc. and/or its affiliates in the United States and certain other countries.

All other trademarks mentioned in this document or website are the property of their respective owners. The use of the word partner does not imply a partnership relationship between Cisco and any other company. (0812R)

About the Authors

Lucien Avramov, CCIE 19945, is a Principal Engineer at Cisco. Lucien specializes in the Nexus data center portfolio and the ACI. Lucien designs datacenter networks worldwide and has wide experience in switch architectures, QoS, ultra-low latency networks, high-performance computing designs, and OpenStack. Lucien is a distinguished Cisco Live speaker and former TAC technical leader, he has several industry certifications, authors RFCs at IETF, and owns an active patent. Lucien holds a master's degree in Computer Science and a bachelor's degree in General Engineering from Ecole des Mines d'Ales, France. In his spare time, Lucien can be found hiking, biking, running marathons around the world, and on Twitter: @flying91.

Maurizio Portolani, Distinguished Technical Marketing Engineer at Cisco Systems, focuses on the design of data center networks. He coauthored *Data Center Fundamentals* for Cisco Press, and holds several patents on current data center technologies. He attended the Politecnico of Torino ("Laurea in Ingegneria") and Ecole Centrale Paris ("Diplôme d'Ingénieur") where he majored in Electronics.

About the Technical Reviewers

Tom Edsall is the Chief Technology Officer of Cisco's Insieme Business Unit, a Cisco Fellow, and a co-founder of Insieme Networks, a developer of application-centric infrastructure products, where he is responsible for system architecture and product evangelism. Insieme Networks was described in *Network World* as "one of the most anticipated events in the networking industry over the past 18 months or so, ever since word leaked that Cisco was funding the spin-in as its response to the software-defined networking trend." At Insieme (recently spun back into Cisco), Edsall has led the development of the Application Centric Infrastructure (ACI), which includes a new line of Nexus 9000 switches that form an application-aware switching fabric along with a centralized controller that manages both virtual and physical network infrastructures.

Tom has been with Cisco since 1993, except for a stint as CTO and co-founder of spin-in Andiamo Systems (building SAN switches). One of Cisco's leading switch architects, he has been responsible for the MDS, Nexus 7000, and Catalyst 5000 and 6000 product lines. Two of his products, the Catalyst 6000 and Nexus 7000, have been the recipients of the prestigious Cisco Pioneer Award. During this time he has been awarded more than 70 patents in the networking industry and was recently an author of "CONGA: Distributed Congestion-Aware Load Balancing for Data Centers," which won the prestigious SIGCOMM 2014 best paper award.

Before joining Cisco, Tom was a co-founder and a member of the senior engineering management team at Crescendo Communications, Cisco's first acquisition. Edsall holds BSEE and MSEE degrees from Stanford, where he has also been a Visiting Scholar and occasional lecturer.

Mike Cohen is Director of Product Management at Cisco Systems. Mike began his career as an early engineer on VMware's hypervisor team and subsequently worked in infrastructure product management on Google and Big Switch Networks. Mike holds a BSE in Electrical Engineering from Princeton University and an MBA from Harvard Business School.

Krishna Doddapaneni is responsible for the switching infrastructure and iNXOS part of ACI. Previously, he served as Director in SAVBU (Cisco) (part of the acquisition of Nuova Systems). In Nuova Systems, he was responsible for the delivery of the first FCoE switch. He was responsible for multiple generations of Nexus 5k/2k product lines. Before Nuova, he was the first employee of Greenfield Networks (acquired by Cisco). He holds an MS degree in Computer Engineering from Texas A&M University. He holds numerous patents in the networking field.

Dedications

Lucien Avramov:

For Regina and Michel, my precious parents who made lifetime sacrifices to give me a better future.

Maurizio Portolani:

This book is dedicated to my friends and my family.

Acknowledgments

We would like to thank Mike Dvorkin, Tom Edsall, and Praveen Jain for founding ACI.

Lucien Avramov:

First, I would like to thank my family, friends, colleagues, customers, and mentors for supporting me during this journey, you know who you are. It means a lot to me. Thank you Mike Dvorkin for sharing your knowledge, philosophy, and friendship. Mike Cohen, thank you for always being available and willing to work hard on the reviews, your opinions, and being a great friend. Tom Edsall, thank you for the quality feedback and time you gave us in this project. Takashi Oikawa, thank you for your kindness and wisdom. Along this journey I made friends and shared incredible memories. Writing a book is a journey mainly with yourself, with a reward comparable to reaching a summit. This journey is stronger when shared with a co-author: I am fortunate to have made a great friend along the way, Maurizio Portolani.

Second, I thank Ron Fuller for introducing me to the pleasure of going into a book project. Thank you to my Cisco colleagues who supported me along the way: Francois Couderc for the great knowledge sharing, time spent thinking about the structure of this book, your advice and reviews; Chih-Tsung Huang, Garry Lemasa, Arkadiy Shapiro, Mike Pavlovich, Jonathan Cornell, and Aleksandr Oysgelt for your encouragement, reviews, and support along the way. A profound acknowledgement and thanks to the Cisco Press team: Brett Bartow, your kindness, availability, and patience have meant a lot to me. Thank you for the opportunity to develop this content and for giving me a chance. Marianne Bartow, thank you for spending so much time with quality reviews. Bill McManus, thank you for the editing. Chris Cleveland, thank you for your support along the way. Mandie Frank, thank you for all the efforts, including keeping this project on time; and Mark Shirar, for design help.

Finally, I thank the people who gave me a chance in my professional career, starting with Jean-Louis Delhaye mentoring me for years at Airbus and being my friend ever since, Didier Fernandes for introducing me and mentoring me in Cisco, Erin Foster for giving me a chance to join Cisco and relocating me to the United States, Ed Swenson and Ali Ali for giving me a full time job in Cisco TAC, John Bunney for taking me along to build the TAC Data Center team and mentoring me. Thank you Yousuf Khan for giving me a chance to join Technical Marketing first, in the Nexus Team, and later in the ACI team, and for coaching me along the way; Jacob Rapp, Pramod Srivatsa, and Tuqiang Cao for your leadership and developing my career.

Maurizio Portolani:

I would personally like to acknowledge many people who opened my eyes to modern software development methodology and technology that I could relate to the changes that ACI is bringing to networking. A special acknowledgment goes to Marco Molteni for his in-depth philosophical views on XML versus JSON and Yaml and for enlightening me on GitHub and Python. I would also like to acknowledge Amine Choukir in particular for his insights on continuous integration, and Luca Relandini for his expertise on automation.

Contents at a Glance

Contents

Command Syntax Conventions

The conventions used to present command syntax in this book are the same conventions used in Cisco's Command Reference. The Command Reference describes these conventions as follows:

- **Boldface** indicates commands and keywords that are entered literally as shown. In actual configuration examples and output (not general command syntax), boldface indicates commands that are manually input by the user (such as a **show** command).

- *Italics* indicate arguments for which you supply actual values.

- Vertical bars (|) separate alternative, mutually exclusive elements.

- Square brackets [ ] indicate optional elements.

- Braces { } indicate a required choice.

- Braces within brackets [{ }] indicate a required choice within an optional element.

Note This book covers multiple operating systems, and different icons and router names are used to indicate the appropriate OS that is being referenced. Cisco IOS and IOS XE use router names such as R1 and R2 and are referenced by the IOS router icon. Cisco IOS XR routers use router names such as XR1 and XR2 and are referenced by the IOS XR router icon.

Foreword

Looking at the history of network control, one can wonder why so much complexity emerged out of so simple concepts. Network management systems have traditionally focused on control of features, without thinking of networks as systems. Any network control scheme, at the heart, aims to solve two things: control of endpoint behaviors, where regulations are imposed on what sets of endpoints can communicate or not, also known as access control, and path optimization problems instrumented through management of numerous network control plane protocols. Unfortunately, this natural separation has rarely been honored, resulting in the control models that are both difficult to consume and operationally fragile.

IT does not exist for the benefit of itself. The purpose of any IT organization is to run business applications. The application owner, architect, and developer all have intimate understanding of their applications. They have a complete picture of the application's infrastructure requirements and full understanding of other application components necessary for communication. However, once it comes to deployment, all this knowledge, the original intent, is forever lost in the implementation detail of the translation between the application requirements and the actual configuration of the infrastructure. The unfortunate consequence of this is that there's no easy way to map resources and configurations back to the application. Now, what if we need to expand the app, add more components, or simply retire it from the data center? What happens to the residual configuration?

When we started Insieme, one of the chief goals was to bring networking into the reach of those who don't need to understand it: an application guy who needs to identify how his application interacts with other application components in the data center, an ops guy who needs to configure cluster expansion, a compliance guy who needs to ensure that no enterprise-wide business rules are violated. We felt that the way operational teams interact with the network needed to change in order for networking to enter the next logical step in the evolution.

Lucien and Maurizio explain the new Policy Driven Data Center and its associated operational model. This book focuses, on one hand, on the architecture, concept, and methodology to build a modern data center solving this paradigm; while also, on the other hand, detailing the Cisco ACI solution.

Mike Dvorkin

Distinguished Cisco Engineer, Chief Scientist, and Co-founder of Insieme Networks

Introduction

Welcome to the Policy Driven Data Center with Application Centric Infrastructure (ACI). You are embarking on a journey to understand the latest Cisco data center fabric and the many innovations that are part of it.

The objective of this book is to explain the architecture design principles, the concepts, and the methodology to build new data center fabrics. Several key concepts in this book, such as the policy data model, programming, and automation, have a domain of applicability that goes beyond the ACI technology itself and forms a core skillset of network engineers and architects.

Cisco Application Centric Infrastructure (ACI) is a data center fabric that enables you to integrate virtual and physical workloads in a highly programmable multi-hypervisor environment that is designed for any multi-service or cloud data center.

To fully appreciate the ACI innovations, one has to understand the key new industry trends in the networking field.

Industry Trends

At the time of this writing, the network industry is experiencing the emergence of new operational models. Many of these changes are influenced by innovations and methodology that have happened in the server world or in the application world.

The following list provides a nonexhaustive collection of trends currently influencing new data center designs:

- Adoption of cloud services.

- New methodology of provisioning network connectivity (namely self-service catalogs).

- Ability to put new applications into production more quickly and to do A/B testing. This concept relates to the ability to shorten the time necessary to provision a complete network infrastructure for a given application.

- Ability to "fail fast"; that is, being able to put a new version of an application into production for a limited time and then to decommission it quickly should bugs arise during the testing.

- Ability to use the same tools that manage servers (such as Puppet, Chef, CFengines, etc.) to manage networking equipment.

- The need for better interaction between server and application teams and operation teams (DevOps).

- Ability to deal with "elephant flows"; that is, the ability to have backups or commonly bulk transfers without affecting the rest of the traffic.

- Ability to automate network configuration with a more systematic and less prone to error programmatic way using scripts.

■ Adoption of software development methodologies such as Agile and Continuous Integration.

Some of these trends are collectively summarized as "application velocity," which refers to the ability to shorten the time to bring an application from development to production (and back to testing, if needed) by spawning new servers and network connectivity in a much faster way than before.

What Is an "Application"?

The meaning of "application" varies depending on the context or job role of the person that is using this term. For a networking professional, an application may be a DNS server, a virtualized server, a web server, and so on. For a developer of an online ordering tool, the application is the ordering tool itself, which comprises various servers: presentation servers, databases, and so on. For a middleware professional, an application may be the IBM WebSphere environment, SAP, and so on.

For the purpose of this book, in the context of Cisco ACI, an application refers to a set of networking components that provides connectivity for a given set of workloads. These workloads' relationship is what ACI calls an "application," and the relationship is expressed by what ACI calls an application network profile, explained after Figure 1.

Figure 1 provides an example illustrating an application that is accessible from a company intranet and that is connected to an external company that provides some business function. This could be, for instance, a travel reservation system, an ordering tool, a billing tool, and so on.

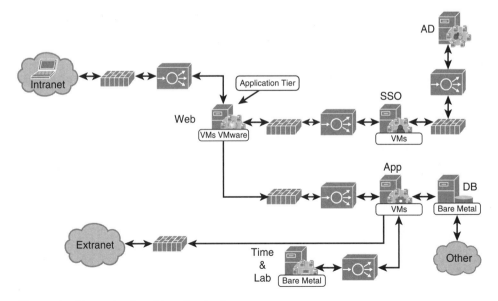

Figure 1   *Example of an "Application"*

This relationship can be expressed in ACI by using the concept of *application network profile* (ANP), which abstracts the specific VLANs or subnets that the building blocks reside on. The configuration of network connectivity is expressed in terms of *policies*, which define which endpoints consume (or provide) services provided by (consumed by) other endpoints.

Using ACI doesn't require deep understanding of these application relationships. These often are implicit in existing networking configurations by means of VLANs and access control lists. Hence, one can just use ANPs and associated policies as containers of existing configurations without the need to map exact server-to-server communication patterns.

The value proposition of using ANPs is that it enables network administrators to express network configurations in a more abstract manner that can be more closely mapped to the building blocks of a business application such as an ordering tool, a travel reservation system, and so on. After the applications are defined, they can be validated in a test environment and immediately moved to a production environment.

The Need for Abstraction

Applications already run in data centers today even without ACI. Network administrators create the connectivity between building blocks by using VLANs, IP addresses, routing, and ACLs by translating the requirements of the IT organization to support a given tool. However, without ACI, administrators have no way to really express such configurations directly in a format that can be mapped to the network, leaving administrators with no choice but to focus primarily on expressing a very open connectivity policy to ensure that servers can talk to each other if they are internal to the company and can talk to the outside if they are on the DMZ or extranet. This requires administrators to harden ACLs and put firewalls to restrict the scope of which service clients and other servers can use from a given set of servers.

This approach results in configurations that are not very portable. They are very much hard-coded in the specific data center environment where they are implemented. If the same environment must be built in a different data center, somebody must perform the tedious job of reconfiguring IP addresses and VLANs and deciphering ACLs.

ACI is revolutionizing this process by introducing the ability to create an application network profile, a configuration template to express relationships between compute segments. ACI then translates those relationships into networking constructs that routers and switches can implement (i.e., in VLANs, VXLANs, VRFs, IP addresses, and so on).

What Is Cisco ACI

The Cisco ACI fabric consists of discrete components that operate as routers and switches but are provisioned and monitored as a single entity. The operation is like a distributed switch and router configuration that provides advanced traffic optimization, security, and telemetry functions, stitching together virtual and physical workloads. The controller, called the Application Policy Infrastructure Controller (APIC), is the central point of management of the fabric. This is the device that distributes ANP policies to the devices that are part of the fabric.

The Cisco ACI Fabric OS runs on the building blocks of the fabric, which are, at time of writing, the Cisco Nexus 9000 Series nodes. The Cisco ACI Fabric OS is object-oriented and enables programming of objects for each configurable element of the system. The ACI Fabric OS renders policies (such as the ANP and its relationships) from the controller into a concrete model that runs in the physical infrastructure. The concrete model is analogous to compiled software; it is the form of the model that the switch operating system can execute.

Cisco ACI is designed for many types of deployments, including public and private clouds, big data environments, and hosting of virtualized and physical workloads. It provides the ability to instantiate new networks almost instantaneously and to remove them just as quickly. ACI is designed to simplify automation and can be easily integrated into the workflow of common orchestration tools.

Figure 2 illustrates the ACI fabric with the spine-leaf architecture and controllers. Physical and virtual servers can be connected to the ACI fabric and also receive connectivity to the external network.

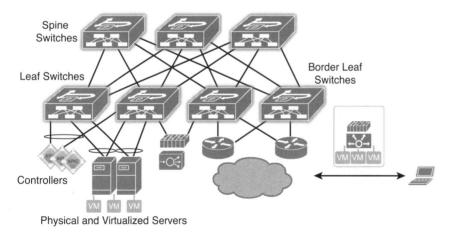

Figure 2   *ACI Fabric*

Cisco ACI Innovations

Cisco ACI introduces many innovations:

- The whole fabric is managed as a single entity but without a centralized control plane.

- The fabric is managed via an object tree with methods and classes that are accessible with REST calls.

- It introduces a new management model based on a declarative approach instead of an imperative approach.

- It allows a clear mapping of application relationships to the network infrastructure.

- It is designed for multi-tenancy.

- It is multi-hypervisor capable.

- It allows the definition of abstract configurations (or templates) that make configurations portable.

- It changes the way that networking configurations are expressed, from VLAN and IP addresses to policies.

- It revolutionizes equal-cost multipathing and quality of service (QoS) with flowlet load balancing, dynamic flow prioritization, and congestion management.

- It introduces new concepts for telemetry, such as the concept of health scores and atomic counters.

Book Structure

Chapter 1: Data Center Architecture Considerations

The goal of this chapter is to describe the network requirements of different server environments and how to meet them in terms of network design.

Chapter 2: Building Blocks for Cloud Architectures

At the time of this writing, most large-scale data center deployments are designed with the principles of cloud computing. This is equally true for data centers that are built by providers or by large enterprises. This chapter illustrates the design and technology requirements of building a cloud.

Chapter 3: The Policy Data Center

The goal of this chapter is to elucidate the Cisco ACI approach to modeling business applications. This approach provides a unique blend of mapping hardware and software capabilities to the deployment of applications either graphically through the Cisco Application Policy Infrastructure Controller (APIC) GUI or programmatically through the Cisco APIC API model. The APIC concepts and principles are explained in detail in this chapter. Finally, the ACI fabric is not only for greenfield deployment. Many users will consider how to deploy an ACI fabric into an existing environment. Therefore, the last part of this chapter explains how to integrate the ACI fabric with an existing network.

Chapter 4: Operational Model

Command-line interfaces (CLI) are great tools for interactive changes to the configuration, but they are not designed for automation, nor for ease of parsing (CLI scraping is neither efficient nor practical) or customization. Furthermore, CLIs don't have the ability to compete with the power of parsing, string manipulation, or the advanced logic that sophisticated scripting languages like Python can offer. This chapter covers the key technologies and tools that new administrators and operators must be familiar with, and it explains how they are used in an ACI-based data center.

Chapter 5: Data Center Design with Hypervisors

This chapter describes the networking requirements and design considerations when using hypervisors in the data center.

Chapter 6: OpenStack

This chapter explains in detail OpenStack and its relation to Cisco ACI. The goal of this chapter is to explain what OpenStack is and present the details of the Cisco ACI APIC OpenStack driver architecture.

Chapter 7: ACI Fabric Design Methodology

This chapter describes the topology of an ACI fabric and how to configure it both as an infrastructure administrator and as a tenant administrator. The chapter covers the configuration of physical interfaces, PortChannels, virtual PortChannels, and VLAN namespaces as part of the infrastructure configurations. The chapter also covers the topics of segmentation, multi-tenancy, connectivity to physical and virtual servers, and external connectivity as part of the tenant configuration.

Chapter 8: Service Insertion with ACI

Cisco ACI technology provides the capability to insert Layer 4 through Layer 7 functions using an approach called a service graph. The industry normally refers to the capability to add Layer 4 through Layer 7 devices in the path between endpoints as service insertion. The Cisco ACI service graph technology can be considered a superset of service insertion. This chapter describes the service graph concept and how to design for service insertion with the service graph.

Chapter 9: Advanced Telemetry

The goal of this chapter is to explain the centralized troubleshooting techniques that ACI offers for isolating problems. It includes topics such as atomic counters and health scores.

Chapter 10: Data Center Switch Architecture

The goal of this chapter is to provide a clear explanation of the data center switching architecture. It is divided into three sections: the hardware switch architecture, the fundamental principles of switching, and the quality of service in the data center.

Terminology

Node: Physical network device.

Spine node: Network device placed in the core part of the data center. Typically it's a device with high port density and higher speed.

Leaf node: Network device placed at the access of the data center. It is the first tier of network equipment defining the data center network fabric.

Fabric: A group of leaf and spine nodes defining the data center network physical topology.

Workload: A virtual machine defining a single virtual entity.

Two-tier topology: Typically defined by a spine-leaf fabric topology.

Three-tier topology: A network topology with access, aggregation, and core tiers.

Services: Category defined by the following (nonexhaustive) group of appliances: load balancers, security devices, content accelerators, network monitoring devices, network management devices, traffic analyzers, automation and scripting servers, etc.

ULL: Ultra-low latency. Characterizes network equipment in which the latency is under a microsecond. Current technology is nanosecond level.

HPC: High-performance compute. Applications using structured data schemes (database) or unstructured data (NoSQL) where performance is important at predictable and low latency and with the capability to scale. The traffic patterns are east-west.

HFT: High-frequency trading. Typically occurs in a financial trading environment, where the latency needs to be minimal on the data center fabric to provide as close as possible to real time information to the end users. Traffic is mainly north-south

Clos: Multistage switching network, sometimes called "fat tree," based on a 1985 article by Charles Leiserson. The idea of Clos is to build a very high-speed, nonblocking switching fabric.

Chapter 1

Data Center Architecture Considerations

This chapter covers data center architecture considerations. It explains the design considerations and methodology used to approach the design process in order to efficiently select the end-to-end network design for a data center fabric project for an architect and provide the needed growth capability for its evolution.

In the data center network design process, there are key considerations for the architecture choice and final design:

- The applications to be hosted in the data center along with the type of storage the applications will use

- The data center needs and constraints, including physical decisions and the pod model

- The different types of data center designs

The virtualized data center represents the majority of data center fabric deployments. The data center's other use cases: big data, ultra-low latency, high-performance compute, and massive scale are also explained. The trend in the data center is toward the spine-leaf architecture, which is a building block for the Application Centric Infrastructure fabric (ACI) explained all along in this book.

Application and Storage

When designing a data center, the most common approach is to use the *three-tier approach*. This comprises the classical access, aggregation, and core layers, commonly referred to as a *three-tier topology*. The data center designs evolve from this three-tier approach into more specific data center trends, the modern trend being toward the two-tier spine-leaf architecture. Understanding the different technical trends in the data center along with the requirements of the project will guide you in triaging the essential aspects of the design. This understanding will give you key knowledge to plan the best type of solution to meet the data center project requirements. This section covers the current recommended methodology to achieve an end-to-end data center design.

This chapter describes how to use the latest design methodologies to address the requirements of the following workload types:

- Virtualized data center

- Big data

- High-performance compute (HPC)

- Ultra-low latency data center

- Massively scalable data centers

Many data centers have a mix of workloads that fall into several of the previous listed catagories. For these types of data centers, you need to build a fabric that is multipurpose; for example, a fabric based on the Cisco Nexus 9000 product family of switches.

Virtualized Data Center

Modern data centers include a significant number of virtualized servers. This chapter explains the design considerations for Virtualized workloads.

Introduction

The virtualized data center represents most of the current data center fabric deployments. These environments include small-, medium-, and commercial-size businesses as well as larger enterprises. The full Cisco data center fabric portfolio is being used from the hypervisor-level switches, such as Nexus 1000v, to the Nexus 9000 product family, including the Cisco Unified Computing System (UCS) servers with blade chassis servers or rack mounts. The Fibre Channel storage is consolidated on the Ethernet wire and coexists with other Ethernet traffic and IP traffic. NFS storage traffic is used as well to store the virtual machines (VMs). FCoE is not mandatory; many deployments in the virtualized data center are with IP storage.

The virtualized data center is built around one or multiple hypervisor types that must coexist and communicate. The data center network needs to handle virtualized traffic, but it must also be highly available. It has to minimize VM interruption when a workload mobility event occurs, such as when a VM needs to move to another host. A key difference in the virtualized data center is the fabric itself. The first cable up to the top-of-rack (ToR) switch is already "fabric" in the sense that it carries traffic from multiple hosts toward the first physical network device, which is a ToR or access switch. The first switch is now a virtual switch device. The letter v is placed in front of each commonly known network element: vSwitch, vEthernet, vNIC, and so forth.

When building the data center network fabric, it is important to consider the number of VMs that will run on each host and the applications that will provide guidance for the oversubscription ratio. The virtualization has multiple layers. For example, a cloud provider that is running a virtual environment may allow its users to also run their own hypervisors. This creates a data center environment, which handles multiple levels of virtualization. Therefore, the number of different encapsulations expands. This creates even further levels inside the hypervisor to reach the first virtual access port where the different properties will be applied (quality of service [QoS], bandwidth restriction, security, port mirroring, etc.).

Within a layer of virtualization, different traffic can run IP or Ethernet application traffic, video, voice, and storage. Therefore, the virtual data center design offers various QoS capabilities to prioritize the various traffic patterns that take the same uplink toward the first ToR switch. The typical type of application running in a virtualized data center is what is often called the *three-tier application model*: consisting of the combination of a specific application, a database, and a web server. Each typically runs on a dedicated virtual machine. In enteprise deployment, databases are often hosted on bare-metal servers.

Definition and Virtualization Concepts

Virtualization in the data center is not restricted to servers. As a result modern data centers use the following technologies:

- Server virtualization

- Storage virtualization

- Services virtualization

- Network virtualization

- Orchestration (management virtualization)

Server Virtualization

Server virtualization is the most common type of hardware virtualization. The current x86 computer hardware is largely underutilized when running a single operating system with its applications. With virtualization, the hardware resources are much better employed, by running multiple VMs and applications on the same physical computer, as shown in Figure 1-1. There is a hypervisor software layer between the physical server and the VMs, emulating a physical dedicated computer logically isolated from the real physical host server. It allows multiple operating systems to share a single hardware host, running simultaneously with their independent functionalities and applications. The VMs are stored as files, making recovery possible on the same or a different physical host. Server virtualization optimizes the data center projects, also called *consolidation projects*, so that the physical servers are used more efficiently.

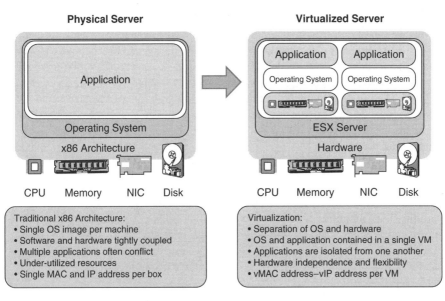

Figure 1-1   *Server Virtualization*

Storage Virtualization

Storage virtualization is a logical and abstracted view of all the physical storage devices in a specific data center project. Users and applications access the storage via the storage virtualization without having to know where the storage is located, how to access it, or how to manage it. This further enables the sharing capability across multiple applications and servers: storage appears as one large pool with no physical boundaries. Storage virtualization applies to large storage-area network (SAN) arrays, logical portioning of a local workstation hard drive, or redundant array of independent disks (RAID). Storage virtualization provides four key benefits:

■ **Optimization of the resources:** The storage devices are no longer dedicated to specific servers or applications, optimizing the use of storage globally available for all the servers and applications in the data center farm. When more storage is needed, physical storage is added to the shared pool.

■ **Lower cost of operation:** The storage configuration is centralized and does not require each server to be configured for its own storage. A storage management tool allows adding, maintaining, and operating the shared storage. The total cost of operation for storage is lowered by this approach, and considerable time is saved.

■ **Increased storage availability:** In a traditional environment, planned or unplanned downtime for maintenance, storage upgrades, power outages, viruses, and so on results in application downtime for the end user. With storage virtualization and redundancy, new storage resources are provisioned quickly, reducing the impact of downtime.

■ **Improved storage performance:** The workload for a storage operation created by an application can be distributed across several different physical storage devices. This improves completion time for the application to perform a read or write operation, as a single task can overwhelm a single storage device.

Services Virtualization

Services virtualization in a data center refers to the use of service devices such as firewalls, load balancers, cache acceleration engines, and so on. A virtual interface, also called a *virtual IP address*, is exposed to the outside of the data center, representing itself as a web server. The virtual interface then manages the connections to and from the web server as needed. A load balancer provides a more robust topology and secure server access, allowing users entry to multiple web servers and applications as a single instance instead of a per-individual-server approach. One server is shown to the outside users, hiding the multiple servers available behind a reverse proxy device. Network services can be physical or virtual. At the time of this writing, several virtual firewalls and virtual load balancers are available on the market.

Network Virtualization

Virtualized servers also require changes to the network infrastructure in order to preserve the segmentation among virtual machines. The main change is the shift of the network access layer inside the server, at the hypervisor level, which contrasts the traditional bare-metal server, where the access layer starts from the first access port to which a physical network cable is connected toward the end server. Network virtualization can leverage one or more of the following technologies:

■ Use of VLANs

■ Use of Virtual Extensible LAN (VXLAN)

■ Use of Virtual Routing and Forwarding (VRF)

Orchestration

Orchestration refers to the coordinated provisioning of virtualized resources pools and virtual instances. This includes static and dynamic mapping of virtual resources to physical resources, along with management capabilities such as capacity planning, analytics, billing, and service-level agreements (SLA). The services are usually abstracted to a customer portal layer, where the end user selects the service and then the service is automatically provisioned using various domain and middleware management systems along with the following (as depicted in Figure 1-2):

■ Configuration management database (CMDB)

■ Service catalog

- Accounting
- SLA management
- Service management
- Service portal

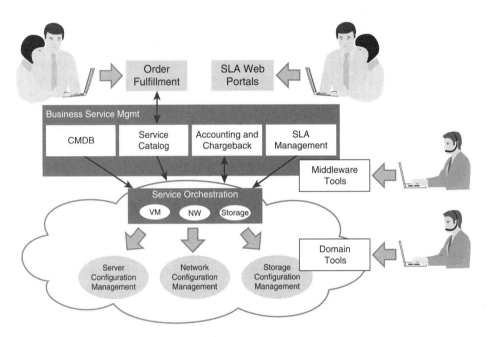

Figure 1-2   *Orchestration*

Network and Design Requirements

The impacts of using a virtualized data center on the network include the following:

- Less physical ports and more virtual ports to manage.
- Increase of risk. A rack has hundreds of VMs, which means a higher impact from outage or upgrade and the need for high availability.
- The need to increase scalability. The more VMs, the more MAC addresses and VLANs.
- Mobility makes capacity planning very difficult. You must overprovision uplinks with higher bandwidth.
- Server evolution to 10-Gigabit Ethernet (GE) at the access layer due to consolidation.
- With overprovisioning, the uplinks move to 40-GE and 100-GE.

- Hypervisor NIC teaming is different from the rack-mount servers' NIC teaming
- 70 to 80 percent of the traffic flow is now east to west (that is, between servers) within the data center.
- The services are now virtual and physical, not only physical.
- The need to adapt to the new multitenancy models with mobility of the VLANs.
- The need for knowledge about the localization of the VM for a physical server.
- Multiple layers of virtualization (cloud offerings).
- Legacy needs to coexist with the virtual environment (mission-critical databases, for example).
- New pay-as-you-grow model, where the growth of the virtualized DC is per rack and not an initial fixed end-to-end data center project.
- Virtualization introduces the need to manage the virtual switch.

Storage Requirements

The virtualization encourages NFS to be used for storing the VMs and Fibre Channel over Ethernet (FCoE) to be used for storing the hypervisors. There is currently a trend to move to IP storage as well for the hypervisor storage. This is why high bandwidth capacity, or QoS, are key to assure the data transfer of storage between the storage arrays and the production compute nodes.

Big Data

This section explains in detail the big data data center trend.

Definition

Big data is loosely defined by its main attributes (as Gartner and other market analysts indicate): volume, velocity, variety, and complexity. Big data is composed of structured and unstructured elements. Although structured data accounts for an enormous number of records, often representing more than petabytes of data, unstructured data, and for the most part human generated, normally makes up a much larger percentage of the total size. This large amount of information is generated as a result of democratization and ecosystem factors such as the following:

- **Mobility trends:** Mobile devices, mobile events and sharing, and sensory integration
- **Data access and consumption:** Internet, interconnected systems, social networking, and convergent interfaces and access models (Internet, search and social networking, and messaging)

- **Ecosystem capabilities:** Major changes in the information processing model and the availability of an open source framework; the general-purpose computing and unified network integration

Big data is a foundational element of social networking and web-based information companies. Consequently, big data, particularly when originated from external sources, tends to contain errors, wrong content, and missing parts. Also, big data usually does not include unique identifiers. These issues generate significant challenges for entity resolution and entity disambiguation. Data generation, consumption, and analytics have provided competitive business advantages for web portals and Internet-centric firms that offer services to customers and services differentiation through correlation of adjacent data.

Some companies with a large Internet presence use big data for the following reasons:

- Targeted marketing and advertising

- Related attached sale promotions

- Analysis of behavioral social patterns

- Metadata-based optimization of workload and performance management for millions of users

Big Data Moves into the Enterprise

The requirements of traditional enterprise data models for application, database, and storage resources have grown over the years, and the cost and complexity of these models have increased along the way to meet the needs of big data. This rapid change prompted changes in the fundamental models that describe the way that big data is stored, analyzed, and accessed. The new models are based on a scaled-out, shared-nothing architecture, bringing new challenges to enterprises to decide what technologies to use, where to use them, and how. One size no longer fits all, and the traditional three-tier network model (access/aggregation/core) is now being expanded to incorporate new building blocks that address the challenges with new information processing frameworks that are purpose-built to meet big data's requirements. However, these systems must also meet the inherent requirement for integration into current business models, data strategies, and network infrastructures.

Big Data Components

Two main building blocks are being added to the enterprise stack to accommodate big data, as shown in Figure 1-3:

- **Hadoop:** Provides storage capability through a distributed, shared file system, and provides analysis capability through a task called *MapReduce*.

- **NoSQL:** Provides the capability to capture, read, and update, in real time, the large influx of unstructured data and data without schemas. Examples include

- Click streams

- Social media

- Log files

- Event data

- Mobility trends

- Sensor and machine data

A trend is to store this data in flash or RAM memory for faster access. NoSQL has become more popular because the volume of data to handle is higher than the SQL type of database structures.

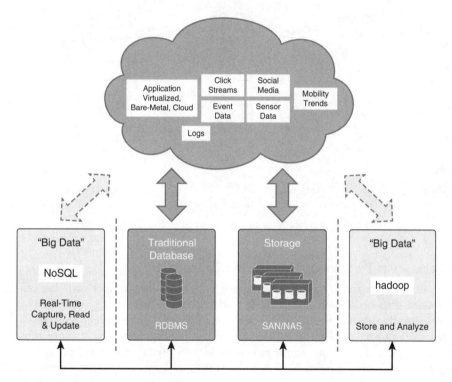

Figure 1-3 *Big Data Enterprise Model*

Network Requirements

Big data components need to integrate alongside the current business models in the enterprise. This integration of new, dedicated big data models can be completely transparent by using Cisco Nexus network infrastructures optimized for big data, as shown in Figure 1-4.

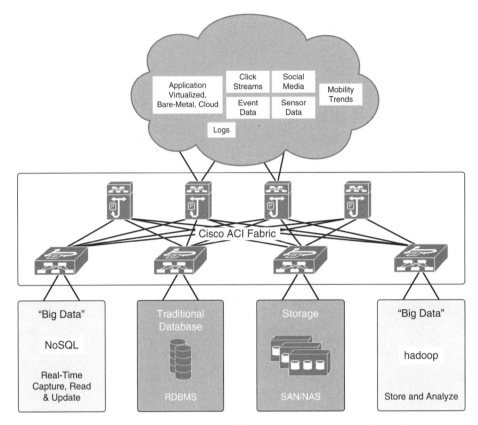

Figure 1-4   *Integration of Big Data Model into Enterprise Network Architecture*

Cluster Design with the Hadoop Building Blocks: the POD

Divide-and-conquer strategies are quite effective for several kinds of workloads that deal with massive amounts of data. A single large workload can be divided or mapped into smaller subworkloads, and the results from the subworkloads can be merged, condensed, and reduced to obtain the final result. The idea behind Hadoop is to exploit this feature of the workload and assign the smaller subworkloads to a large cluster of inexpensive nodes built with general-purpose hardware, rather than use expensive, fault-tolerant hardware. Further, handling massive amounts of data requires storage. Hadoop has a distributed, cluster file system that scales to warehouse these massive amounts of data. The cluster is built so that the entire infrastructure is resilient and fault tolerant, even though individual components can fail, dramatically lowering the system-wide MTBF (mean time between failure) rate despite having a higher component MTBF rate, as shown in Figure 1-5.

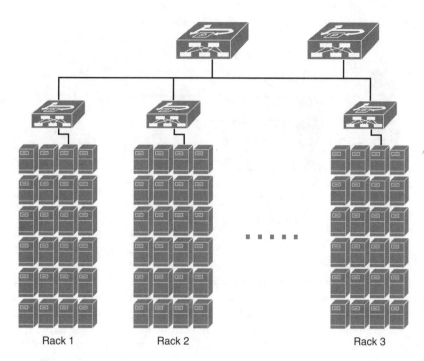

Figure 1-5 *Cluster Design*

Storage Requirements

Big data applications use a distributed IP storage. It is a shared file system, typically NFS or direct attach storage (DAS). The storage is located on each server node. Some performance applications in big data are similar to the ultra-low latency type of application storage located on the volatile memory of each node instead of a hard drive. Flash hard drives are also expanding in this environment.

Design Considerations

A functional and resilient network is crucial to an effective big data cluster. However, analysis has proven that factors other than the network have a greater influence on the performance of the cluster. Nevertheless, consider some of the relevant network characteristics and their potential effects. Figure 1-6 shows the relative importance of the primary parameters validated during extensive testing.

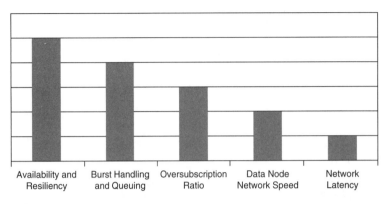

Figure 1-6   *Relative Importance of Parameters to Job Completion*

Availability and Resiliency

The failure of a networking device can affect multiple data nodes of a Hadoop cluster. The tasks on the affected nodes may then need to be rescheduled on other functioning nodes, increasing their load. Further, the Hadoop infrastructure may start certain maintenance activities such as data rebalancing and replication factor to compensate for the failed nodes, increasing the load on the cluster even more. These events are critical factors in degradation of the cluster performance. Project completion will take longer, impairing the ability to schedule new jobs.

It is important to build a network that is available and resilient. First, focus on the network architecture: deploy architectures that provide the required redundancy and that can also scale as the cluster grows. Technologies that allow network designs with multiple redundant paths between the data nodes are inherently better than technologies that have one or two points of failure.

After the architectural framework is laid out, consider the availability aspects of individual devices. Switches and routers that run operating systems that are proven in the industry to be resilient provide better network availability to servers. Switches and routers that can be upgraded without any disruption to the data nodes provide higher availability. Further, devices that are proven to be easy to manage, troubleshoot, and upgrade help ensure less network downtime and increase the availability of the network and, hence, the cluster.

Burst Handling and Queue Depth

In Hadoop-type big data jobs, several operations and phases are bursty. A network that cannot handle bursts effectively drops packets, so optimal buffering is needed in devices to absorb bursts. Any packet dropped because a buffer is not available results in retransmission, which if excessive leads to longer job completion times. Be sure to choose switches and routers with architectures that employ buffer and queuing strategies that can handle bursts effectively. An example of burst and buffer utilization is shown in Chapter 10, "Data Center Switch Architecture."

Oversubscription Ratio

A good network design must consider the possibility of unacceptable congestion at critical points in the network under realistic loads. A ToR device that accepts 20 Gbps of traffic from the servers but has only two 1-Gbps uplinks (a total of 2 Gbps) provisioned (a 20:2 [or 10:1] oversubscription ratio) can drop packets, leading to poor cluster performance. However, overprovisioning the network can be costly. Generally accepted oversubscription ratios are around 4:1 at the server access layer and 2:1 between the access layer and the aggregation layer or core. Lower oversubscription ratios should be considered if higher performance is required. How does oversubscription increase when certain devices fail? Be sure to provision critical points in the network (such as the core) adequately. Multipathing technologies, such as Layer 3 Equal Cost Multipath [ECMP] with or without VXLAN or ACI, deliver a linear increase in oversubscription with each device failure and are better than architectures that degrade dramatically during failures.

Data Node Network Speed

Be sure to provision data nodes with enough bandwidth for efficient job completion. Also remember the price-to-performance ratio entailed in adding more bandwidth to nodes. The recommendations for a cluster depend on workload characteristics. Typical clusters are provisioned with one or two 1-Gbps uplinks per data node. Cluster management is made easier by choosing network architectures that are proven to be resilient and easy to manage and that can scale as your data grows. The use of 10-Gbps server access is largely dependent on the cost/performance trade-off. The workload characteristics and business requirement to complete the job in required time drives the 10-Gbps server connectivity. As 10-Gbps Ethernet LAN-on-motherboard (LOM) connectors become more commonly available on servers in the future, more clusters are more likely to be built with 10-Gigabit Ethernet data node uplinks. The Nexus 2000 Fabric Extender (FEX) is not a common best practice in Hadoop environments.

Network Latency

Variations in switch and router latency are shown to have only limited impact on cluster performance. From a network point of view, any latency-related optimization must start with a network-wide analysis. "Architecture first, and device next" is an effective strategy. Architectures that deliver consistently lower latency at scale are better than architectures with higher overall latency but lower individual device latency. The latency contribution to the workload is much higher at the application level, contributed to by the application logic (Java Virtual Machine software stack, socket buffer, etc.), than at the network level. In any case, slightly more or less network latency does not noticeably affect job completion times. Layer 2 is not mandatory. Some designs find L3 with BGP or OSPF protools running down to the compute node.

High-Performance Compute

This section explains in detail the high-performance compute data center trend.

Definition

High-performance compute (HPC) refers to the practice of aggregating compute capability to provide higher performance than a typical workstation to solve large problems in engineering, industry, science, business, and so on.

Network Requirements

The network traffic is usually an east-to-west traffic pattern and contained within a single data center. The scale is achieved using a pod model, discussed in detail in the "Design Considerations" section. Predictability and ultra-low latency are key. A data center fabric providing similar low latency (regardless of whether a server is connected in the same rack, same cluster, or same row) reduces the compute time for the HPC applications. Adequate throughput and buffering (while capable of elastically scaling with the growth of the compute nodes) is key.

HPC and big data are very similar in terms of network requirements and designs, with one major difference: big data is IP based, whereas HPC is usually Ethernet and non-IP. This restricts the options to build a data center fabric for HPC compared to doing so for big data. The other network properties remain similar. Layer 2 data center fabric protocols such as Cisco vPC and VXLAN are leverages to build an HPC cluster at scale.

The network requirements for HPC can be summarized as follows:

- L2 network
- 90+ percent of the traffic is east to west
- No virtualization
- 1-GE NICs moving to 10-GE and 40-GE
- Core network running at 10-GE or 40-GE

Storage Requirements

Storage is contained on each host; it's called a distributed storage model. The storage is handled by the HPC application. There is typically no Fibre Channel requirement for the HPC storage, nor any specific storage network constraint to address on the switches.

Design Considerations

The traffic can be IP but also non-IP (running over Ethernet). The non-Ethernet supercomputing capabilities are not discussed in this book. Today's Ethernet technology enables non-Ethernet traffic to be encapsulated and transported over standard Ethernet media and to be moved over a standard consolidated Ethernet data center by using, for example, Cisco Nexus products. The Cisco approach is to build Ethernet-based HPC clusters.

Typical HPC environments use clusters of 32 nodes each. A node represents a logical entity with 24 core CPUs and one 10-GE NIC, in a rack-mount server. This provides 768 cores per rack. A typical environment for HPC can start with a rack of only 32 nodes. Deployments commonly have four racks at least, representing 128 nodes.

It's important to define the size of the POD. This is the critical initial size for the project. As the project grows, the POD concept is repeated to add more HPC clusters. The example provided in this section illustrates a POD that consists of the 128-node servers and the appropriate switches forming a logical compute entity.

The Cisco approach for HPC is to leverage the UCS-C rack-mount servers along with the specific HPC NIC card called *usNIC*. Cisco userspace NIC (usNIC) provides direct access to the NIC hardware from the Linux userspace. It uses an operating system bypass via the linux Verbs API (UD) and OpenMPI. This NIC provides a back-to-back latency of 1.7 us, while offering up to 89.69% of HPL efficiency across 512 cores. The benefit of this NIC is to rely on Ethernet standards versus the use of an RDMA network media. It is to note that RDMA solutions can be accomodated across Cisco Nexus switches and ACI with the RDMA over Ethernet protocol. iWarp is another TCP protocol to allow acceleration; its performance is slower than usNIC.

The HPC network needs to be as fast as possible to provide the lowest possible latency between nodes. The lowest-latency product at the moment of writing is the Cisco Nexus 3548 switch, providing line-rate forwarding with 190-ns latency. It can be used as a ToR, defining the leaf layer, and also at the spine layer when the oversubscription ratio is sufficient. The network fabric needs to carry Ethernet traffic; therefore, fabric technologies such as Cisco vPC and Cisco VXLAN are well suited to build an Ethernet fabric capable of carrying HPC traffic from any host to another. A typical network oversubscription ratio for an HPC design is 2:1. To achieve lower-cost designs, the oversubscription ratio can be raised, up to typically a 5:1 ratio.

Design Topologies

In HPC topologies, the typical design is a one- or two-tier network infrastructure. It also can be referred to as a *spine/leaf* type of design, where the spine plays the role of an aggregation device. The goal of the design topology is to provide the necessary port count at a given service NIC speed. Most common are 10-GE designs from the access to the network; 40-GE uplinks can be used toward the aggregation device. You must consider the end-to-end latency when choosing the design. Figure 1-7 depicts the different topologies possible for an HPC cluster, divided into 10-GE fabric and 40-GE fabric. These are nonblocking fabrics with end-to-end, nonoversubscribed 10-GE or 40-GE speeds. It is possible and a good practice to aggregate 10-GE server access connections with 40-GE spine switches.

Figure 1-7 depicts an example of an HPC cluster with 160 server nodes where an over-subscription ratio of 2:1 is used.

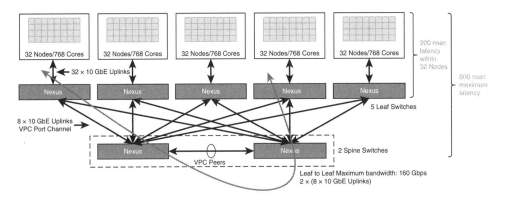

Figure 1-7   *Example of an HPC Cluster of 160 Nodes with a 2:1 Oversubscription Ratio*

Ultra-Low Latency

This section explains in detail the ultra-low latency data center trend.

Definition

Ultra-low latency (ULL) data center design is the race to zero. In these data centers, the goal is to design the fastest possible Ethernet-based network with the lowest possible end-to-end latency.

Port density is reduced to the minimum and the applications are clustered to decrease the number of network devices for each environment to the strict minimum. Most of the typical ULL designs are under the 500 server port count for the whole ULL data center. In the high-frequency trading (HFT) environment, which is the most representative of the ULL data center trend, typically 24 to a maximum of 48 ports per rack are used. The data center is collocated at an exchange data center facility to reduce the latency of the information coming from the exchange itself to the HFT firm.

In HFT data centers, it is imperative to provide the information from the stock exchanges as quickly as possible, with minimum delay. Being able to build the fastest possible network allows the HFT companies to offer a more competitive solution to their clients; therefore, the main criteria for HFT customers to adopt one firm versus another is the latency of their data center.

HFT data center designs are very different from the other designs. For example, there is no virtualization in this environment, and NICs with kernel bypass technologies are used to reduce at maximum the latency on the server-processing side and avoid the CPU delays. On the network side, CX-1 (twinax) cables are preferred over optical fiber up to 5 meters. The design is often nonblocking and provides end-to-end 10-GE to 40-GE speeds. The congestion and queuing impacts on the data center switch are reduced as much as possible. To reduce the need for buffering, factors such as speed mismatch or the many-to-one conversation on the network devices are reduced by dividing the applications across different servers. The traffic patterns east to west and north to south are therefore separated in the network and very often even on different data center topologies. This removes the need for QoS on the network side. In an ULL environment, everything is designed to avoid the need for QoS.

The latency now is relatively close to zero, with performances of IP/Ethernet switching as low as 50 ns, which is the serialization delay of the smallest possible frame on the wire: 64 bytes at 10-GE speed, and the main efforts to reduce the data center switching equipment latency have reached maturity. This moves the paradigm to look now into NICs, servers, flash storage, and, foremost, application optimization.

Figure 1-8 illustrates the order of magnitude of latency for different components on the network side and also for middleware and applications. It is not an exhaustive list, but rather an overview to understand the level of latency.

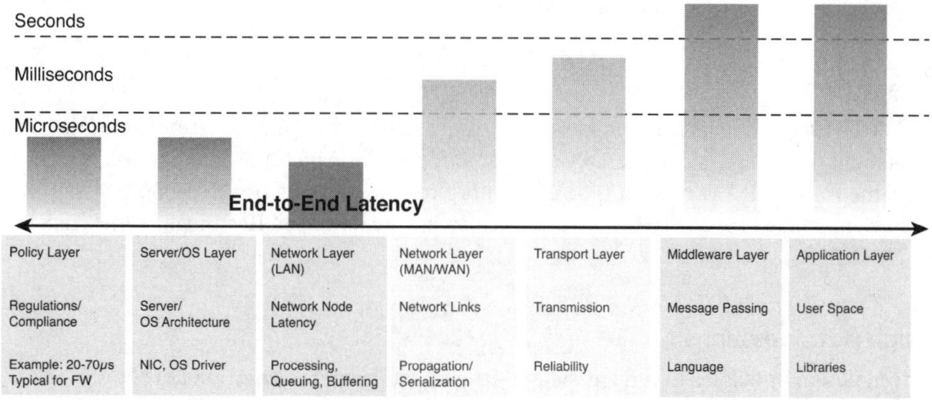

Seconds							
Milliseconds							
Microseconds							

End-to-End Latency

Policy Layer	Server/OS Layer	Network Layer (LAN)	Network Layer (MAN/WAN)	Transport Layer	Middleware Layer	Application Layer
Regulations/ Compliance	Server/ OS Architecture	Network Node Latency	Network Links	Transmission	Message Passing	User Space
Example: 20-70μs Typical for FW	NIC, OS Driver	Processing, Queuing, Buffering	Propagation/ Serialization	Reliability	Language	Libraries

Figure 1-8 *Latency Order of Magnitude*

Network Requirements

For ultra-low latency, the network requirements are as follows:

- Fastest possible network with the bare minimum feature set providing the best possible performance. Line-rate equipment (nonblocking switching) is preferred when available.

- Uniform speed in the end design; no speed mismatch (for example, 1 GE–10-GE). Most commonly the speed is end-to-end 10-GE for the network equipment all the way to the server port. There is a trend for higher speed, which can be adopted as the switch latency reduces with 40-GE/100-GE and 40-GE/100-GE NICs becoming more common in the industry.

- No queuing, no QoS.

- Layer 3–capable data center switching devices, Layer 3 data center fabrics.

- Multicast at Layer 2 and Layer 3.

- Network Address Translation (NAT).

- Traffic replication as fast as possible.

- Analytics and scripting.

This latency reduction also develops a new area for the data center architect: the analytics. Because it's not possible to improve what cannot be measured, and a short congestion event of even 1.5 Mb creates a delay of 1 ms of network latency, which is already 1 million times more than the switch latency during noncongestion, monitoring is becoming a requirement. Production environments running at such ultra-low latency need to be monitored. When an application issue presents itself, the data center operation team must examine the network and determine if this issue occurred in the network environment (switch buffering, for example). This is why the network monitoring and application-centric view become very important.

Storage Requirements

In HFT environments the storage is local to the hosts, following a distributed model. The amount of storage is considerably small and, for performance reasons, stays on the host in the form of RAM or flash type of memory for the duration of the data process. The backup storage for the HFT network can also use a centralized IP storage model such as NFS/CIFS.

Design Considerations

Ten design principles to reduce the end-to-end data center latency are as follows:

- **Speed:** The faster the network, the lower the serialization delay and latency.

- **Physical media type:** Copper twinax cables are faster today than fiber optic, and microwave can be a faster media than fiber for interconnects for certain speeds and distances; for example, interconnecting Chicago and NYC with microwave saves a considerable latency compared to the traditional dark fiber between the two cities, because dark fiber is not in line of sight and therefore takes a longer distance between the two cities.

- **Switching mode:** Cut-through switching provides a predictable performance across packet size, versus store-and-forward switching.

- **Buffer amount in the network:** What is the right buffer amount to provide high performance? Buffer bloat affects data center latency numbers. Large, throughput-sensitive TCP flows build up queue depth and cause delays for smaller, latency-sensitive flows.

- **Feature set used on the network equipment:** This has a direct impact on the end-to-end latency. For example, protocols such as CDP, STP, and LLDP contribute up to 2.5 times more latency than when they are not used.

- **Rack-mount servers:** These are lower latency than blades, and the nonvirtualized OS also saves latency.

- **The CPU/memory choice:** This does matter in the server because it dictates the performance of the compute.

- **Network adapter card and protocol used:** This has impact that can lower latency by up to four times (from 20 usec to 5 usec).

- **Visibility and analytics:** These are key in understanding the effects of latency. Precision Time Protocol (PTP), IEEE 1588 v2, helps provide a precise clock across networking and compute devices to gain insight.

- **Security:** Security measures increase latency considerably, to a level at which the solution is far from being ultra-low latency or even low latency. There are ways to get around this in the network.

Design Topologies

The two main design topologies that are covered in this section are feed replication and HFT.

Feed Replication

Feed replication provides the fastest possible replication of market data information destined to different servers handling the market data, called *feed handlers*. With the Cisco Nexus 3548, it is possible to deliver north-to-south traffic replication at 50 ns. The feed handlers therefore receive the traffic from the exchange feed with a network-added latency of only 50 ns. The return traffic, south to north, which is used for order transactions, is achieved at 190 ns. In such a design, the goal is to minimize as much as possible the number of switches, cable length, and so forth between the exchange feeds and the feed handler servers. Figure 1-9 depicts a feed replication design example with Nexus 3548 where the switch latency can be as low as 50 ns for north-to-south traffic coming from the exchange feeds. With the Cisco Nexus 9000 standalone Top of Rack switches, the performance would be around 0.600 us; with the ACI switches, it would be in the range of 1 us.

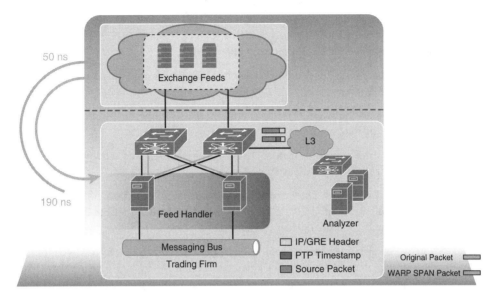

Figure 1-9   *Feed Replication Design Example*

HFT Example

In HFT topologies, the typical design is a one- or two-tier network infrastructure. This is also referred to as a *spine/leaf* type of design, where the spine plays the role of an aggregation device. The goal of the design topology is to provide the necessary port count at a given service NIC speed. Most common are 10-GE designs from the access to the network. 40-GE uplinks can be used toward the aggregation device. Consider the end-to-end latency when choosing your design. Figure 1-10 depicts the different topologies possible for an HFT cluster, divided in 10-GE fabric and 40-GE fabric. These are nonblocking fabrics with end-to-end, nonoversubscribed 10-GE or 40-GE speeds. It is possible and a good practice to aggregate 10-GE server access connections with 40-GE spine switches. However, there is a speed change introduced that creates an in-cast buffering scenario, which increases burst impact on the network. Therefore, this type of design should be considered only when it provides the fastest end-to-end latency. Currently the fastest solution is with the Nexus 3548 two-tier 10-GE fabric design.

Figure 1-10 has design topologies for HFT; first with up to 12 servers and second with up to 48 servers at 10-GE, nonblocking, with two NICs in each.

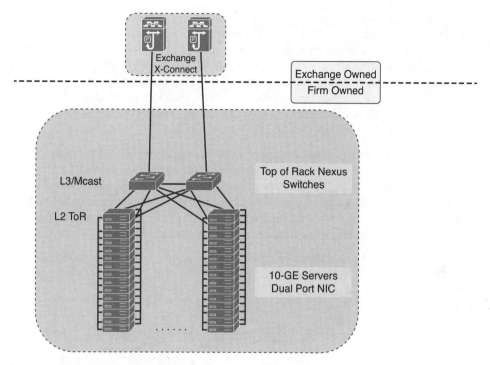

Figure 1-10 *HFT Colocation Design*

Massively Scalable Data Center

This section explains in detail the MSDC data center trend.

Definition

Massively scalable data center (MSDC) is not an industry-standard term, but rather a name used by Cisco to cover this data center type. The MSDC system is a reference architecture based on a Clos fabric (topology) built using Cisco platforms. The MSDC system targets very large data centers that have hundreds of thousands of servers with 10-GE interfaces connected to a network with Layer-3 adjacencies in a nonblocking fashion. It is even possible to have routing protocols peering into the network equipment from the host machine itself, in order to provide the capability to arbitrate and optimize the path selection from the host. Typically this type of data center is found in the field of web search engines, social networks, and cloud-hosting devices that have structured and unstructured data schemes.

The MSDC architecture is driven by two key application segments: content serving and big data analytics.

Content delivery applications include Akamai's Technologies and Limelight Networks' content delivery network (CDN), Apple's iTunes, YouTube's video, Facebook photos, and so forth. The scalability challenge in serving media to millions of users over tens of thousands of devices necessitates the use of tools and techniques that normally are not available off-the-shelf. Service providers build these clusters or grids in house. Today these home-grown infrastructures serve as differentiators for these service providers. Some of them, such as LinkedIn, Facebook, and Google, have open sourced the infrastructure to seed an ecosystem.

Big data analytics is a new application that has taken parallel storage and processing to analyze large data warehouses with unstructured (no metadata) data. There are multiple frameworks to process big data. However, open source Hadoop is now seen as a clear winner. In a social application these technologies are used to generate customized web pages for the visitors to a website. The back-end analytics to populate various sections of the page are accomplished using Hadoop or a related parallel processing infrastructure.

Figure 1-11 shows the workflow of a typical social application web infrastructure solution.

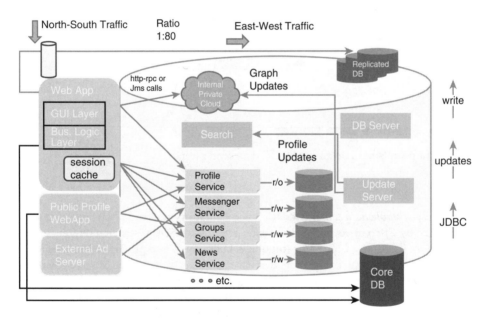

Figure 1-11 *Typical Social Network Application*

The MSDC customer system characteristics are summarized in Table 1-1.

Table 1-1 *Characteristics of MSDC Customer-Designed Systems*

MSDC System Characteristic	Description
Multiroot, multipath network topology	The traditional network architecture optimized for traffic in/out of a data center does not suffice for these data centers. The majority of the traffic in these data centers is among the servers. To optimize on this east-to-west traffic (bi-sectional bandwidth), the customer adopts topologies that previously were used only in the HPC market segment. For instance, a web search customer uses a flattened butterfly topology in its search engine application that has approximately 20,000 servers.
Distributed computing on scale-out compute cluster	These customers exploit the parallelism in the application to improve on latency and throughput. Cluster-based computing is the standard with distributed application components.
Parallel and distributed database with NoSQL, sharding, and caching	The databases that provide persistence to these applications are so large that they cannot be bottlenecked with serial queries and SQL semantics. The data is stored in Bigtables or sharded across many nodes, then retrieved using parallel frameworks such as MapReduce or cached in distributed caching stores such as memcached.
In-memory computing	To fulfill the large number of requests that arrive at these data centers for the same data set, the customers have deployed in-memory databases and caches to improve on the latency of a page view.
Power cost conservation	The data center operations budget allocates sufficient funds to power to enable these customers to seek, fund, and deploy innovations that can reduce the power/thermal/carbon footprint of the data center.

Network Requirements

The following three main requirements drive the networking in the data center to adapt to the MSDC systems:

- **Scale exceeds the current limits:** The industry is in the midst of a fundamental transition toward consolidation of application delivery via concentrated and dense computing data centers. The sites are designed on a scale that far exceeds the published configuration limits of today's data center networking equipment and protocols.

- **Change in traffic flow direction:** Data center applications have changed the dominant direction of network traffic from north–south (in/out of data center) to east–west (among servers in a cluster). The new pattern requires a scale-out architecture for the network akin to scale-out architecture in compute/storage infrastructure.

- **Scale-out with multirooted topology with fewer tiers:** MSDC is among the few scale-out architectures that have found traction in industry. The key feature of this architecture is a distributed core architecture using a multistage Clos topology that uses Layer 3 protocols as the control plane. Clos topology is also known as nonblocking topology, or fat-tree topology.

For MSDC systems, the network requirements are summarized as follow:

- Scale (size of the nonblocking network)

- Port density

- Bandwidth

- 1 GE, mainly 10-GE to the leaf switch and higher speed from the leaf to the spine

- Variable oversubscription, capability to adapt the oversubscription over time

- IP transport: TCP/UDP

- Layer 3 fabric down to the host (mainly OSPF and/or BGP; EIGRP can be found)

- IPv6

Research and development in the area of more advanced congestion control, transport mechanisms, and advanced load-balancing algorithms (PFC, DCTCP, etc.) is active. However, the most common features are the host-based Equal Cost Multipath (ECMP) for uplink forwarding path selection and simple drop-and-tail queuing.

Storage Requirements

MSDC storage is typically distributed and hosted directly on the servers. In some cases it is hosted on a dedicated storage facility.

Design Considerations

The key design considerations for the MSDC type of data center include the following:

- Spine and leaf topologies

- Layer 3 control plane

- Open hardware and open software

- Multi-tenancy includes tenant based and application based

Design Topologies

Figure 1-12 shows an MSDC system that uses a three-stage Clos topology and can scale to connect up to 12,288 node ports with 1:1 oversubscribed *or* 36,864 node ports with 3:1 oversubscription. All hosts are physical nodes with 10-GE interfaces. It also supports up to 122,880 (1:1) and 368,640 (3:1) physical nodes using 1-Gbps links in a Layer 3 adjacent manner. The system does not rely on Spanning Tree Protocol for resiliency. Instead, it manages multiple paths using ECMP, which runs as a function of the routing protocol on the leaf switches. The network provides for a Layer 3 lookup that is available at every hop (beginning at the leaf). The network has border gateways or border leafs that provide 10-Gbps throughput to the public Internet or a DCI link.

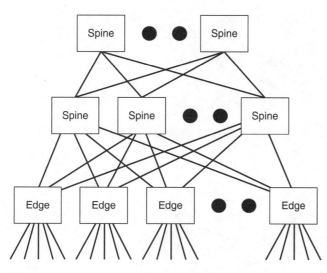

Figure 1-12   *MSDC Design Topology*

Design Topologies Examples

The virtualized data center, big data, HPC, ULL, and MSDC (spine-leaf) design topologies can be achieved with Cisco ACI or standalone Cisco Nexus 9000 switches. Three examples are summarized in Figure 1-13 for a CLOS nonblocking architecture, where each 10G host facing port can send line rate traffic. This design example is based on a choice of the Cisco Nexus 9396 leaf switch and the Cisco Nexus 9336, 9508, and 9516 spine switches, each with 36x40GE spine linecard. The example is given with N spines; the goal here is to show an example of a small/medium to large scale. The calculation is based on the number of spines, N, the number of ports in a spine, or spine card: 36x40GE ports and the leaf having 12x40GE uplinks for 48x10GE ports down. There is an immediate correlation between the type of spine and the potential number of nonblocking leaf ports depicted in the formula displayed in Figure 1-13. The interconnect between spine and leaf here uses a 40-GE speed. It is expected to have 40-GE at the leaf port facing level and 100-GE in the spine leaf interconnect in the future. The same methodology would apply for the design, the port densities would be then subject to change.

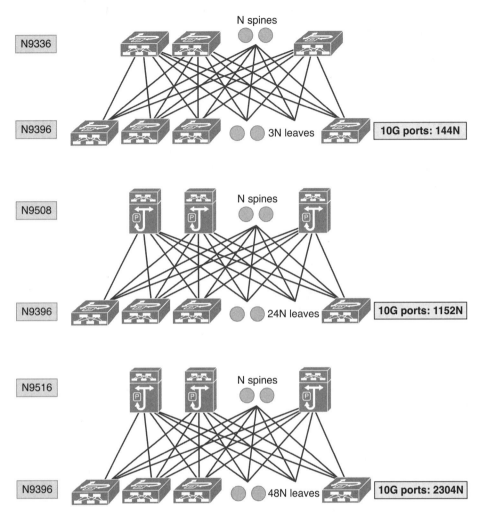

Figure 1-13   *ACI Fabric/N9K CLOS Fabric Examples with 40-GE Interconnect*

The POD-based Designs

This section explains the concept of the POD and looks specifically at the FlexPod architecture from Cisco and NetApp.

The POD Model or the Data Model for Shared Infrastructure and Cloud Computing

The way in which data is consumed has evolved and is dynamic. Today, data center projects have a fixed budget and specific scope and requirements. Once the design is finalized, the requirements translate into a network topology, the number of switches, and so forth. Most projects have a goal of not only meeting initial requirements but also including the capacity to expand in the future as needed, with the same site or a different physical location. The current industry trends indicate a vast data center transformation toward shared infrastructure and cloud computing. Therefore, the way of consuming information in the data center is a "pay as you grow model," where the compute, storage, and network components have the potential to be added over time.

Understanding that the requirements and data center plans may change over time, Cisco designed the Cisco Nexus Series switches to allow incremental growth along with migration—coexistence of different generations of data center fabrics such as the Cisco Nexus 7000, 6000-5000, 2000 series three-tier design, the latest Cisco Nexus 9000 Standalone or with Application Centric Infrastructure software. An alternative to manually using all the Cisco Nexus network equipment is to make a design to support this consumption model; there is the all-in-one solution with compute, storage, and network. There are different types of all-in-one, pay-as-you-grow solutions, such as for example FlexPod and Vblock. The goal is to provide a model that allows incremental growth by repeating the same block model or "POD" and extending this toward the data center. By introducing such standardization, the POD helps customers mitigate the risk and uncertainty involved in planning, designing, implementing, and automating the expansion of a data center or a new data center infrastructure. This results in a more predictive and adaptable architecture with the capacity to meet future growth.

A key difference between the FlexPod model and Vblock model is the storage: FlexPod uses NetApp storage, whereas Vblock uses EMC storage. Both solutions use Cisco UCS for the compute and the Cisco Nexus series switches for the network. When choosing a model, it is critical to understand the number of VMs required and the applications to be used in the data center, as these factors will dictate solutions that are either storage intensive or CPU intensive. For example, Oracle Database is storage intensive, whereas Big Data is CPU intensive. In the storage selection, a key technical decision is the type of storage to use for the application: centralized shared storage or distributed local storage on the hosts? Fibre Channel type of storage or IP-based storage? It is possible to have different applications and types of PODs for each purpose running in the same data center fabric.

This POD model addresses the following design principles and architecture goals:

- **Application availability:** Ensures that the services are accessible and ready to use
- **Scalability:** Addresses increasing demands with appropriate resources
- **Flexibility:** Provides new services or recovers resources without infrastructure modification requirements
- **Manageability:** Facilitates efficient infrastructure operations through open standards and APIs
- **Performance:** Assures that the required application or network performance is met
- **Comprehensive security:** Facilitates different organizations to have their own specific policies and security models

With FlexPod, Vblock, and Hitachi, the solution architecture and its many use cases have been thoroughly validated and verified while creating a portfolio of detailed documentation, information, and references to assist customers in transforming their data centers to this shared infrastructure model. This portfolio includes, but is not limited to, the following items:

- Best practice architectural design

- Workload sizing and scaling guidance

- Implementation and deployment instructions

- Technical specifications (rules for what is, and what is not, a FlexPod configuration)

- Frequently asked questions (FAQs)

- Cisco Validated Designs (CVDs) and NetApp Validated Architectures (NVAs) focused on a variety of use cases

The FlexPod Design

FlexPod is a best-practice data center architecture that includes three components:

- Cisco Unified Computing System (Cisco UCS)

- Cisco Nexus switches

- NetApp Fabric-Attached Storage (FAS) systems

These components are connected and configured according to best practices of both Cisco and NetApp. FlexPod can scale up for greater performance and capacity (adding compute, network, or storage resources individually as needed), or it can scale out for environments that need multiple consistent deployments (rolling out additional FlexPod stacks). This model delivers a baseline configuration and also has the flexibility to be sized and optimized to accommodate many different use cases.

Typically, the more scalable and flexible a solution is, the more difficult it becomes to maintain a single unified architecture capable of offering the same features and functionalities across each implementation. This is one of the key benefits of FlexPod. Each of the component families offers platform and resource options to scale the infrastructure up or down, while supporting the same features and functionalities that are required under the configuration and connectivity best practices of FlexPod.

The POD approach enables a data center project to grow on demand, keeping the same initial architecture with compute, network, and storage, and add more scale as the project needs to expand.

Data Center Designs

Designing a data center network infrastructure consists of defining how the switches are interconnected and how data communication is assured in the network. There is the three-tier approach, access, aggregation, and core, where Cisco vPC is the most commonly deployed technology in the data centers. There is also the newly emerging two-tier fabric method called *spine-leaf*. Both approaches are discussed in the "Logical Data Center Design with the Spine-Leaf ACI Foundation Architecture" section later in the chapter.

There are three fundamental approaches to physical data center design: end of row (EoR), middle of row (MoR), and top of rack (ToR). The naming convention represents the placement of the network switches in the data center row.

These deployment models are selected depending on the data center project requirements:

- Failure domain size
- Power available for the racks and the data center
- Number of servers per rack
- Number of NICs per server
- NIC speed
- Cabling constraints
- Operational constraints
- Switch form factors available on the market
- Budget available
- Oversubscription ratio

This list is not meant to be exhaustive but rather is intended to explain the concept behind the final decision of mainly middle-of-row or top-of-rack approaches. Currently, the trend is to design data centers with the ToR approach. This doesn't mean that ToR is the only design approach to follow, as the requirements differ for data centers, but it is the most common current deployment.

End of Row

EoR is the classical data center model, with the switches located at the end of the row of the data center. There is cabling from each rack running to the end-of-row network equipment, as depicted in Figure 1-14. The EoR model reduces the number of network devices to manage and optimizes the port utilization of the network. With this model, the server placement decisions are less constrained in the racks. For a redundant design, it is possible to have two bundles of copper to each rack, both running to opposite EoR network infrastructure. The drawback of this model is the necessity of large preinstalled cabling running horizontally on each row and from each end of row either on aerial trays or under the floor. Additionally, it creates a significant network failure domain for each row. This is even further impacted when the servers are virtualized and each runs tens to hundreds of VMs. These drawbacks discourage the EoR model in modern data centers, where racks are deployed in various fashions and the speed and cabling requirements may change from one rack to another, which requires recabling. The EoR model is well suited for highly available chassis switches, where the server access ports are in fact connected to the modular chassis switches.

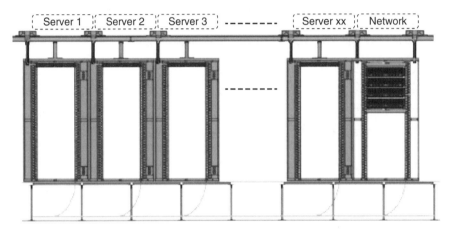

Figure 1-14   *EoR Connection Model*

Middle of Row

MoR is a variant of the EoR model. The MoR model defines an architecture in which servers are connected to the switches that are located in the middle of the row. The MoR model reduces the need for longer cables from one extremity of the row to the other end, because with MoR the network is located in the middle. MoR reduces cable cost not only by the length but also by the type of cable. CX-1 twinax cables 7 m to 10 m long can be used to interconnect devices to the MoR network equipment, instead of longer fiber runs with patch panel.

Top of Rack: The Modern Data Center Approach

As previously mentioned, the ToR approach is currently the most common. It is better suited for the pod design and contains a failure domain. The ToR model defines an architecture in which servers are connected to switches that are located within the same racks. These switches are connected to aggregation switches, typically using horizontal fiber-optic cabling. This model offers a clear access-layer migration path to an optimized high-bandwidth network and cabling facilities architecture that enables low capital and operating expenses. It also supports a pay-as-you-grow computer deployment model, which increases business agility. The data center's access layer presents the biggest challenge to architects because they need to choose the cabling architecture to support the data center computer connectivity needs.

The ToR network architecture and cabling model suggest the use of fiber as the backbone cabling to the rack, with mainly copper or fiber media for server connectivity at the rack level. The use of fiber from each rack also helps protect infrastructure investments as evolving standards, including 40-GE and 100-GE, are more likely to be implemented using fiber before any other transmission mechanism. For example, 40-GE is now capable of running on existing multimode 10-GE fiber cable infrastructure with the Cisco QSFP BiDi optics as transceivers. By limiting the use of copper within racks, the ToR model isolates the cabling that changes most often to the parts of the data center that are modified most frequently: the racks themselves. The use of fiber runs from racks provides a flexible data center cabling infrastructure that supports the transition from Gigabit Ethernet to 10-GE and 40-GE now, while enabling transition to 100-GE and higher in the future. The main drawback with the ToR approach is the number of switches to manage. This is not an issue with the Cisco Nexus 2000 approach, which centralizes the management. Furthermore, with the Cisco ACI fabric, this is even less of a concern, as all the fabric is application defined and controlled. ACI fabric is extensively covered in this book.

With the ToR approach, the leaf, spine, or aggregation can still be connected at the EoR (see Figure 1-15) or MoR (see Figure 1-16) while drastically reducing the amount of cabling and providing a scalable pay-as-you-grow model at the rack level.

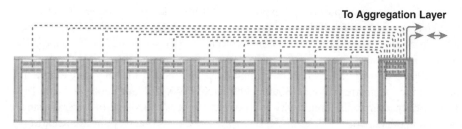

Figure 1-15 *ToR Deployment with EoR Aggregation/Spine/Leaf*

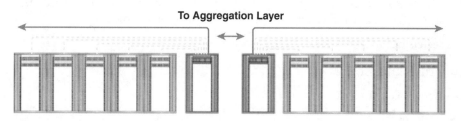

Figure 1-16 *ToR Deployment with MoR Aggregation/Spine/Leaf*

A typical oversubscription ratio is 5:1 between the servers and the uplink bandwidth on the ToR. This motivates the initial 48-port-based nonblocking switches for ToR, where 40 ports are server facing and 8 ports are used for uplinks. Depending on deployment requirements, nonblocking ToR design or high oversubscription design can be achieved. For example, an HFT environment requires a nonblocking and nonoversubscribed network, whereas a highly dense virtualized environment or virtual desktop demands a higher ratio. Depending on whether or not the environment is virtualized, dual-homed or single-homed servers are utilized with either 1-GE, 10-GE, or 40-GE NIC cards. The same principles apply whenever 100-GE or higher-speed NICs become available.

The rack sizes are evolving from the standard 42 rack units (RU) and 19-inch wide slot to denser and taller models. There are many options in rack sizes, currently up to 23 inches wide with height options ranging from 44 RU to extra-tall customized rack designs with 57 RU. One RU represents 1.75 inches in height. In current designs, the size of 48 RU is becoming more common as it stretches the 42 RU size to a denser format, while still staying practical for transport trucks, doorway sizes, and so forth.

It is common to find 2 to 4 RU used for the management of out-of-band network, the patch panel, console cables, and so on. This leaves 4 to 6 RU for ToR switches, as it is a common requirement to be able to fit 40 RU of server density. The airflow for ToR switches is front-to-back. and there is no need to add spaces between the switches. They should be stacked on the servers. It is possible to reverse the airflow to back-to-front by replacing the fan trays and power supplies in the Cisco Nexus switches. A back-to-front airflow can be found in end-of-row type of designs.

Single-Homed Servers Design

A single ToR switch is typically deployed in a rack for single-homed servers. The ToR switch has switch ports for the servers as well as uplink ports going to the aggregation layer, which can be MoR, EoR, and so on. Typically, the ToR switches' ports all have the same functionality. There is no specific dedicated uplink port except for the Cisco Nexus 2000 product family, where the uplink ports are specific and only they can be connected to the upstream Nexus 5000, 5500, 6000, 7000, 7700, or 9000 products. The fabric technology or connectivity technology can be with Layer 2 or Layer 3, using upstream in the network vPC, VXLAN, IP, or the latest end-to-end application-centric infrastructure fabric ACI.

A pair of ToR switches is deployed in a rack for the dual-homed servers. In this scenario, for each NIC on a given server, the connectivity is to a different ToR switch.

The servers can operate in the following scenarios:

- Active/active Layer 2
- Active/active Layer 3
- Active/passive

The fabric or connectivity technology can have either Layer 2 and Layer 3 redundancy to the fabric with the ToR or Layer 2 redundancy with vPC technology. From the ToR upstream, the technologies used are similar to the single-homed server designs.

Logical Data Center Design with the Spine-Leaf ACI Foundation Architecture

Traditional networks have been built using a redundancy model with Spanning Tree Protocol. Later, leveraging vPC provided an active/active type of connectivity that enhanced by a factor of two the bandwidth available compared to an STP active/standby topology. The vPC design and topologies have been used most commonly in the data centers in the past five years, and are not covered in this section. The new trend of designing a data center is using a spine-and-leaf two-tier design, and this is the design the ACI fabric also relies on. This section explains the spine-leaf architecture and design and then covers the ACI spine-leaf benefits.

A data center network is typically physically collocated and under a single administrative domain. Unlike traditional enterprise networks, the majority of the traffic in a data center is east to west (between servers within the data center) rather than north to south (between the servers within the data center and the outside). The equipment in a data center tends to be homogenized (servers, networking gear, NIC, storage, and connectivity). In terms of server ports, data center networks range anywhere from 3000 ports to upward of 100,000 ports. They are also more cost sensitive, and not as feature rich as traditional enterprise networks. Finally, most of the applications in a data center are tailored to take advantage of these regular characteristics.

The spine-leaf data center architecture is designed to meet these requirements and consists of a topology, a set of open protocols, and a minimal set of functionality in each network node. The physical topology, in its simplest form, is based on a two-tier, "fat-tree" topology, also known as a *Clos* or *nonblocking* topology. This topology consists of a set of leaf edge devices connected to a set of spine devices in a full bipartite graph—that is, each leaf edge device is connected to each spine and vice versa, as shown in Figure 1-17.

This architecture has four fundamental characteristics:

- Fat-tree topology
- Fine-grained redundancy to get very high network availability
- Based on open, interoperable, standard technologies
- Relies on homogeneity, regularity, and simplicity for scaling management

The benefits of this architecture are

- Scalability
- Flexibility
- Reliability
- Availability today
- Open, interoperable components
- Low CAPEX and OPEX

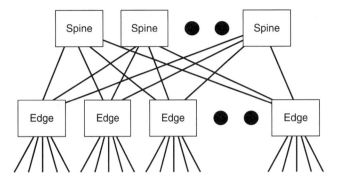

Figure 1-17   *Spine-Leaf Architecture*

Each node is a fully functional switch. For instance, each node can receive a standard network packet and forward it as you expect a typical switch or router to do. In addition, each node has a control plane associated with it that determines the forwarding state of that node.

This topology makes heavy use of multipathing to achieve the desired bandwidth between the nodes. The forwarding paradigm used with a spine-leaf architecture can be based on Layer 2 forwarding (bridging) or Layer 3 forwarding (routing) depending on the requirements of a particular customer. Each of these has real (and perceived) advantages and disadvantages. This section does not discuss the trade-offs. For instance, the ACI architecture relies on a routed host approach, or Layer 3 for the spine-leaf architecture.

The spine-leaf architecture provides the advantage of *fine-grained redundancy*, meaning many elements are working in parallel such that the failure of any one component or a small number of components does not have much effect on the total function of the network. If a switch fails, it is not critical to the network administrator. This is a subtle yet very powerful concept. The benefits of fine-grained redundancy are best illustrated with a comparative example. With the traditional data center network design that has two switches at the top of a tree, if you lose, for whatever reason, one of those switches, 50 percent of the capacity of the network becomes lost. The probability of losing that one switch is related to its reliability, and the typical reliability goal is five 9s, meaning that you have a 0.001 percent chance of losing 50 percent of your network capacity. Although this is a small chance, your customers would clearly like better.

Contrast this with a spine-leaf based network with 20 switches in the spine. To lose the same amount of bandwidth, 50 percent, you would have to lose ten switches simultaneously. It is obvious that this is very unlikely, but to put some concrete numbers on it, let's make an assumption and a simple calculation. Assume that for some reason you have very poor reliability in the switches, only two 9s; that is, the chance of a switch failing is 1%. The chance of ten of these miserable switches failing simultaneously is 0.01^{10} or 0.000000000000000001 percent. Not bad compared to the highly reliable switch's 0.00001 percent chance. The basic idea here is to design your network with the assumption that things will fail, rather than trying to make the components of your network flawless. No component is "too big to fail." For example, this approach should be taken by the MSDC customers to compute resources as well as for the infrastructure. It is much easier to convince someone that their network is designed to handle failure gracefully than it is to convince them that any single component's failure is so unlikely that they can sleep well at night.

The same arguments can be applied to operational aspects of the network. When the software of a switch must be upgraded, even when that switch supports Cisco In-Service Software Upgrade (ISSU), there is usually a significant concern about the impact of that upgrade on the network service. With fine-grained redundancy, the administrator simply takes the switch out of service, upgrades it, reboots it, or does whatever else is necessary without a concern for the impact on the overall network service. With the spine-leaf architecture, high availability is handled by the whole fabric, without the need to have a single device to support ISSU to prevent application disruption.

And finally, the latency characteristics are very low and constant port to port. Many MSDC customers desire consistent any-port to any-port latency, assuming zero queuing delay. The maximum latency of a packet going from one port to any other port in the spine-leaf architecture is the same regardless of the network size. That latency is twice the latency of the edge device plus the latency of the spine. As the industry and Cisco develop new switches that are more and more latency optimized, the spine-leaf architecture will seamlessly take advantage of those advancements. As it is, it is easy to see a way to achieve a maximum of 1.5 microseconds of latency for 100,000 nonblocking ports of 10-GE using switches currently under development at Cisco. Thus, this network can even meet low-latency network requirements. Similar considerations apply to buffering and forwarding table size. These are functions of the implementation of the switches used. If larger buffers are needed, then use switches with bigger buffers. The same goes for table sizes. This freedom to design each network element according to the particular trade-offs and market considerations that a development group may have is a nice flexibility of the spine-leaf architecture. Very large scale, fixed per-port cost, and low, consistent latency are all compelling characteristics of the spine-leaf architecture.

The ACI architecture relies on the spine-leaf model described in this section. The ACI fabric also leverages a central point of management while keeping an independent device distributed control plane. This allows the fabric to provide a single switch type of operation while having all the benefits of the spine-leaf architecture.

Summary

In the data center network design process, there are key considerations for the architecture choice and final design:

- The applications to be hosted in the data center along with the type of storage the applications use

- The data center needs and constraints, including the pod model design

- The different types of data center designs

The trend is toward the spine-leaf architecture, which addresses the considerations and data center requirements. The ACI fabric relies on the spine-leaf architecture and ToR approach depicted in this chapter. This fabric approach is suitable for all trends of application and storage types of design, providing a degree of flexibility in the data center design, where one technology can be used for different application and storage use cases.

Table 1-2 summarizes the five different application trends and the fabric choices. The new spine-leaf ACI architecture is suitable for all use cases, and the benefits of ACI are described in the chapters that follow.

Table 1-2   *Summary of the Five Different Application Trends and the Network Choices for Each*

Application Category	Storage	Fabric	Fabric Technologies	Port Count	Oversubscription Ratio
ULL	Distributed IP	L2, L3	ACI, vPC, Routing	<100	1:1
Big Data	Distributed IP	L2, L3	ACI, vPC, VXLAN Routing	<100 to 2000	High
HPC	Distributed non-IP	L2	ACI, vPC, FabricPath	<100 to 1000	2:1 to 5:1
MSDC	Distributed IP	L3	ACI, Routing, OTV	1000 to 10,000	High
Virtual DC	Centralized FC or IP Distributed IP for smaller size	L2, L3	ACI,vPC, VXLAN, Routing, OTV	<100 to 10,000	High

Note: Figure 1-1 and Figure 1-2 are courtesy of Cisco Press publication: 'Cloud Computing: Automating the Virtualized Data Center'

Chapter 2

Building Blocks for Cloud Architectures

At the time of this writing, most large-scale data center deployments are designed with the principles of cloud computing at the forefront. This is equally true for data centers that are built by providers or by large enterprises. This chapter illustrates the design and technology requirements for building a cloud.

Introduction to Cloud Architectures

The National Institute of Technology and Standards (NIST) defines cloud computing as "a model for enabling convenient, on-demand network access to a shared pool of configurable computing resources (e.g., networks, servers, storage, applications, and services) that can be rapidly provisioned and released with minimal management effort or service provider interaction." (See http://csrc.nist.gov/groups/SNS/cloud-computing.)

Data center resources, such as individual servers or applications, are offered as *elastic* services, which means that capacity is added on demand, and when the compute or application is not needed, the resources providing it can be decommissioned. Amazon Web Services (AWS) is often regarded as the pioneer of this concept and many similar services that exist today.

Cloud computing services are often classified according to two different categories:

- **Cloud delivery model:** Public cloud, private cloud, or hybrid cloud

- **Service delivery model:** Infrastructure as a Service, Platform as a Service, or Software as a Service

The cloud delivery model indicates where the compute is provisioned. The following terminology is often used:

- **Private cloud:** A service on the premises of an enterprise. A data center designed as a private cloud offers shared resources to internal users. A private cloud is shared by tenants, where each tenant is, for instance, a business unit.

- **Public cloud:** A service offered by a service provider or cloud provider such as Amazon, Rackspace, Google, or Microsoft. A public cloud is typically shared by multiple *tenants*, where each tenant is, for instance, an enterprise.

- **Hybrid cloud:** Offers some resources for workloads through a private cloud and other resources through a public cloud. The ability to move some compute to the public cloud is sometimes referred to as *cloud burst*.

The service delivery model indicates what the user employs from the cloud service:

- **Infrastructure as a Service (IaaS):** A user requests a dedicated machine (a virtual machine) on which they install applications, some storage, and networking infrastructure. Examples include Amazon AWS, VMware vCloud Express, and so on.

- **Platform as a Service (PaaS):** A user requests a database, web server environment, and so on. Examples include Google App Engine and Microsoft Azure.

- **Software as a Service (SaaS) or Application as a Service (AaaS):** A user runs applications such as Microsoft Office, Salesforce, or Cisco WebEx on the cloud instead of on their own premises.

The cloud model of consumption of IT services, and in particular for IaaS, is based on the concept that the user relies on a self-service portal to provide services from a catalog and the provisioning workflow is completely automated. This ensures that the user of the service doesn't need to wait for IT personnel to allocate VLANs, stitch load balancers or firewalls, and so on. The key benefit is that the fulfillment of the user's request is quasi-instantaneous.

Until recently, configurations were performed via the CLI to manipulate on a box-by-box basis. Now, ACI offers the ability to instantiate "virtual" networks of a very large scale with a very compact description using Extensible Markup Language (XML) or JavaScript Object Notation (JSON).

Tools such as Cisco UCS Director (UCSD) and Cisco Intelligent Automation for Cloud (CIAC) orchestrate the ACI services together with compute provisioning (such as via Cisco UCS Manager, VMware vCenter, or OpenStack) to provide a fast provisioning service for the entire infrastructure (which the industry terms a *virtual private cloud*, a *virtual data center*, or a *container*).

The components of the cloud infrastructure are represented at a very high level in Figure 2-1. The user (a) of the cloud service (b) orders a self-contained environment (c) represented by the container with firewall load balancing and virtual machines (VM). CIAC provides the service catalog function, while UCSD and OpenStack operate as the element managers.

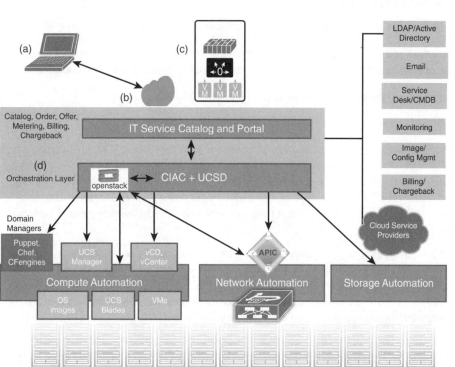

Figure 2-1 *Building Blocks of a Cloud Infrastructure*

This request is serviced by the service catalog and portal via the orchestration layer (d). The orchestration layer can be composed of several components. Cisco, for instance, offers CIAC, which interacts with various element managers to provision compute, network, and storage resources.

Figure 2-1 also explains where Application Centric Infrastructure (ACI) and, more precisely, the Cisco Application Policy Infrastructure Controller (APIC), fit in the cloud architecture.

Network Requirements of Clouds and the ACI Solution

The network infrastructure that provides support for cloud deployments must meet several requirements, such as:

- Scale for a very large number of virtual machines
- Support Layer 2 adjacency between workloads
- Support multi-tenancy

- Be highly programmable
- Support the insertion of load balancers and firewalls
- Support the insertion of virtual load balancers and virtual firewalls

The first and second requirements are almost incompatible because if the data center were built with traditional spanning-tree technologies, it would incur two problems:

- Spanning-tree scalability limits on the control plane
- Exhaustion of the MAC address tables

To address these requirements, the ACI fabric is built based on a VXLAN overlay, which allows switches to maintain perceived Layer 2 adjacency on top of a Layer 3 network, thus removing the control plane load associated with spanning tree from the switching infrastructure. To address the mobility requirements over a Layer 3 infrastructure, the forwarding is based on host-based forwarding of full /32 addresses combined with the mapping database.

This overlay, like most, requires the data path at the edge of the network to map from the tenant end point address in the packet, a.k.a. its *identifier*, to the location of the endpoint, a.k.a. its *locator*. This mapping occurs in a function called a *tunnel endpoint* (TEP). The challenge with this mapping is having to scale for very large data centers, because the mapping state must exist in many network devices.

The second problem with scale is that when an endpoint moves (that is, its locator changes), the mapping state must be updated across the network in all TEPs that have that mapping.

The ACI solution addresses these problems by using a combination of a centralized database of the mappings implemented in the packet data path, at line rate, and a caching mechanism, again in the data path, at the TEP. (Chapter 7, "ACI Fabric Design Methodology," explains the traffic forwarding in ACI in detail.)

The other key requirement of building a cloud solution is to be able to instantiate networks in a programmatic way. If the network is managed box by box, link by link, the script or the automation tool must access individual boxes and trace where a workload is in order to enable VLAN trunking on a number of links. It must also ensure that the end-to-end path is provisioned according to the abstraction model. ACI solves this issue by providing a centralized configuration point, the APIC controller, while still maintaining individual control plane capabilities on each node in the fabric. The controller exposes the entire network as a hierarchy of objects in a tree. It describes network properties related to workloads as logical properties instead of physical properties. So, to define connectivity requirements for workloads, you don't have to express which physical interface a particular workload is on.

Furthermore, the fabric exposes the networking properties of all the switches so that they can all be configured and managed via Representational State Transfer (REST) calls as a single giant switch/router. The APIC REST API accepts and returns HTTP or HTTPS messages that contain JSON or XML documents. Orchestration tools can easily program the network infrastructure by using REST calls. (Chapter 4, "Operational Model," illustrates this new model and how to automate configurations with REST calls and scripting.)

Multi-tenancy is conveyed in the management information model by expressing all configurations of bridge domains, VRF contexts, and application network profile as children of an object of type fvTenant. The segmentation on the network transport is guaranteed by the use of different VXLAN VNIDs.

Insertion of firewall and load balancers is also automated to simplify the creation of virtual containers comprising physical or virtual firewall and load balancing services. (Chapter 8, "Service Insertion with ACI," illustrates in more detail the modeling of services and how they are added to the fabric.)

Amazon Web Services Model

This section describes some of the services offered by Amazon Web Services and some of the AWS naming conventions. AWS offers a very wide variety of services, and the purpose of this section is not to describe all of them. Rather, this section is useful to the network administrator for two reasons:

- As a reference for a popular IaaS service

- The potential need to extend a private cloud into the Amazon Virtual Private Cloud

The following list provides some key AWS terminology:

- **Availability Zone:** A distinct location within a region that is insulated from failures in other Availability Zones, and provides inexpensive, low-latency network connectivity to other Availability Zones in the same region.

- **Region:** A collection of Availability Zones, such as us-west, us-east-1a, eu-west, etc., in the same geographical region

- **Access credentials:** A public key that is used to access AWS resources allocated to a given user

- **Amazon Machine Image (AMI):** The image of a given virtual machine (which Amazon calls an *instance*)

- **Instance:** A virtual machine that is running a given AMI image

- **Elastic IP address:** A static address associated with an instance

Amazon Elastic Compute Cloud (EC2) services enable you to launch an AMI in a region of the user's choice and in an Availability Zone of the user's choice. Instances are protected by a firewall. The instance also gets an IP address and a DNS entry. The EC2 services can also be accompanied by the Elastic Load Balancing, which distributes traffic across EC2 compute instances. Auto Scaling helps with provisioning enough EC2 instances based on the utilization. Amazon CloudWatch provides information about CPU load, disk I/O rate, and network I/O rate of each EC2 instance.

> **Note**   More information can be found at:
>
> http://docs.aws.amazon.com/general/latest/gr/glos-chap.html
>
> http://docs.aws.amazon.com/AmazonCloudWatch/latest/DeveloperGuide/Using_Query_API.html

Amazon Simple Storage Service (S3) is accessed via web services API based on SOAP or with the HTTP API that uses the standard HTTP verbs (GET, PUT, HEAD, and DELETE). The objects are identified by using the protocol name, the S3 endpoint (s3.amazonaws.com), the object key, and what is called the *bucket name*.

All resources can be created and manipulated by using Amazon SDKs available for various programming languages, such as the Python and PHP SDKs available at the following respective URLs:

> http://aws.amazon.com/sdk-for-python/
>
> http://aws.amazon.com/sdk-for-php/

With this approach, you can fully automate tasks such as the following:

- Locating the server resources
- Attaching storage
- Providing Internet connectivity
- Setting up switching and routing
- Booting the server
- Installing the OS
- Configuring applications
- Assigning IP addresses
- Configuring firewalling
- Scaling up the infrastructure

> **Note**   For more information, please refer to the book *Host Your Web Site in the Cloud: Amazon Web Services Made Easy*, by Jeff Barr (SitePoint, 2010).

You can access the AWS-hosted Amazon Virtual Private Cloud (VPC) in multiple ways. One way is to set a jumphost to which you log in over SSH with the public key that

AWS generates. Another approach is to connect the enterprise network to the Amazon VPC via VPNs.

Automating Server Provisioning

In large-scale cloud deployments with thousands of physical and virtual servers, administrators must be able to provision servers in a consistent and timely manner.

This section is of interest to the network administrator for several reasons:

- Some of these technologies can also be used to maintain network equipment designs.

- Cisco ACI reuses some of the concepts from these technologies that have proven to be effective to the task of maintaining network configurations.

- A complete design of ACI must include support for these technologies because the compute attached to ACI will use them.

The high-level approach to automating server provisioning consists of performing the following:

- PXE booting a server (physical or virtual)

- Deploying the OS or customized OS on the server with Puppet/Chef/CFEngine agents

Because of the above reasons, a typical setup for a cloud deployment requires the following components:

- A DHCP server

- A TFTP server

- An NFS/HTTP or FTP server to deliver the kickstart files

- A master for Puppet or Chef or similar tools

PXE Booting

In modern data centers, administrators rarely install new software via removable media such as DVDs. Instead, administrators rely on PXE (Preboot eXecution Environment) booting to image servers.

The booting process occurs in the following sequence:

1. The host boots up and sends a DHCP request.

2. The DHCP server provides the IP address and the location of the PXE/TFTP server.

3. The host sends a TFTP request for pxelinux.0 to the TFTP server.

4. The TFTP server provides pxelinux.0.

5. The host runs the PXE code and requests the kernel (vmlinuz).

6. The TFTP server provides vmlinuz code and provides the location of the kickstart configuration files (NFS/HTTP/FTP and so on).

7. The host requests the kickstart configuration from the server.

8. The HTTP/NFS/FTP server provides the kickstart configuration.

9. The host requests to install packages such as the RPMs.

10. The HTTP/NFS/FTP server provides the RPMs.

11. The host runs Anaconda, which is the post-installation scripts.

12. The HTTP/NFS/FTP server provides the scripts and the Puppet/Chef installation information.

Deploying the OS with Chef, Puppet, CFengine, or Similar Tools

One of the important tasks that administrators have to deal with in large-scale data centers is maintaining up-to-date compute nodes with the necessary level of patches, the latest packages, and with the intended services enabled.

You can maintain configurations by creating VM templates or a golden image and instantiating many of them, but this process produces a monolithic image, and replicating this process every time a change is required is a lengthy task. It is also difficult, if not impossible, to propagate updates to the configuration or libraries to all the servers generated from the template. The better approach consists of using a tool such as Chef, Puppet, or CFengine. With these tools, you create a bare-bones golden image or VM template and you push servers day-2.

These tools offer the capability to define the node end state with a language that is abstracted from the underlying OS. For instance, you don't need to know whether to install a package with "yum" or "apt"; simply define that a given package is needed. You don't have to use different commands on different machines to set up users, packages, services, and so on.

If you need to create a web server configuration, define it with a high-level language. Then, the tool creates the necessary directories, installs the required packages, and starts the processes listening on the ports specified by the end user.

Some of the key characteristics of these tools are that they are based on principles such as a "declarative" model (in that they define the desired end state) and idempotent configurations (in that you can rerun the same configuration multiple times and it always yields the same result). The policy model relies on the declarative approach. (You can find more details about the declarative model in Chapter 3, "The Policy Data Center.")

With these automation tools, you can also simulate the result of a given operation before it is actually executed, implement the change, and prevent configuration drifting.

Chef

The following list provides a reference for some key terminology used by Chef:

- **Node:** The server (but could be a network device).

- **Attributes:** The configuration of a node.

- **Resources:** Packages, services, files, users, software, networks, and routes.

- **Recipe:** The intended end state of a collection of resources. It is defined in Ruby.

- **Cookbook:** The collection of recipes, files, and so on for a particular configuration need. A cookbook is based on a particular application deployment and defines all the components necessary for that application deployment.

- **Templates:** Configuration files or fragments with embedded Ruby code (.erb) that is resolved at run time.

- **Run list:** The list of recipes that a particular node should run.

- **Knife:** The command line for Chef.

- **Chef client:** The agent that runs on a node.

Normally the administrator performs configurations from "Knife" from a Chef workstation, which has a local repository of the configurations. The cookbooks are saved on the Chef server, which pushes them to the nodes, as shown in Figure 2-2.

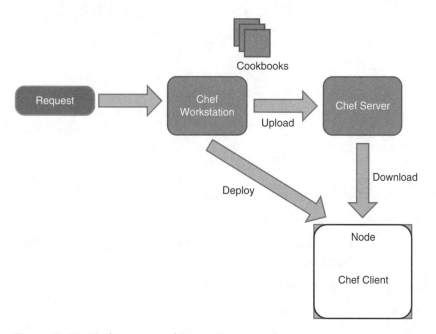

Figure 2-2 *Chef Process and Interactions*

The recipe that is relevant to the action to be performed on the device is configured on the Chef workstation and uploaded to the Chef server.

Puppet

Figure 2-3 illustrates how Puppet operates. With the Puppet language, you define the desired state of resources (users, packages, services, and so on), simulate the deployment of the desired end state as defined in the manifest file, and then apply the manifest file to the infrastructure. Finally, it is possible to track the components deployed, track the changes, and correct configurations from drifting from the intended state.

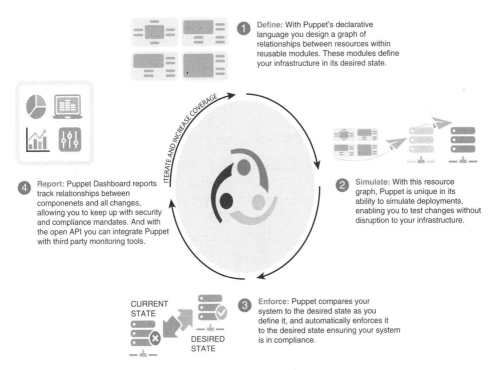

1 Define: With Puppet's declarative language you design a graph of relationships between resources within reusable modules. These modules define your infrastructure in its desired state.

4 Report: Puppet Dashboard reports track relationships between componenets and all changes, allowing you to keep up with security and compliance mandates. And with the open API you can integrate Puppet with third party monitoring tools.

2 Simulate: With this resource graph, Puppet is unique in its ability to simulate deployments, enabling you to test changes without disruption to your infrastructure.

3 Enforce: Puppet compares your system to the desired state as you define it, and automatically enforces it to the desired state ensuring your system is in compliance.

ITERATE AND INCREASE COVERAGE

CURRENT STATE

DESIRED STATE

Figure 2-3 *Puppet*

The following is a list of some key terminology used in Puppet:

- **Nodes:** The servers, or network devices
- **Resource:** The object of configuration: packages, files, users, groups, services, and custom server configuration.
- **Manifest:** A source file written using Puppet language (.pp)
- **Class:** A named block of Puppet code
- **Module:** A collection of classes, resource types, files, and templates, organized around a particular purpose

■ **Catalog:** Compiled collection of all resources to be applied to a specific node, including relationships between those resources

Orchestrators for Infrastructure as a Service

Amazon EC2, VMware vCloud Director, OpenStack, and Cisco UCS Director are IaaS orchestrators that unify the provisioning of virtual machines, physical machines, storage, and networking and can power up the entire infrastructure for a given user environment (called a *container*, *virtual data center*, or *tenant*).

The following common operations are enabled by these tools:

■ Creating a VM

■ Powering up a VM

■ Powering down a VM

■ Power cycling a VM

■ Changing ownership of a server

■ Taking a snapshot of an image

vCloud Director

VMware supports the implementation of clouds with the use of vCloud Director. vCloud Director builds on top of vCenter, which in turn coordinates VMs across a number of hosts that are running vSphere. Figure 2-4 illustrates the features of vCloud Director, which provides tenant abstraction and resource abstraction and a vApp Catalog for users of the cloud computing service.

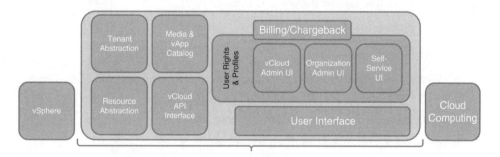

Figure 2-4 *vCloud Director Components*

Figure 2-5 shows how vCloud Director organizes resources in a different way and provides them as part of a hierarchy where the Organization is at the top. Inside the Organization there are multiple vDCs.

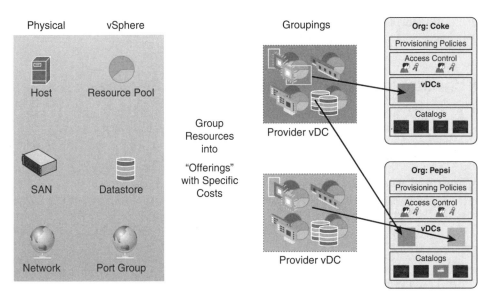

Figure 2-5   *vCloud Director Organization of Resources*

OpenStack

Chapter 6, "OpenStack," covers the details of OpenStack as it relates to ACI. The purpose of this section is to explain how OpenStack fits in cloud architectures.

Project and Releases

Each functional area of OpenStack is a separate project. For the purpose of cloud deployments, you don't have to use the entire OpenStack set of capabilities; you can, for instance, just leverage the APIs of a particular project.

The list of projects is as follows:

- Nova for compute
- Glance, Swift, and Cinder for image management, object storage, and block storage, respectively
- Horizon for the dashboard, self-service portal, and GUI
- Neutron for networking and IP address management
- Telemetry for metering
- Heat for orchestration

The release naming is very important because different releases may have significant changes in capabilities. At the time of this writing, you may encounter the following releases:

- Folsom (September 27, 2012)

- Grizzly (April 4, 2013)

- Havana (October 17, 2013)

- Icehouse (April 17, 2014)

- Juno (October 2014)

- Kilo (April 2015)

Note   You can find the list of releases at:

http://docs.openstack.org/training-guides/content/
associate-getting-started.html#associate-core-projects

The releases of particular interest currently for the network administrator are Folsom, because it introduced the Quantum component to manage networking, and Havana, which replaced the Quantum component with Neutron. Neutron gives more flexibility to manage multiple network components simultaneously, especially with the ML2 architecture, and is explained in detail in Chapter 6.

The concept of the plug-in for Neutron is significant. It is how networking vendors plug into the OpenStack architecture. Neutron provides a plug-in that can be used by OpenStack to configure their specific networking devices through a common API.

Multi-Hypervisor Support

OpenStack manages compute via the Nova component, which controls a variety of compute instances, such as the following:

- Kernel-based Virtual Machine (KVM)

- Linux Containers (LXC), through libvirt

- Quick EMUlator (QEMU)

- User Mode Linux (UML)

- VMware vSphere 4.1 update 1 and newer

- Xen, Citrix XenServer, and Xen Cloud Platform (XCP)

- Hyper-V

- Baremetal, which provisions physical hardware via pluggable subdrivers

Installers

The installation of OpenStack is a big topic because installing OpenStack has been complicated historically. In fact, Cisco took the initiative to provide an OpenStack rapid scripted installation to facilitate the adoption of OpenStack. At this time many other installers exist.

When installing OpenStack for proof-of-concept purposes, you often hear the following terminology:

- **All-in-one installation:** Places the OpenStack controller and nodes' components all on the same machine

- **Two-roles installation:** Places the OpenStack controller on one machine and a compute on another machine

To get started with OpenStack, you typically download a devstack distribution that provides an all-in-one, latest-and-greatest version. Devstack is a means for developers to quickly "stack" and "unstack" an OpenStack full environment, which allows them to develop and test their code. The scale of devstack is limited, naturally.

If you want to perform an all-in-one installation of a particular release, you may use the Cisco installer for Havana by following the instructions at http://docwiki.cisco.com/wiki/OpenStack:Havana:All-in-One, which use the git repo with the code at https://github.com/CiscoSystems/puppet_openstack_builder. Chapter 6 provides additional information regarding the install process.

There are several rapid installers currently available, such as these:

- Red Hat OpenStack provides PackStack and Foreman

- Canonical/Ubuntu provides Metal as a Service (MaaS) and JuJu

- SUSE provides SUSE Cloud

- Mirantis provides Fuel

- Piston Cloud provides one

Architecture Models

When deploying OpenStack in a data center, you need to consider the following components:

- A PXE server/Cobbler server (Quoting from Fedora: "Cobbler is a Linux installation server that allows for rapid setup of network installation environments. It glues together and automates many associated Linux tasks so you do not have to hop between lots of various commands and applications when rolling out new systems, and, in some cases, changing existing ones.")

- A Puppet server to provide image management for the compute nodes and potentially to image the very controller node of OpenStack

- A node or more for OpenStack controllers running keystone, Nova (api, cert, common, conductor, scheduler, and console), Glance, Cinder, Dashboard, and Quantum with Open vSwitch

■ The nodes running the virtual machines with Nova (common and compute) and Quantum with Open vSwitch

■ The nodes providing the proxy to the storage infrastructure

Networking Considerations

Cisco products provide plug-ins for the provisioning of network functionalities to be part of the OpenStack orchestration. Figure 2-6 illustrates the architecture of the networking infrastructure in OpenStack.

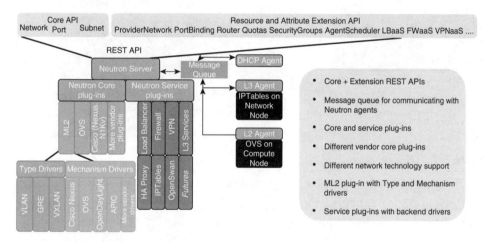

Figure 2-6 *OpenStack Networking Plug-ins*

Networks in OpenStack represent an isolated Layer 2 segment, analogous to VLAN in the physical networking world. They can be mapped to VLANs or VXLANs and become part of the ACI End Point Groups (EPGs) and Application Network Policies (ANP). As Figure 2-6 illustrates, the core plug-ins infrastructure offers the option to have vendor plug-ins. This topic is described in Chapter 6.

Note For more information about OpenStack, visit http://www.openstack.org.

UCS Director

UCS Director is an automation tool that allows you to abstract the provisioning from the use of the element managers and configure compute, storage, and ACI networking as part of an automated workflow in order to provision applications. The workflow provided by UCS Director is such that the administrator defines server policies, application network policies, storage policies, and virtualization policies, and UCSD applies these policies across the data center as shown in Figure 2-7.

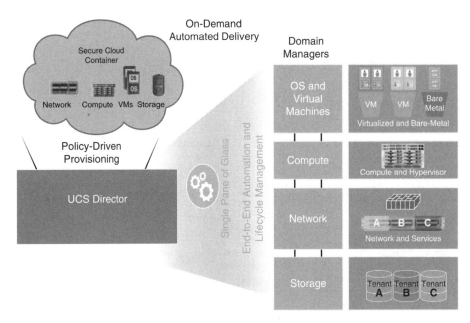

Figure 2-7 *UCS Director*

The workflow can be defined in a very intuitive way via the graphical workflow designer.

UCSD has both a northbound API and a southbound API. The southbound API allows UCSD to be an extensible platform.

Note For additional information on UCS Director, visit: https://developer.cisco.com/site/data-center/converged-infrastructure/ucs-director/overview/

Cisco Intelligent Automation for Cloud

Cisco Intelligent Automation for Cloud is a tool that enables a self-service portal and is powered by an orchestration engine to automate the provisioning of virtual and physical servers. Although there are some blurred lines between UCSD and CIAC, CIAC uses the UCSD northbound interface and complements the orchestration with the ability to standardize operations such as offering a self-service portal, opening a ticket, doing chargeback, and so on. CIAC orchestrates across UCSD, OpenStack, and Amazon EC2, and integrates with Puppet/Chef. It also provides measurement of the utilization of resources for the purpose of pricing. Resources being monitored include vNIC, hard drive usage, and so on.

Figure 2-8 illustrates the operations performed by CIAC for PaaS via the use of Puppet.

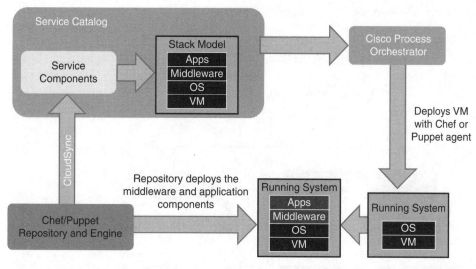

Figure 2-8 *CIAC Operations*

Figure 2-9 illustrates more details of the provisioning part of the process.

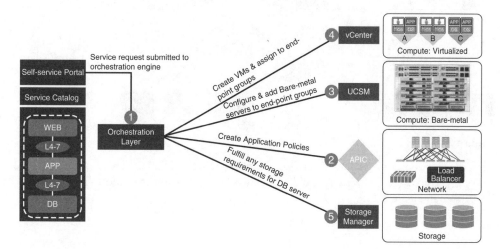

Figure 2-9 *CIAC Workflow*

CIAC organizes the data center resources with the following hierarchy:

- Tenants

- Organization within tenants

- Virtual data centers

- Resources

Figure 2-10 illustrates the hierarchy used by CIAC.

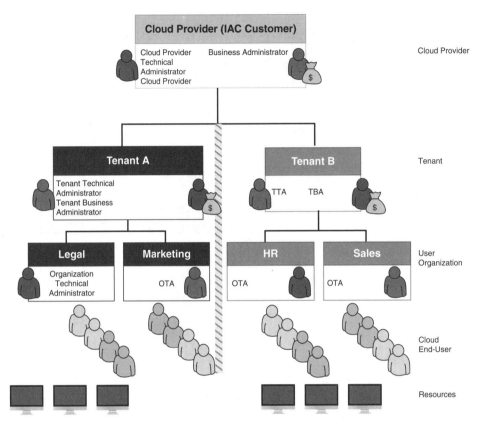

Figure 2-10   *Hierarchy in CIAC*

The user is offered a complete self-service catalog that includes different options with the classic Bronze, Silver, and Gold "containers" or data centers to choose from, as illustrated in Figure 2-11.

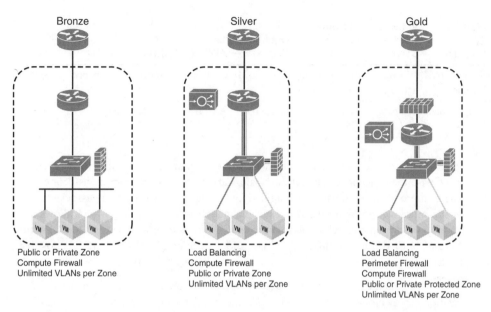

Figure 2-11 *Containers*

Conciliating Different Abstraction Models

One of the tasks of an administrator is to create a cloud infrastructure that maps the abstraction model of the service being offered to the abstractions of the components that make the cloud.

A typical offering may consist of a mix of VMware-based workloads, OpenStack/ KVM-based workloads with an ACI network, and UCSD/CIAC orchestration. Each technology has its own way of creating hierarchy and virtualizing the compute and network.

Table 2-1 provides a comparison between the different environments.

Table 2-1 *Differences Among VMware vCenter Server, VMware vCloud Director, OpenStack, Amazon EC2, UCS Director, CIAC, and ACI*

Platform Type/ Property	VMware vCenter Server	VMware vCloud Director	OpenStack (Essex)	Amazon AWS (EC2)	UCS Director	CIAC	ACI
Compute POD	Data center	Organization	OpenStack PE ID	Account	Account	Server	N/A
Tenant	Folder	Organization	N/A	Account	N/A	Tenant	Security domain
Organization	Folder	N/A	N/A	N/A	Group	Organization	Tenant
VDC	Resource pool	Organization VDC	Project	Account	VDC	VDC	Tenant

Platform Type/ Property	VMware vCenter Server	VMware vCloud Director	OpenStack (Essex)	Amazon AWS (EC2)	UCS Director	CIAC	ACI
VLAN Instance	vCenter network	Org network/ network pool	Network ID	Network ID	Network policy	Network	Subnet
VM Template	Full path	VM template HREF	Image ID	AMI ID	Catalog	Server template	N/A

In ACI the network is divided into tenants, and the administration of the tenants is organized with the concept of a security domain. Different administrators are associated with one or more security domains and, similarly, each tenant network can be associated with one or more security domains. The result is a many-to-many mapping, which allows creating sophisticated hierarchies. Furthermore, if two tenant networks represent the same "tenant" in CIAC but two different organizations within the same "tenant," it is possible to share resources and enable the communication between them.

In CIAC, a tenant can contain different organizations (e.g., departments) and each organization can own one or more virtual data centers (aggregates of physical and virtual resources). Network and other resources can be either shared or segregated, and the API exposed by the ACI controller (APIC) to the orchestrator makes it very easy.

Note   For more information regarding Cisco's development in the OpenStack area, visit these links:

http://www.cisco.com/web/solutions/openstack

http://docwiki.cisco.com/wiki/OpenStack

Summary

This chapter described the components of a cloud infrastructure and how ACI provides network automation for the cloud. It explained the Amazon Web Services approach. This chapter also described the role of the various orchestration tools, such as OpenStack, Cisco UCS Director, and Cisco Intelligent Automation for Cloud. It also introduced some key concepts regarding how to automate the provisioning of servers and how to get started with OpenStack. It explained the OpenStack modeling of the cloud infrastructure and compared it to similar modeling by CIAC and ACI. It also discussed the administrator's task of mapping the requirements of IaaS services onto the models of these technologies.

Chapter 3

The Policy Data Center

The goals of this chapter are to help understand the Cisco Application Centric Infrastructure (ACI) approach to modeling business applications to the Cisco ACI network fabric and to show how to apply consistent, robust policies to these applications. The Cisco ACI approach provides a unique blend of mapping hardware and software capabilities to the deployment of applications either graphically through the Cisco Application Policy Infrastructure Controller (APIC) GUI or programmatically through the Cisco APIC API model, a RESTful (Representational State Transfer) interface. The APIC model offers a type of controller that is unique in the industry. The APIC concepts and principles are explained in detail in this chapter. Finally, the Cisco ACI fabric is not only for greenfield deployment. Many users are interested in deploying the ACI fabric into an existing environment. The last part of this chapter explains how to integrate the ACI fabric with an existing network.

Why the Need for the Policy-Based Model?

The current enterprise customers, service providers, cloud providers, and (more generally) data center environment customers are required to deploy applications faster and faster in their respective environments. The applications that a data center is hosting can multiply in an exponential fashion. At the same time, the hardware complexity of the network devices is expanding as more features need to be compressed into smaller-size chipsets while increasing the port density, port throughput, and functionalities. The network environments also become more diverse because there are different devices used for spine, leaf, and various generations of the products in the same data center environment. This further segregates the application owners' needs and the network team's capability to implement the new applications in a timely fashion. Figure 3-1 depicts this barrier of communication that needs to be addressed by the network and application owners in order to deploy a new solution on the infrastructure.

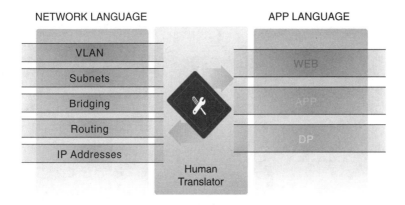

NETWORK LANGUAGE   APP LANGUAGE

VLAN

Subnets

Bridging

Routing

IP Addresses

WEB

APP

DP

Human
Translator

Figure 3-1 *Language Difference Between Network and Application*

To deploy a new application in the network, the network team needs to execute the following:

■ Locate a VLAN and subnet

■ Assure the security with access control lists (ACL)

■ Determine whether a quality of service (QoS) map is needed for the new application in the end-to-end network QoS model, which will vary in terms of capability depending on the hardware it is deployed on

The bottom line is that to achieve a new application deployment, the network team must become true experts of the network infrastructure, in addition to understanding the long processes for certification of the network changes and the testing environment. Naturally, the same issues will arise for troubleshooting an application. Correlating the application events such as latency, bandwidth, and drops to the network operation (where packets need to be traced down to each hardware to confirm if it is a network issue) is very time consuming and difficult in larger-scale environments.

This brings us to the idea of a level of abstraction: human translation between network and application language shouldn't be necessary. Furthermore, the resources should be optimized. Systems should be capable to deploy applications where the infrastructure is ready to accept them without disruption to other traffic, as well as optimizing the available hardware network resources. This is the value of the Policy Driven Data Center approach.

This Policy Driven Data Center brings a declarative approach model leveraged by the policy to supersede the older, imperative control model, as depicted in Figure 3-2. With the declarative control model, the switches are educated and instructed from the application requirements (called *endpoint groups* in Cisco ACI) and deploy the application where and when they are capable, instead of manually hard-coding with a set of basic instructions. For example, the control tower instructs an airplane where to take off. The pilot of the plane, not the control tower, handles the take-off. This is the essence of using a declarative control model from the promise theory.

Baggage handlers follow sequences
of simple, basic instructions

Air traffic control tells where to take off from,
but not how to fly the plane

Figure 3-2 *Policy Data Center Declarative Control Model*

With the policy data center approach, there is a new level of abstraction between the hardware and the software and a methodology to adapt networking across various hardware platforms, capabilities, and future evolutions. This allows automation between networking and application teams and reduces the time of deployment for applications from months to seconds or less.

The Policy Theory

The Cisco APIC policy model is defined from the top down as a policy enforcement engine focused on the application itself and abstracting the networking functionality underneath.

The Cisco APIC policy model is an object-oriented model based on promise theory. *Promise theory* is based on declarative, scalable control of intelligent objects, in comparison to legacy imperative control models.

An imperative control model is a big-brain system or top-down style of management. In these systems, the central manager must be aware of both the configuration commands of underlying objects and the current state of those objects, as shown in Figure 3-3.

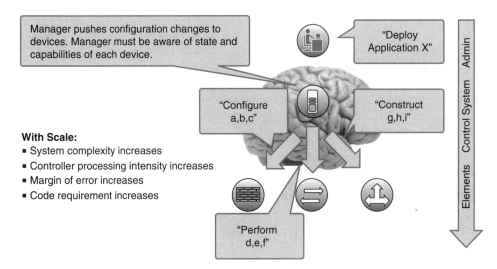

Figure 3-3 *Configuration to Underlying Components*

Promise theory, in contrast, relies on the underlying objects to handle configuration state changes initiated by the control system as desired state changes. The objects are in turn also responsible for passing exceptions or faults back to the control system. This lightens the burden and complexity of the control system and allows for greater scale. These systems scale further by allowing for methods of underlying objects to in turn request state changes from one another and/or lower-level objects. Figure 3-4 depicts promise theory.

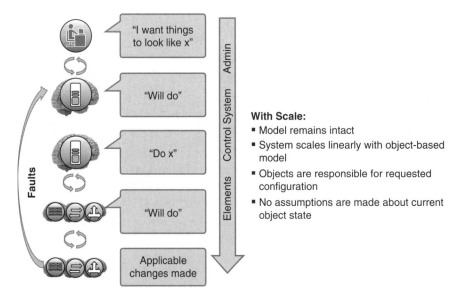

Figure 3-4 *Promise Theory Approach to Large-Scale System Control*

Cisco APIC Policy Object Model

Traditionally applications have been restricted by capabilities of the network. Concepts such as addressing, VLAN, and security have been tied together, limiting the scale and mobility of the application itself. Because today's applications are being redesigned for mobility and web scale, this is not conducive to rapid and consistent deployment.

The physical Cisco ACI fabric is built on a spine-leaf design; its topology is illustrated in Figure 3-5. It uses a bipartite graph where each leaf is a switch that connects to each spine switch, and no direct connections are allowed between leaf switches and between spine switches. The leaves act as the connection point for all external devices and networks, and the spine acts as the high-speed forwarding engine between leaves. Cisco ACI fabric is managed, monitored, and administered by the Cisco APIC.

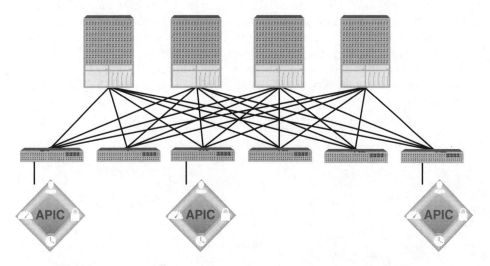

Figure 3-5 *Cisco ACI Fabric Design*

At the top level, the Cisco APIC policy model is built on a series of one or more tenants that allow segregation of the network infrastructure administration and data flows. These tenants can be used for customers, business units, or groups, depending on organizational needs. For instance, a given enterprise might use one tenant for the entire organization, while a cloud provider might have customers using one or more tenants to represent their organization.

Tenants further break down into private Layer 3 networks, which directly relate to a Virtual Route Forwarding (VRF) instance or separate IP space. Each tenant may have one or more private Layer 3 networks depending on their business needs. Private Layer 3 networks provide a way to further separate the organizational and forwarding requirements below a given tenant. Because contexts use separate forwarding instances, IP addressing can be duplicated in separate contexts for the purpose of multitenancy.

A *tenant* is a logical container or a folder for application policies. It can represent an actual tenant, an organization, or a domain, or can just be used for the convenience of organizing information. A normal tenant represents a unit of isolation from a policy perspective, but it does not represent a private network. A special tenant named *common* has sharable policies that can be used by all tenants. A *context* is a representation of a private Layer 3 namespace or Layer 3 network. It is a unit of isolation in the Cisco ACI framework. A tenant can rely on several contexts. Contexts can be declared within a tenant (contained by the tenant) or can be in the "common" tenant. This approach provides both multiple private Layer 3 networks per tenant and shared Layer 3 networks used by multiple tenants. This way, you do not dictate a specific rigidly constrained tenancy model. The endpoint policy specifies a common Cisco ACI behavior for all endpoints defined within a given virtual ACI context.

Below the context, the model provides a series of objects that define the application itself. These objects are called endpoint groups (EPG). EPGs are a collection of similar endpoints representing an application tier or set of services. EPGs are connected to each other via policies. It is important to note that policies in this case are more than just a set of ACLs and include a collection of inbound/outbound filters, traffic quality settings, marking rules/redirection rules, and Layers 4–7 service device graphs. This relationship is shown in Figure 3-6.

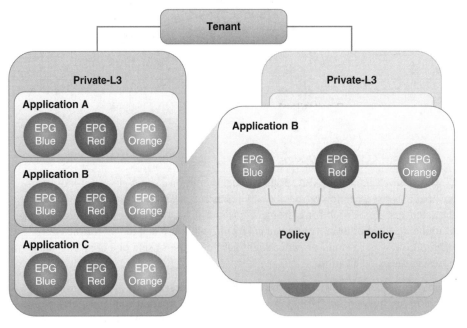

Figure 3-6   *Cisco APIC Logical Object Model*

Figure 3-6 depicts two contexts under a given tenant and the series of applications that make up that context. The EPGs shown are groups of endpoints that make up an application tier or other logical application grouping. For example, Application B (shown expanded on the right of Figure 3-6) could be a blue web tier, red application tier, and orange database tier. The combination of EPGs and the policies that define their interaction is an application network profile on the Cisco ACI fabric.

Endpoint Groups

EPGs provide a logical grouping for objects that require similar policy. For example, an EPG could be the group of components that make up an application's web tier. Endpoints themselves are defined using NIC, vNIC, IP address, or DNS name with extensibility for future methods of identifying application components.

EPGs are also used to represent other entities such as outside networks, network services, security devices, network storage, and so on. They are collections of one or more endpoints providing a similar function. They are a logical grouping with varying use options depending on the application deployment model in use. Figure 3-7 depicts the relationship between endpoints, EPGs, and applications.

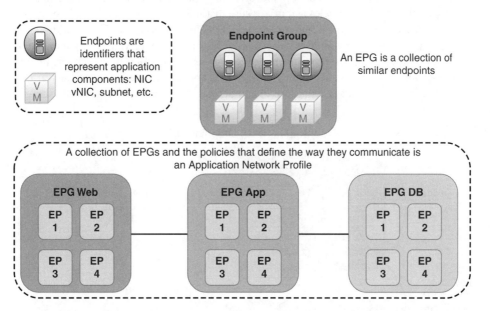

Figure 3-7 *Endpoint Group Relationships*

EPGs are designed for flexibility, allowing their use to be customized to one or more deployment models a given customer might choose. The EPGs are then used to define where policy is applied. Within the Cisco ACI fabric, policy is applied between EPGs, therefore defining how EPGs communicate with one another. This is designed to be extensible in the future to policy application within an EPG itself.

Some example uses of EPGs are as follows:

- **EPG defined by traditional network VLANs:** All endpoints connecting to a given VLAN are placed in an EPG

- **EPG defined by a VxLAN:** All endpoints connecting to a given VLAN are placed in an EPG

- **EPG mapped to a VMware port group**

- **EPG defined by IPs or subnet:** For example, 172.168.10.10 or 172.168.10*

- **EPG defined by DNS names or DNS ranges:** For example, example.web.networks.com or *.web.networks.com

The use of EPGs is intentionally left both flexible and extensible. The model is intended to provide tools to build an application's network representation that maps to the actual environment's deployment model. Additionally, the definition of endpoints is intended to be extensible to provide support for future product enhancements and industry requirements.

The implementation of EPGs within the fabric provides several valuable benefits. EPGs act as a single policy enforcement point for a group of contained objects. This simplifies configuration of these policies and makes sure that it is consistent. Additional policy is applied based not on subnet, but rather on the EPG itself. This means that IP addressing changes to the endpoint do not necessarily change its policy, which is common in the case of traditional networks (the exception here is an endpoint defined by its IP). Alternatively, moving an endpoint to another EPG applies the new policy to the leaf switch that the endpoint is connected to and defines new behavior for that endpoint based on the new EPG.

Figure 3-8 displays the relationship between endpoints, EPGs, and policies.

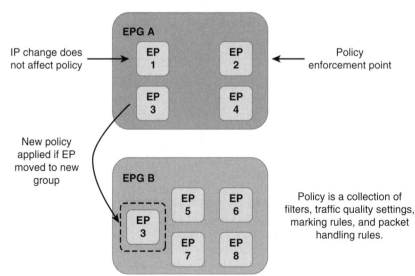

Figure 3-8 *Relationship Between EPGs and Policies*

The final benefit provided by EPGs is in the way in which policy is enforced for an EPG. The physical ternary content-addressable memory (TCAM) where policy is stored for enforcement is an expensive component of switch hardware and therefore tends to lower policy scale or raise hardware costs. Within the Cisco ACI fabric, policy is applied based on the EPG rather than the endpoint itself. This policy size can be expressed as $n * m * f$, where n is the number of sources, m is the number of destinations, and f is the number of policy filters. Within the Cisco ACI fabric, sources and destinations become one entry for a given EPG, which reduces the number of total entries required. An EPG is different from a VLAN: an EPG can be restricted to a VLAN in a specific bridge domain. However the EPG can be much more than VLANs, it can be collection vNICs, MAC addresses, subnets, and so on, as explained in the "Endpoint Groups" section. Figure 3-9 displays the EPG role in policy table size reduction.

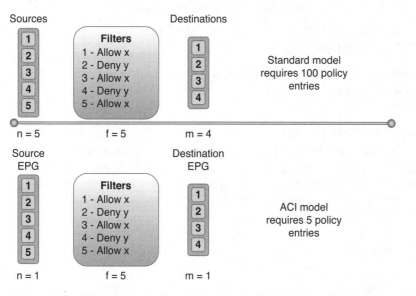

Figure 3-9 *EPG Role in Policy Table Size Reduction*

As discussed, policy within a Cisco ACI fabric is applied between two EPGs. They can be utilized in either a unidirectional or bidirectional mode between any given pair of EPGs. These policies then define the allowed communication between EPGs, as shown in Figure 3-10.

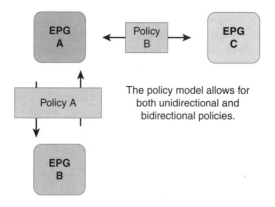

Figure 3-10   *Unidirectional and Bidirectional Policy Enforcement*

Cisco APIC Policy Enforcement

This section covers the concept of Cisco APIC policy enforcement, including unicast and multicast enforcement.

Unicast Policy Enforcement

The relationship between EPGs and policies can be thought of as a matrix with one axis representing source EPGs (sEPG) and the other destination EPGs (dEPG), as shown in Figure 3-11. One or more policies are placed in the intersection between appropriate sEPGs and dEPGs. The matrix becomes sparsely populated in most cases because many EPGs have no need to communicate with one another.

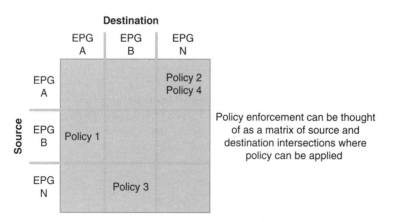

Figure 3-11   *Policy Enforcement Matrix*

Policies break down into a series of filters for quality of service, access control, and so on. Filters are specific rules that make up the policy between two EPGs. Filters are composed of inbound and outbound: permit, deny, redirect, log, copy (separate from

SPAN), and mark functions. Policies allow for wildcard functionality within the definition. The enforcement of policy typically takes an approach of most specific match first. The wildcard enforcement rules are illustrated in Figure 3-12.

sEPG	dEPG	Application ID	Comments
Fully Qualified	Fully Qualified	Fully Qualified	Fully Qualified (S, D, A) rules
Fully Qualified	Fully Qualified	*	(S, D, *) rules
Fully Qualified	*	Fully Qualified	(S, *, A) rules
*	Fully Qualified	Fully Qualified	(*, D, A) rules
Fully Qualified	*	*	(S, *, *) rules
*	Fully Qualified	*	(*, D, *) rules
*	*	Fully Qualified	(*, *, A) rules
*	*	*	Default (for example, implicit deny)

Enforcement

Figure 3-12 *Wildcard Enforcement Rules*

Enforcement of policy within the fabric is always guaranteed; however, policy can be applied in one of two places. Policy can be enforced opportunistically at the ingress leaf; otherwise, it is enforced on the egress leaf. Policy can be enforced at ingress only if the destination EPG is known. The source EPG is always known, and policy rules pertaining to that source as both an sEPG and a dEPG are always pushed to the appropriate leaf switch when an endpoint attaches. After policy is pushed to a leaf, it is stored and enforced in hardware. Because the Cisco APIC is aware of all EPGs and the endpoints assigned to them, the leaf to which the EPG is attached always has all policies required and never needs to punt traffic to a controller, as might be the case in other systems. Figure 3-13 displays the summary of the application of a policy to the leaf nodes.

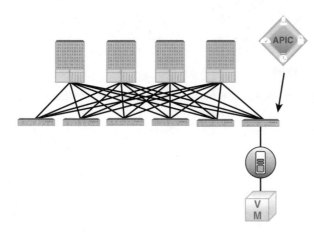

1) Endpoint attaches to fabric

2) APIC detects endpoint and its designated EPG

3) APIC pushes required policy (policies with EPG listed as src/dest) to leaf switch

Figure 3-13 *Applying Policy to Leaf Nodes*

As mentioned, if the destination EPG is not known, policy cannot be enforced at ingress. Instead, the source EPG is tagged, and the policy applied bits are not marked. Both of these fields exist in the reserved bits of the VxLAN header. The packet is then forwarded to the forwarding proxy, typically resident in the spine. The spine is aware of all destinations in the fabric; therefore, if the destination is unknown, the packet is dropped. If the destination is recognized, the packet is forwarded to the destination leaf. The spine never enforces policy; this is handled by the egress leaf.

When a packet is received by the egress leaf, the sEPG and the policy applied bits are read (these were tagged at ingress). If the policy applied bits are marked as applied, the packet is forwarded without additional processing. If instead the policy applied bits do not show that policy has been applied, the sEPG marked in the packet is matched with the dEPG (always known on the egress leaf), and the appropriate policy is then applied. Figure 3-14 displays the enforcement of the policy on the whole fabric.

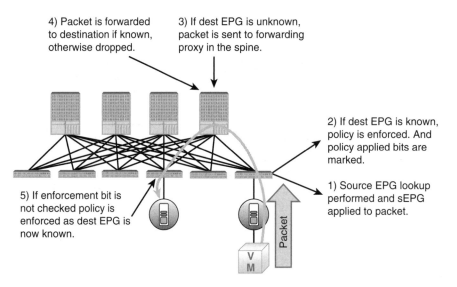

Figure 3-14   *Enforcing Policy on Fabric*

The opportunistic policy application allows for efficient handling of policy within the fabric. This application is further represented in Figure 3-15.

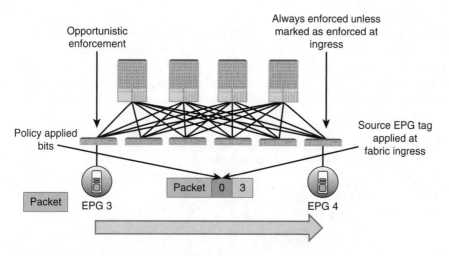

Figure 3-15 *Opportunistic Ingress Enforcement of Policy*

Multicast Policy Enforcement

The nature of multicast makes the requirements for policy enforcement slightly different. Although the source EPG is easily determined at ingress because it is never a multicast address, the destination is an abstract entity; the multicast group may consist of endpoints from multiple EPGs. In multicast cases the Cisco ACI fabric uses a multicast group for policy enforcement. These groups are defined by specifying a multicast address range or ranges. Policy is then configured between the sEPG and the multicast group as shown in Figure 3-16.

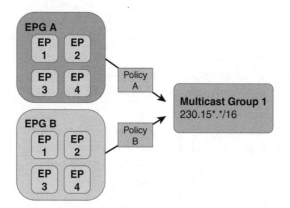

Figure 3-16 *Multicast Group (Specialized Multicast EPG)*

The multicast group (EPG group corresponding to the multicast stream) is always the destination and never used as a source EPG. Traffic sent to a multicast group is either from the multicast source or a receiver joining the stream through an Internet Group Management Protocol (IGMP) join. Because multicast streams are nonhierarchical and the stream itself is already in the forwarding table (using IGMP join), multicast policy is always enforced at ingress. This prevents the need for multicast policy to be written to egress leaves, as shown in Figure 3-17.

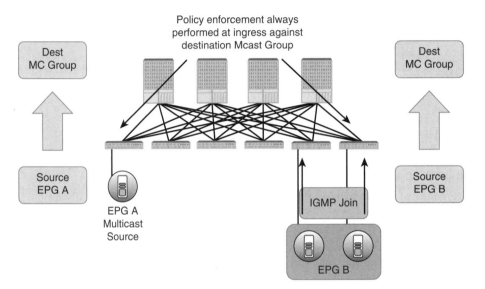

Figure 3-17   *Multicast Policy Enforcement*

Application Network Profiles

As stated earlier, an application network profile (ANP) within the fabric is a collection of the EPGs, their connections, and the policies that define those connections. ANPs become the logical representation of the entire application and its interdependencies on the Cisco ACI fabric.

ANPs are designed to be modeled in a logical fashion, which matches the way applications are created and deployed. The configuration and enforcement of the policies and connectivity are then handled by the system itself using the Cisco APIC rather than through an administrator. Figure 3-18 illustrates the ANP concept.

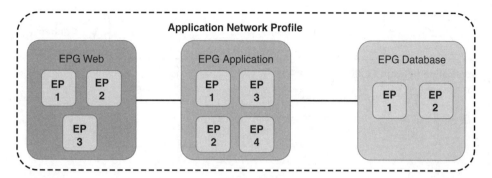

Figure 3-18 *Application Network Profile*

Creating ANPs requires three general steps:

- Creation of EPGs (as discussed earlier)

- Creation of policies that define connectivity, including:

  - Permit

  - Deny

  - Log

  - Mark

  - Redirect

  - Copy to

  - Service graphs

- Creation of connection points between EPGs using policy constructs known as *contracts*

Contracts

Contracts define inbound and outbound permits, denies, QoS, redirects, and service graphs. They allow for both simple and complex definition of how a given EPG communicates with other EPGs dependent on the requirements of a given environment.

In Figure 3-19 notice the relationship between the three tiers of a web application defined by EPG connectivity and the contracts that define their communication. The sum of these parts becomes an ANP. Contracts also provide reusability and policy consistency for services that typically communicate with multiple EPGs. Figure 3-20 uses the concept of network file system (NFS) and management resources.

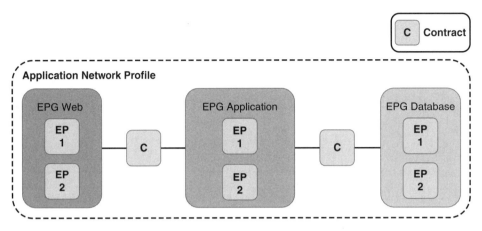

Figure 3-19 *Contracts with Application Network Profiles*

Figure 3-20 shows the basic three-tier web application used previously with some additional connectivity that is usually required. Notice the shared network services, NFS, and management, which is used by all three tiers as well as other EPGs within the fabric. In these cases the contract provides a reusable policy defining how the NFS and MGMT EPGs produce functions or services that can be consumed by other EPGs.

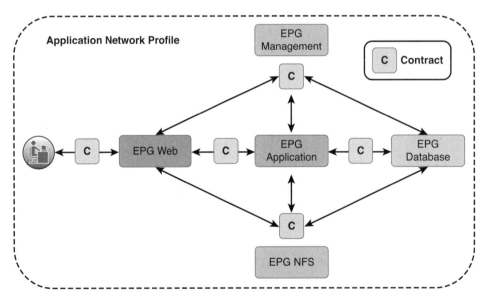

Figure 3-20 *Complete Application Network Profile*

Within the Cisco ACI fabric, the "what" and "where" of policy application have been intentionally separated. This allows policy to be created independently of how it is applied and reused where required. The actual policy configured in the fabric is determined based on the policy defined as a *contract* (the what) and the intersection of EPGs and other contracts with those policies (the where).

In more complex application deployment environments, contracts are further broken down using *subjects*, which can be thought of as applications or subapplications. To better understand this concept, think of a web server. Although it might be classified as web, it might be producing HTTP, HTTPS, FTP, and so on, and each of these subapplications might require different policies. Within the Cisco APIC model, these separate functions or services are defined using subjects, and subjects are combined within contracts to represent the set of rules that define how an EPG communicates with other EPGs, as shown in Figure 3-21.

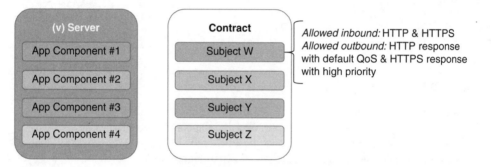

Figure 3-21 *Subjects Within Contract*

Subjects describe the functions that an application exposes to other processes on the network. Think of it as producing a set of functions: that is, the web server produces HTTP, HTTPS, and FTP. Other EPGs then consume one or more of these functions; which EPGs consume these services are defined by creating relationships between EPGs and contracts, which contain the subjects defining applications or subapplications. Full policy is defined by administrators defining groups of EPGs consuming what other EPGs provides. Figure 3-22 illustrates how this model offers functionality for hierarchical EPGs, or more simply EPGs that are groups of applications and subapplications.

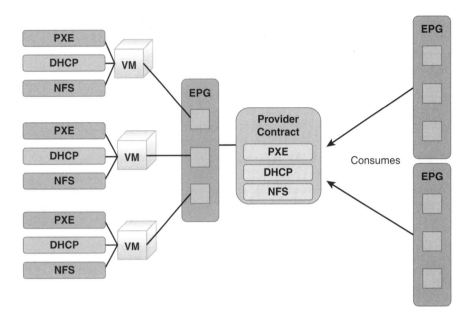

Figure 3-22   *Detail View of Subjects Within Contract*

Additionally, this model provides the capability to define a disallow list on a per-EPG basis. These disallows, known as *taboos*, override the contract itself, making sure that certain communications are denied on a per-EPG basis. This capability provides a blacklist model within the Cisco ACI fabric, as shown in Figure 3-23.

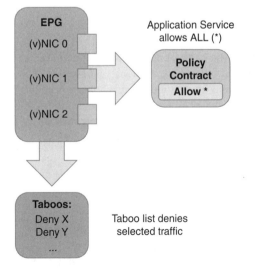

Figure 3-23   *Use of Taboos to Create Blacklist Behavior*

Figure 3-23 shows that a contract can be defined allowing all traffic from all EPGs. The allow is then refined by creating a taboo list of specific ports or ranges that are undesirable. The model provides a transitional method for customers desiring to migrate over time from a blacklist model, which is typically in use today, to the more desirable whitelist model. In a blacklist model, all communication is open unless explicitly denied, whereas a whitelist model requires communication to be explicitly defined before being permitted. It is important to remember that disallow lists are optional, and in a full whitelist model they are rarely needed.

Contracts provide a grouping for the descriptions and associated policies that define those application services. They can be contained within a given scope, tenant, context, or EPG as a local contract. An EPG is also capable of subscribing to multiple contracts, which provide the superset of defined policies.

Although contracts can be used to define complex real-world application relationships, they can also be used very simply for traditional application deployment models. For instance, if a single VLAN or VxLAN is used to define separate services, and those VLANs or VxLANs are tied to port groups within VMware, a simple contract model can be defined without unneeded complexity.

However, in more advanced application deployment models such as PaaS, SOA 2.0, and Web 2.0 models, where more application granularity is required, complex contract relationships are used. These relationships are implemented to define detailed relationships between components within a single EPG and to multiple other EPGs.

Although contracts provide the means to support more complex application models, they do not dictate additional complexity. As stated, for simple application relationships, simple contracts can be used. For complex application relationships, the contract provides a means for building those relationships and reusing them where required.

Contracts break down into subcomponents:

- **Subjects:** Group of filters that apply to a specific app or service
- **Filters:** Used to classify traffic
- **Actions:** Such as permit, deny, mark, and so on to perform on matches to those filters
- **Labels:** Used optionally to group objects such as subjects and EPGs for the purpose of further defining policy enforcement

In a simple environment, the relationship between two EPGs is similar to that in Figure 3-24. Here web and app EPGs are considered a single application construct and defined by a given set of filters. This is a very common deployment scenario. Even in complex environments, this model is preferred for many applications.

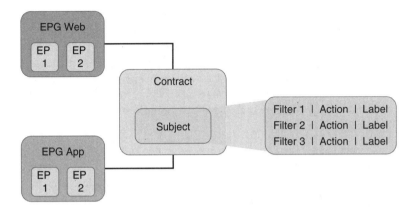

Figure 3-24   *Simple Policy Contract Relationships*

Many environments require more complex relationships; some examples include

- Environments using complex middleware systems

- Environments in which one set of servers provides functionality to multiple applications or groups (for example, a database farm providing data for several applications)

- PaaS, SOA, and Web 2.0 environments

- Environments where multiple services run within a single OS

In these environments the Cisco ACI fabric provides a more robust set of optional features to model actual application deployments in a logical fashion. In both cases, the Cisco APIC and fabric software are responsible for flattening the policy down and applying it for hardware enforcement. This relationship between the logical model, which is used to configure application relationships, and the concrete model, which is used to implement the application relationships on the fabric, simplifies design, deployment, and change within the fabric.

An example of this would be an SQL database farm providing database services to multiple development teams within an organization, such as a red team, blue team, and green team each using separate database constructs supplied by the same farm. In this instance, a separate policy might be required for each team's access to the database farm, as shown in Figure 3-25.

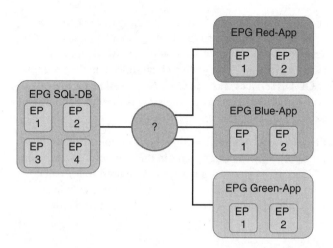

Figure 3-25 *Single Database Farm Serving Three Separate Groups Requiring Separate Policy Controls*

The simple models discussed previously do not adequately cover this more complex relationship between EPGs. In these instances, you need the ability to separate policy for the three separate database instances within the SQL-DB EPG, which can be thought of as *subapplications* and are referred to within the Cisco ACI fabric as *subjects*.

The Cisco ACI fabric provides multiple ways to model this application behavior depending on user preference and application complexity. The first way is to use three contracts, one for each team. Remember that an EPG can inherit more than one contract and receives the superset of rules defined there. In Figure 3-26 each app team's EPG connects to the SQL-DB EPG using its own specific contract.

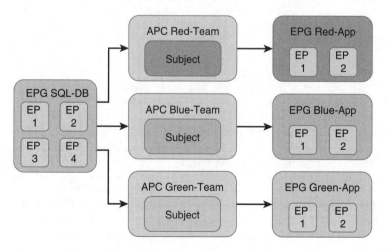

Figure 3-26 *Utilizing Three Contracts to Define Separate Consumer Relationships*

As shown, the SQL-DB EPG inherits the superset of policies from three separate contracts. Each application team's EPG then connects to the appropriate contract. The contract designates the policy, while the relationship defined by the arrows denotes where the policy will be applied or who is providing/consuming which service. In this example the Red-App EPG consumes SQL-DB services with the QoS, ACL, marking, redirect, and so on behavior defined within the Red-Team APC. The same is true for the blue and green teams.

In many instances, groups of contracts get applied together. For example, if multiple DB farms are created that all require access by the three teams in this example, development, test, and production farms are used. In these cases, a bundle can be used to logically group the contracts. Bundles are optional; a bundle can be thought of as a container for one or more contracts for the purpose of ease of use. The utilization of bundles is depicted in Figure 3-27.

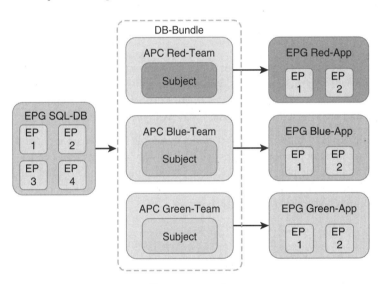

Figure 3-27   *Using Bundles to Group Contracts*

In Figure 3-27 it is very important to note the attachment points of the arrows showing relationship. In this example you want SQL-DB EPG to provide all contracts within the contract bundle, so attach the bundle itself to the EPG. For each of the three application teams, you want access defined only by its specific contract, so attach each team to consume the corresponding contract itself within the bundle.

This same relationship can optionally be modeled in another way using labels. Labels provide an alternative grouping function for use within application policy definition. In most environments labels are not required, but they are available for deployments with advanced application models and teams who are familiar with the concept.

When employing labels, a single contract can be used to represent multiple services or components of applications provided by a given EPG. In this case the labels represent the DB EPG providing database services to three separate teams. By labeling the subjects and the EPGs using them, separate policy is applied within a given contract even if the traffic types or other classifiers are identical. Figure 3-28 shows this relationship.

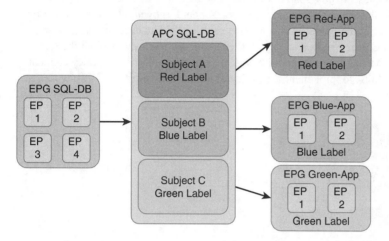

Figure 3-28 *Using Labels to Group Objects Within Policy Model*

In Figure 3-28 the SQL-DB EPG provides services using a single contract called *SQ-DB*, which defines the database services it supplies to three different teams. Each of the three teams' EPGs that will consume these services are then attached to the same traffic. By using labels on the subjects and the EPGs, specific rules are defined for each team. The rules within the contract that matches the label are the only ones applied for each EPG. This holds true even if the classification within the construct is the same: for example, the same Layer 4 ports and so on.

Labels provide a very powerful classification tool that allows objects to be grouped together for the purpose of policy enforcement. This also permits applications to be moved quickly through various development life cycles. For example, if the red label service Red-App represents a "development environment" that needs to be promoted to "test environment," which is represented by the blue label, the only required change would be to the label assigned to that EPG.

Understanding Cisco APIC

This section explains the architecture and components of the Cisco APIC: Application Policy Infrastructure Controller.

Cisco ACI Operating System (Cisco ACI Fabric OS)

Cisco has taken the traditional Cisco Nexus OS (NX-OS) developed for the data center and pared it down to the essential features required for a modern data center deploying

Cisco ACI. Cisco has also made deeper structural changes so that the Cisco ACI Fabric OS can easily render policy from the APIC into the physical infrastructure. A Data Management Engine (DME) in the ACI Fabric OS provides the framework that serves read and write requests from a shared lockless data store. The data store is object oriented, with each object stored as chunks of data. A chunk is owned by one ACI Fabric OS process, and only the owner of this process can write to the data chunk. However, any ACI Fabric OS process can read any of the data simultaneously through the CLI, Simple Network Management Protocol (SNMP), or an API call. A local policy element (PE) enables the APIC to implement the policy model directly in the ACI Fabric OS, as illustrated in Figure 3-29.

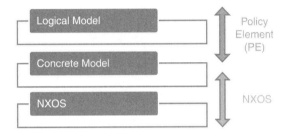

Figure 3-29   *Cisco ACI Fabric OS*

Architecture: Components and Functions of the Cisco APIC

The APIC consists of a set of basic control functions, displayed in Figure 3-30, which include

- Policy Manager (policy repository)

- Topology Manager

- Observer

- Boot Director

- Appliance Director (cluster controller)

- VMM Manager

- Event Manager

- Appliance Element

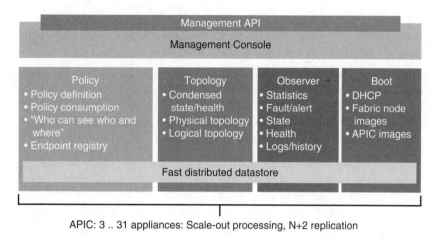

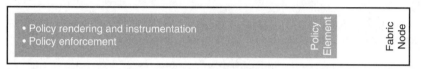

Figure 3-30 *Cisco APIC Component Architecture*

Policy Manager

The Policy Manager is a distributed repository responsible for the definition and deployment of the policy-based configuration of Cisco ACI. This is a collection of policies and rules applied to existing or hypothetical (not yet created) endpoints. The endpoint registry is a subset of the Policy Manager that tracks endpoints connecting to Cisco ACI and their assignment to endpoint groups as defined by the policy repository.

Topology Manager

The Topology Manager maintains up-to-date Cisco ACI topology and inventory information. Topology data is reported to the APIC by the leaf and spine switches. The physical topology is based on the information discovered by the Link Layer Discovery Protocol (LLDP) and the routing topology of the fabric as reported by protocols (modified Intermediate System-to-Intermediate System [IS-IS]) running within the fabric infrastructure space.

A global view of time-accurate topology information is available in the Topology Manager and includes

- Physical topology (Layer 1; physical links and nodes)
- Logical path topology (reflection of Layer 2 + Layer 3)

Topology data, along with associated aggregated operational state, is asynchronously updated in the Topology Manager upon detection of topology changes, and is available for queries via the APIC API, CLI, and UI.

A subfunction of the Topology Manager performs inventory management for the APIC and maintains a complete inventory of the entire Cisco ACI. The APIC inventory management subfunction provides full identification, including model and serial number, as well as user-defined asset tags (for ease of correlation with asset and inventory management systems) for all ports, line cards, switches, chassis, and so forth.

Inventory is automatically pushed by the DME-based policy element/agent embedded in the switches as soon as new inventory items are discovered or removed or transition in state occurs in the local repository of the Cisco ACI node.

Observer

The Observer is the monitoring subsystem of the APIC, and it serves as a data repository of the Cisco ACI operational state, health, and performance, which includes

- Hardware and software state and health of ACI components

- Operational state of protocols

- Performance data (statistics)

- Outstanding and past fault and alarm data

- Record of events

Monitoring data is available for queries via the APIC API, CLI, and UI.

Boot Director

The Boot Director controls the booting and firmware updates of the Cisco spine and leaf and the APIC controller elements. It also functions as the address allocation authority for the infrastructure network, which allows the APIC and the spine and leaf nodes to communicate. The following process describes bringing up the APIC and cluster discovery.

Each APIC in Cisco ACI uses an internal private IP address to communicate with the ACI nodes and other APICs in the cluster. APICs discover the IP address of other APICs in the cluster using an LLDP-based discovery process.

APICs maintain an appliance vector (AV), which provides a mapping from an APIC ID to an APIC IP address and a universally unique identifier (UUID) of the APIC. Initially, each APIC starts with an AV filled with its local IP address, and all other APIC slots are marked unknown.

Upon switch reboot, the PE on the leaf gets its AV from the APIC. The switch then advertises this AV to all of its neighbors and reports any discrepancies between its local AV and neighbors' AVs to all the APICs in its local AV.

Using this process, APICs learn about the other APICs in Cisco ACI via switches. After validating these newly discovered APICs in the cluster, APICs update their local AV and program the switches with the new AV. Switches then start advertising this new AV. This process continues until all the switches have the identical AV and all APICs know the IP address of all the other APICs.

Appliance Director

The Appliance Director is responsible for formation and control of the APIC appliance cluster. The APIC controller runs on server hardware ("bare metal"). A minimum of three controllers are initially installed for control of the scale-out ACI. The ultimate size of the APIC cluster is directly proportionate to the ACI size and is driven by the transaction rate requirements. Any controller in the cluster is able to service any user for any operation, and a controller can be seamlessly added to or removed from the APIC cluster. It is important to understand that, unlike an OpenFlow controller, none of the APIC controllers are ever in the data path. The Appliance Director is illustrated in Figure 3-31.

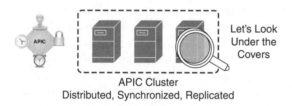

APIC Cluster
Distributed, Synchronized, Replicated

Figure 3-31 *Appliance Director*

VMM Manager

The VMM Manager acts as an agent between the policy repository and a hypervisor. It is responsible for interacting with hypervisor management systems such as VMware's vCenter and cloud software platforms such as OpenStack and CloudStack. VMM Manager inventories all of the hypervisor elements (pNICs, vNICs, VM names, etc.) and pushes policy into the hypervisor, creating port groups and so forth. It also listens to hypervisor events such as VM mobility.

Event Manager

The Event Manager is a repository for all the events and faults initiated from the APIC or the fabric nodes. It is detailed in Chapter 9, "Advanced Telemetry."

Appliance Element

The Appliance Element is a monitor for the local appliance. It manages the inventory and state of the local APIC appliance.

Architecture: Data Management with Sharding

The Cisco APIC cluster uses a technology from large databases called *sharding*. To understand the sharding concept, consider the concept of database partitioning. Sharding is a result of the evolution of what is called *horizontal partitioning of a database*. In this partitioning, the rows of the database are held separately instead of being normalized and split vertically into columns. Sharding goes further than horizontal partitioning, also partitioning the database across multiple instances of the schema. In addition to increasing redundancy, sharding increases performance because the search load for a large partitioned table can be split across multiple database servers, not just multiple indexes on the same logical server. With sharding, large partitionable tables are split across the servers, and smaller tables are replicated as complete units. After a table is sharded, each shard can reside in a completely separated logical and physical server, data center, physical location, and so forth. There is no ongoing need to retain shared access between the shards to the other unpartitioned tables located in other shards.

Sharding makes replication across multiple servers easy, unlike horizontal partitioning. It is a useful concept for distributed applications. Otherwise, a lot more interdatabase server communication is needed because the information wouldn't be located in a separated logical and physical server. Sharding, for example, reduces the number of data center interconnect links needed for database querying. It requires a notification and replication mechanism between schema instances, to help ensure that the unpartitioned tables remain as synchronized as the applications require. In situations where distributed computing is used to separate loads between multiple servers, a shard approach offers a strong advantage.

Effect of Replication on Reliability

Figure 3-32 shows the proportion of data that is lost when the nth appliance is lost out of a total of five appliances and there is a variable replication factor of K. When $K = 1$, no replication occurs, and each shard has one copy; when $K = 5$, full replication occurs, and all appliances contain a copy. N indicates the number of Cisco APIC appliances lost. When $n = 1$, one appliance has been lost; when $n = 5$, the last appliance has been disconnected.

Consider the example of K = 1: just one copy is made. Therefore, for every appliance lost, the same amount of data is lost from n = 1 to n = 5. As the replication factor K increases, no data loss occurs unless at least K appliances are lost; also, the data loss is gradual and starts at a smaller value. For example, with three appliances (K = 3), no data is lost until the third appliance (n = 3) is lost, at which point only 10 percent of the data is lost. Cisco APIC uses a minimum of three appliances (n = 3) for this reason.

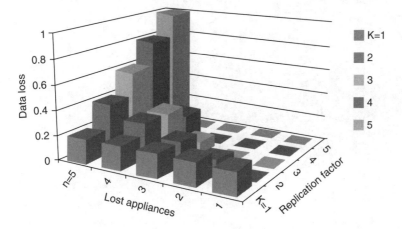

Figure 3-32 *Effect of Replication on Reliability*

Effect of Sharding on Reliability

In Figure 3-33, L represents the number of appliances, starting with a minimum of three. By maintaining a replication factor of K = 3, no data loss occurs as long as the three appliances are not missing at the same time. Only when the third Cisco APIC appliance is lost does data loss occur, and it is a complete loss. Increasing the number of appliances significantly and rapidly improves resilience. For example, with four appliances, as shown in Figure 3-32, losing the third appliance means a loss of 25 percent of the data. With 12 appliances, the loss of the third appliance means only a 0.5 percent data loss. With sharding, increasing the number of appliances can very quickly reduce the likelihood of data loss. Full replication is not needed to achieve a very high rate of data protection.

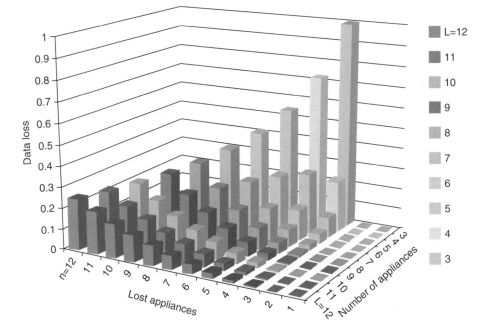

Figure 3-33   *Effect of Sharding on Reliability*

Sharding Technology

The sharding technology provides scalability and reliability to the data sets generated and processed by the distributed policy repository, the endpoint registry, the Observer, and the Topology Manager. The data for these Cisco APIC functions is partitioned into logically bounded subsets called *shards* (analogous to database shards). A shard is a unit of data management, and all of the above data sets are placed into shards.

The sharding technology illustrated in Figure 3-34 has the following characteristics:

■ Each shard has three replicas.

■ Shards are evenly distributed.

■ Shards enable horizontal (scale-out) scaling.

■ Shards simplify the scope of replications.

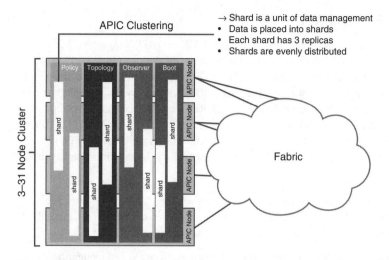

Figure 3-34   *Sharding*

One or more shards are located on each Cisco APIC appliance and processed by a controller instance located on that appliance. The shard data assignments are based on a predetermined hash function, and a static shard layout determines the assignment of shards to appliances. Each replica in the shard has a use preference, and writes occur on the replica that is elected leader. Other replicas are followers and do not allow writes. In the case of a split-brain condition, automatic reconciliation is performed based on time stamps. Each Cisco APIC has all Cisco APIC functions; however, processing is evenly distributed throughout the Cisco APIC cluster.

User Interface: Graphical User Interface

The GUI is an HTML5-based web UI that works with most modern web browsers. The GUI provides seamless access to both the APIC and the individual nodes.

User Interface: Command-Line Interface

A full stylistic and semantic (where it applies) compatibility with Cisco NX-OS CLI is provided. The CLI for the entire Cisco ACI is accessed through the APIC and supports a transactional mode. There is also the ability to access specific Cisco ACI nodes with a read-only CLI for troubleshooting. An integrated Python-based scripting interface is supported that allows user-defined commands to attach to the command tree as if they were native platform-supported commands. Additionally, the APIC provides a library for any custom scripts.

User Interface: RESTful API

The Cisco APIC supports a comprehensive RESTful API over HTTP(S) with XML and JSON encoding bindings. Both class-level and tree-oriented data access are provided by the API. Representational state transfer (REST) is a style of software architecture for distributed systems such as the World Wide Web. REST has emerged over the past few years as a predominant web services design model. REST has increasingly displaced other design models such as SOAP and Web Services Description Language (WSDL) because of its simpler style. The uniform interface that any REST interface must provide is considered fundamental to the design of any REST service, and thus the interface has these guiding principles:

- **Identification of resources:** Individual resources are identified in requests, for example, using URIs in web-based REST systems. The resources are conceptually separate from the representations that are returned to the client.

- **Manipulation of resources through these representations:** When a client holds a representation of a resource, including any metadata attached, it has enough information to modify or delete the resource on the server, provided it has permission.

- **Self-descriptive messages:** Each message includes enough information to describe how to process the message. Responses also explicitly indicate their cache ability.

An important concept in REST is the existence of resources (sources of specific information), each of which is referenced with a global identifier (such as a URI in HTTP). In order to manipulate these resources, components of the network (user agents and origin servers) communicate via a standardized interface (such as HTTP) and exchange representations of these resources (the actual documents conveying the information).

Any number of connectors (clients, servers, caches, tunnels, etc.) can mediate the request, but each does so without "seeing past" its own request (referred to as *layering*, another constraint of REST and a common principle in many other parts of information and networking architecture). Thus, an application can interact with a resource by knowing two things: the identifier of the resource and the action required. The application does not need to know whether there are caches, proxies, gateways, firewalls, tunnels, or anything else between it and the server actually holding the information. The application must understand the format of the information (representation) returned, which is typically an HTML, XML, or JSON document of some kind, although it may be an image, plain text, or any other content. The document model in XML and JSON is described in Chapter 4, "Operational Model."

System Access: Authentication, Authorization, and RBAC

The Cisco APIC supports both local and external authentication and authorization (TACACS+, RADIUS, Lightweight Directory Access Protocol [LDAP]) as well as role-based administrative control (RBAC) to control read and write access for **all** managed objects and to enforce Cisco ACI administrative and per-tenant administrative separation as shown in Figure 3-35. The APIC also supports domain-based access control, which enforces where (under which subtrees) a user has access permissions.

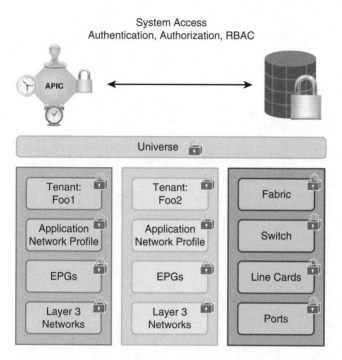

Figure 3-35 *Authentication, Authorization, and RBAC*

Summary

The Cisco ACI policy model enables the configuration and management of a scalable architecture of network and service objects. The policy model provides robust repeatable controls, multitenancy, and minimal requirements for detailed knowledge of the underlying network infrastructure as this information is known by the Cisco APIC. The model is designed for multiple types of data centers including private and public clouds.

ACI provides a logical model for laying out applications, which is then applied to the fabric by Cisco APIC. It helps to bridge the gaps in communication between application requirements and the network constructs that enforce them. The Cisco APIC model is designed for rapid provisioning of applications on the network that can be tied to robust policy enforcement while maintaining a workload-anywhere approach.

The Cisco APIC is a modern, highly scalable distributed control system that manages the Cisco ACI switch elements and offers policy-driven network provisioning that is implicitly automated. The APIC is designed to accomplish all of this while remaining out of the data path, thus allowing extremely high performance of Cisco ACI.

Chapter 4

Operational Model

RFC 3535 (http://tools.ietf.org/html/rfc3535) is an informational RFC initiated in 2002 that captures the status of the industry in terms of network management and the requests of operation teams to networking gear manufacturers. The document highlights the shortcomings of existing technologies such as the Simple Network Management Protocol (SNMP) and the command-line interface (CLI). It also calls for networks to be configured as a whole, and for configurations to be text based so that revision control can be easily applied to them with tools such as Apache Subversion (SVN), Mercurial, or Git.

CLIs are great tools for interactive changes to the configuration, but they are not designed for automation, ease of parsing (CLI scraping is neither efficient nor practical), or customization. Furthermore, CLIs don't have the capability to compete with the power of parsing, string manipulation, and the advanced logic that sophisticated scripting languages such as Python can offer.

The operational model introduced by Cisco Application Centric Infrastructure (ACI) technology is intended to address the network management requirements described in RFC 3535. An operator can configure Cisco ACI using specialized scripts or graphical user interfaces that execute Representational state transfer (REST) calls. This operational model is designed to replace or complement the traditional CLI.

This chapter covers the key technologies and tools that new administrators and operators need to be familiar with to work in a Cisco ACI environment, and it explains how those tools and technologies are used in a Cisco ACI–based data center.

Introduction to Key Technologies and Tools for Modern Data Centers

In a data center based on the Cisco ACI fabric, the operator can use

- The Graphical User Interface

- Custom Python scripts that perform complex operations on the entire fabric

- Native REST calls via tools such as Postman

The administrator of a modern data center must be familiar with the following:

- **REST:** RESTful APIs used with an Extensible Markup Language (XML) or JavaScript Object Notation (JSON) payload have become the preferred web service model, replacing previous models such as SOAP and WSDL. Modern controllers such as the Cisco APIC can be managed entirely via REST calls.

- **Python:** Python is becoming one of the preferred scripting languages for operations including data center management and configuration.

- **Git (or similar tools):** Git is a revision control system built to facilitate distributed software development. Git is used by enterprises to manage revisions of configuration scripts.

Network Management Options

The networking industry has developed various approaches to network management. Table 4-1 outlines the differences among the industry's network management technologies and protocols that are currently used the most: REST, Network Configuration Protocol (NETCONF), and Simple Network Management Protocol (SNMP).

Table 4-1 *Comparison of REST, NETCONF, and SNMP*

	REST	NETCONF	SNMP
Transport	HTTP/HTTPS	SSH	UDP
Payload formatting	XML, JSON	XML	BER
Schema		YANG	MIBs
Identification of resources	URLs	Paths	OIDs

The following are the key requirements for management protocols as expressed in RFC 3535:

- The payload must be human readable.

- The payload must be text based for ease of revision control.

- Transactions must follow the ACID rules: they must be atomic, consistent, independent, and durable.

The Cisco ACI implementation is based on REST, which meets the first two requirements in the list. Cisco ACI is designed to ensure that transactions meet the ACID rules.

REST Protocol

A RESTful web service (also called a *RESTful web API*) is implemented using HTTP and the principles of REST. A RESTful web service is a collection of resources that includes the following:

- The base universal resource identifier (URI) for the web service, such as https://<IP of controller>/resources/.

- The Internet media type of the data supported by the service, typically XML or JSON.

- The set of operations supported by using the HTTP methods GET, POST, and DELETE. Standard HTTP requests have the following semantics:

  - **POST:** Used to perform configurations. Target domain name, class, and options specify roots of subtrees at which modifications are applied. Data carried in the request is in the form of structured text (XML or JSON) subtrees.

  - **DELETE:** Used to delete objects; for example, to delete configurations.

  - **GET:** Used to perform queries. It specifies the retrieval of objects in the scope of the URL.

The typical sequence of configuration is shown in the following steps:

Step 1. Authenticate: Call **https://<IP of controller>/login.xml** with a payload that in XML could look similar to **<user name='username' pwd= 'password'/>**. This call returns a cookie value that the browser uses for the next calls.

Step 2. Send HTTP POST to apply the configuration: The URL of the POST message varies depending on the object; for example: **https://<IP of controller>/api/ mo/uni.xml**, where **api** indicates that this call is to the API, **mo** indicates that this call is to modify a managed object, **uni** (universe) refers to the root of the object tree, and **.xml** indicates that the payload is in XML format. If the end of the URL were **.json**, that would mean that the payload is in JSON format.

Step 3. Verify the HTTP status code: You want a response of 200 OK.

Most automation tools include the native capability to perform REST calls and use XML or JSON payloads. This makes it easy to integrate REST-capable network devices into an automation workflow.

Various tools enable you to test REST calls individually. One convenient tool is Postman (http://www.getpostman.com). Postman makes sending REST calls easy: just choose the

HTTP method (POST, DELETE, or GET), enter the URL, enter the XML payload, and click the Send button to send the post to the controller. You can also use Python (or any other scripting language) by creating a simple script that transforms XML files into REST calls, or you can use a software development kit (SDK) that makes REST calls directly.

XML, JSON, and YAML

XML and JSON are formats to structure data. Both enable you to serialize objects for the purpose of transferring data (name/value pairs) between clients and servers. Their structuring formats differ in their syntax and how they provide a representation of such things as hierarchy and arrays of data.

The XML format is very similar to HTML.

The JSON format has the following characteristics:

■ Each object is delimited by curly brackets.

■ Key-value pairs are separated by a colon (:).

■ Arrays are enclosed in square brackets and a comma follows each element of the array.

Note   For additional information on the JSON syntax, visit http://json.org/.

Examples 4-1 and 4-2 show the same tenant configuration in the Cisco ACI fabric in XML format and JSON format, respectively. The configuration creates a tenant called NewCorp in a bridge domain called bridgedomain1.

Example 4-1   *Tenant Configuration in Cisco ACI Formatted in XML*

```
<fvTenant descr="" dn="uni/tn-NewCorp" name="NewCorp" >
  <fvCtx name="router1" >
  </fvCtx>
  <fvBD arpFlood="no" descr="" mac="00:22:BD:F8:19:FF" name="bridgedomain1"
unicastRoute="yes" unkMacUcastAct="proxy" unkMcastAct="flood">
    <fvRsCtx tnFvCtxName="router1"/>
  </fvBD>
</fvTenant>
```

Example 4-2   *Tenant Configuration in Cisco ACI Formatted in JSON*

```
{
    "fvTenant": {
        "attributes":{
            "dn":"uni/tn-NewCorp",
```

```
                "name":"NewCorp"
            },
            "children":[
                {
                    "fvCtx":{
                        "attributes":{
                            "name":"router1"
                        }
                    }
                },
                {
                    "fvBD":{
                        "attributes":{
                            "arpFlood":"no",
                            "name":"bridgedomain1",
                            "unicastRoute":"yes"
                        },
                        "children":[
                            {
                                "fvRsCtx":{
                                    "attributes":{
                                        "tnFvCtxName":"router1"
                                    }
                                }
                            }
                        ]
                    }
                }
            ]
        }
    }
}
```

YAML defines a format that is as powerful as JSON or XML in that it enables you to create hierarchical structures, arrays, and so on, but it is more compact and human-readable than JSON and XML.

Example 4-3 shows a configuration file formatted in YAML, which defines "tests" as an array of two elements, where each element includes three key-value pairs.

Example 4-3 *Using YAML Format for Configuration Files*

```
host:    192.168.10.1:7580
name:    admin
passwd:  password
```

```
tests:
  - type: xml
    path:  /api/node/mo/.xml
    file: tenant1.xml

  - type: xml
    path:  /api/node/mo/.xml
    file: application.xml
```

REST calls used to perform configurations in Cisco ACI carry either an XML-formatted payload or a JSON-formatted payload.

This chapter describes the use of YAML to format text files used as configuration files for Python scripts.

Python

This chapter isn't intended to be a comprehensive guide on Python. For most operators, the minimum knowledge of Python required may be to simply type

```
python code.py
```

But because you may want to either create a customized script or modify an existing one using Python, this section gives you an overview of Python and provides some basic knowledge in case you haven't used Python before.

Python is an interpreted programming language; it is not compiled into a standalone binary code. It is translated into bytecode that is automatically executed within a Python virtual machine. Python also offers a prompt from which to execute scripts in an interactive manner via the interpreter. This feature is useful for testing each individual line of a script. When you run the interpreter by invoking **python** from the prompt, you get this prompt: >>>. Because the examples in this chapter are often based on the use of the interpreter, all configuration lines that start with >>> refer to the use of the Python interpreter.

Python Basics

A good place to start learning Python is the online tutorial at https://docs.python.org/2/tutorial/inputoutput.html.

The following are some of the key characteristics of Python scripting:

- Indentation is mandatory.

- It is case sensitive.

- Python doesn't distinguish between "D" and 'D'.

- Comments start with #.

- Libraries in Python are called *modules*.

- The typical script starts with **import** followed by the modules that are needed.

- The module named sys is almost always needed because, among other things, it provides the capability to parse the command-line options with sys.argv[1], sys.argv[2], and so on.

- You don't need to declare the type of variables because this is done dynamically (you can check the type by using the command **type(n)**).

- It's possible to define new functions with the command **def function (abc)**.

- Python offers data structures that make data handling very convenient: lists, tuples, dictionaries (dict).

- Python checks errors at run time.

Where Is the **main()** Function?

In Python, there's no strict need for a **main()** function. But in a well-structured script, you may want to define the equivalent of a **main()** function as follows. Python invokes standard methods, which are defined with a double underscore (__) at the beginning. One example of such methods is __main__. When you call the Python script directly, __name__ is set to __main__. If this function is imported, then __name__ takes the name of the filename of that module.

```
def main()
if __name__ == '__main__':
  main()
```

Functions Definition

Basic functions in Python are created by using the keyword **def**, as shown in Example 4-4.

Example 4-4 *Defining a Function*

```
def myfunction (A):
    If A>10:
     Return "morethan10"

    If A<5:
      Return "lessthan5"
```

The **import math** command brings the module math into the current script. Use the command **dir** to see which classes and methods are defined in this module, as shown in Example 4-5.

Example 4-5 *Importing a Module*

```
>>> import math
>>> dir (math)
['__doc__', '__name__', '__package__', 'acos', 'acosh', 'asin', 'asinh', 'atan',
'atan2', 'atanh', 'ceil', 'copysign', 'cos', 'cosh', 'degrees', 'e', 'erf',
'erfc', 'exp', 'expm1', 'fabs', 'factorial', 'floor', 'fmod', 'frexp', 'fsum',
'gamma', 'hypot', 'isinf', 'isnan', 'ldexp', 'lgamma', 'log', 'log10', 'log1p',
'modf', 'pi', 'pow', 'radians', 'sin', 'sinh', 'sqrt', 'tan', 'tanh', 'trunc']
>>> math.cos(0)
1.0
```

You can import a specific function or method from a module; for example, from the argparse module, you can import the **ArgumentParser** function. In this case, you can invoke the function by its name directly without having to prepend the name of the module; in other words, you can call **ArgumentParser** instead of **argparse. ArgumentParser.**

Useful Data Structures

Python offers several types of data structures:

- **Lists:** A list is a number of connected items. For example the list a: a= [1, 2, 3, 4, 'five', [6, 'six']]. You can modify an element of a list; for instance, you can change a[0] from the value of 1 to "one" by entering **a[0]='one'**.

- **Tuples:** A tuple is similar to a list but cannot be modified: for example, a=(1, 2, 3, 4, 'five').

- **Dictionaries:** A dictionary is a collection of key-value pairs; for instance, you can define **protocols = {'tcp': '6', 'udp': '17'}**.

- **Sets:** A set is an unordered list of elements; for instance, you can define **protocols = {'tcp', '6', 'udp', '17'}**.

- **Strings:** A string is a linear sequence of characters, words, or other data; for instance, you can define **'abcdef'**.

Example 4-6 shows a list.

Example 4-6 *List*

```
>>> a = [1, [2, 'two']]
>>> a
[1, [2, 'two']]
>>> a[0]
1
>>> a[-1]
[2, 'two']
```

The following configuration shows a dictionary:

```
>>> protocols = {'tcp': '6', 'udp': '17'}
>>> protocols['tcp']
'6'
```

Example 4-7 shows a set.

Example 4-7 *Set*

```
>>> a = {'a', 'b', 'c'}
>>> a[0]
Traceback (most recent call last):
  File "<stdin>", line 1, in <module>
TypeError: 'set' object does not support indexing
```

Strings offer the option to concatenate string elements by using **%s**, which can be used regardless of whether the variables are numbers or strings. For instance, if a=10, then "foo%s"%a is Foo10.

You can perform sophisticated operations on strings. You can index individual elements, or select ranges of elements. Example 4-8 shows a string.

Example 4-8 *String*

```
>>> a ='abcdef'
>>> a[3]
'd'
>>> a[4:]
'ef'
```

Parsing Files

Parsing the content of files is made simple by using libraries offered by Python. The content of files (for instance, configuration files) can be parsed into a dictionary or a list depending on the configuration needs. A common human-readable format is YAML. One can import YAML libraries and parse files using existing functions.

Note   More information can be found at https://docs.python.org/2/library/configparser.html.

Example 4-9 shows how Python parses a YAML-formatted file into a dictionary. It shows the use of YAML parsing modules in Python.

Example 4-9   *Using YAML Libraries*

```
>>> import yaml
>>> f = open('mgmt0.cfg', 'r')
>>> config = yam.safe_load(f)
Traceback (most recent call last):
  File "<stdin>", line 1, in <module>
NameError: name 'yam' is not defined
>>> config = yaml.safe_load(f)
>>> config
{'leafnumber': 101, 'passwd': 'ins3965!', 'name': 'admin', 'url':
  'https://10.51.66.243', 'IP': '172.18.66.245', 'gateway': '172.18.66.1/16'}
```

YAML is not included by default in Python, so you need to install this library separately.

Python offers the capability to easily parse JSON-formatted files (https://docs.python.org/2/library/json.html). Example 4-10 shows the use of JSON parsing modules in Python.

Example 4-10   *Using JSON-Formatted Files*

```
{
  "name" : "ExampleCorp",
  "pvn"  : "pvn1",
  "bd"   : "bd1",
  "ap"   : [ {"name" : "OnlineStore",
              "epgs" : [{"name" : "app"},
                        {"name" : "web"},
                        {"name" : "db"}
                       ]
            }
          ]
}

>>> import json
>>> f = open('filename.json', 'r')
>>> dict = json.load(f)
>>> dict
{u'bd': u'bd1', u'ap': {u'epgs': [{u'name': u'app'}, {u'name': u'web'}, {u'name':
u'db'}], u'name': u'OnlineStore'}, u'name': u'ExampleCorp', u'pvn': u'pvn1'}
>>> dict['name']
u'ExampleCorp'
```

Verifying Python Scripts

Python code is not compiled, so you discover errors in the code when the code is executing. You can use **pylint <file name> | grep E** to find errors before you execute the code. You can install Pylint with **pip** as follows:

```
sudo pip install pylint
```

The errors start with the letter *E*.

Where to Run Python

Support for Python varies depending on the host operating system that you are running. If, for example, you have an Apple OS X–based machine, Python support is built-in. All the examples in this chapter are based on the use of Python on an Apple MacBook. If you are using an OS X machine, you may need to install Xcode (https://developer.apple.com/xcode/). Many operating systems support python, but they are not covered.

Pip, EasyInstall, and Setup Tools

In general, it is convenient to have pip installed to install other Python packages, known as *eggs*. Think of an egg as being similar to a Java JAR file.

If you need to run Python on a Linux machine, use yum or apt-get to install the Python setup tools (https://pypi.python.org/pypi/setuptools or **wget https://bootstrap.pypa.io/ez_setup.py -O - | sudo python**), then use easy_install (which is part of the setup tools) to install pip, and then use pip to install other packages:

- **yum** (or **apt-get**) **install python-setuptools**

- **easy_install –i http://pypi.gocept.com/simple/ pip**

If you run Python on an OS X machine, first install Homebrew (http://brew.sh/) to install the setup tools, then use Homebrew or easy_install to install pip, and then use pip to install Python packages.

In the case of the Python egg for ACI, use easy_install to install it.

Which Packages Do I Need?

Python calls libraries *modules*. Some modules are installed by default, while others come as part of packages. The common tool used to install Python packages is pip (https://pypi.python.org/pypi/pip), with the syntax **pip install –i <url>**.

This is a list of common packages that you should install:

- **CodeTalker:** https://pypi.python.org/pypi/CodeTalker/0.5

- **Websockets:** https://pypi.python.org/pypi/websockets

This is a common list of libraries that you need to import in Python:

- import sys

- import os

- import json

- import re

- import yaml

- import requests

The following configuration shows how to set the path in a Python script so that it can find the proper libraries:

```
sys.path.append('pysdk')
sys.path.append('vmware/pylib')
sys.path.append('scvmm')
```

virtualenv

Virtual Env is a way to create separate Python environments with different packages installed. Imagine that you need to run Python applications that have different dependencies. One application requires library version 1, and the other requires library version 2, so you need to choose which version to install. Virtual Env scopes the installation of the packages to individual and separate Python environments so that you don't have to choose.

> **Note**   Additional information about Virtual Env is available at https://pypi.python.org/pypi/virtualenv.

Example 4-11 shows how to create a new virtualenv. First, install virtualenv with **sudo pip install virtualenv**. Next, **virtualenv cobra1** creates a virtual environment called cobra1. Enter cobra1 by using **cd cobra1**, and then activate it with **source bin/activate**. You now can install packages that are specific to this environment. If you want to leave the virtual environment, just enter **deactivate**.

Example 4-11   *Creation of a Virtual Environment*

```
prompt# sudo pip install virtualenv
prompt# virtualenv cobra1
prompt# cd cobra1
prompt# source bin/activate
(cobra1)prompt# pip install requests
[...]
(cobra1)prompt# deactivate
```

You can run Python scripts with this virtual environment from any folder on the host. If you want to switch to a different virtual environment, use **source <newvenv>/bin/ activate**, then run the scripts, and then enter **deactivate**.

You can also compress the virtual environment with tar and share it with other administrators.

Git and GitHub

Centralized version control systems have been available since the early days of software development. Distributed version control systems are newer to the market, so you may be more familiar with the centralized type of system. Git is a distributed version/revision control system. Because Git is one of the most popular version control systems currently in use, every network administrator should be familiar with its key concepts.

Revision control is used for managing software development projects or documentation.

GitHub is a Git-based repository that offers a cloud-based centralized repository. Cisco has several repositories on GitHub. You can find the Cisco ACI repository at https:// github.com/datacenter/ACI.

Basic Concepts of Version Control

The following are some of the key services of a version control system:

- Synchronization of the changes performed on the same code by different developers

- Tracking of the changes

- Backup and restore capabilities

Key terminology that you should be familiar with includes the following:

- **Repository (repo):** Where the files are stored

- **Trunk, master, main, or mainline:** The main location of the code in the repository

- **Working set:** The local copy of the files from the central repository

Version control systems are used in networking to control the development of scripts that will be used to manage the network. As a network administrator, you need to be able to perform the following key version control system operations:

- Cloning a repository or checking out; for example, creating a local copy of the entire repository

- Pulling from a repository or rebasing; for example, updating the local repository with the changes from the central repository

- Adding a new file to a repository (if permitted)

■ Pushing changes (checking in or committing) to the central repository (if permitted): for example, sending the modifications that you performed on your local copy of the script back to the main repository

If you contribute changes to the main repository, your changes will conflict with other administrators' changes or with the existing repository, and those conflicts will have to be resolved before your changes are merged and become effective.

Centralized Versus Distributed

Popular version control systems such as Apache Subversion (SVN) use a centralized repository, which means that after you make changes to a local copy of the main code and want to check in those changes, you need to be online and connected to the centralized repository. In a distributed version control system such as Git or Mercurial, each developer has a local copy of the central repository and makes local commits before pushing the changes to the central repository. This offers the advantage of having a local system with the history of the changes and enabling the developer to defer synchronizing the changes to the central repository. Clearly, if many people are contributing to the same code, it is practical to rebase the local copy frequently so that only minor conflicts have to be resolved before the commit to the central repository.

Enhanced patching is among the improvements that Git has brought to the development of code. Previously, after a developer made local changes to the code on his machine, the patch process required the developer to use the **diff** utility to create a file showing the changes between the new code and the original code, and then send the file as an email attachment to the owner of the code so that the owner could review and apply the changes. Git solves this problem by having on the main repository a fork (now called a *repository mirror*) of the central code to which the developer can push changes. This generates a "pull request," which is then handled by the person who owns the main repository.

In most cases, you would work with a central repository from which all the people on the team pull changes, but Git also provides the capability to work with a fully distributed version control system without a central repository.

Overview of Basic Operations with Git

As a network administrator, you won't need to manage sophisticated handling of branches, but you should know how to get a local copy of the scripts that Cisco makes available and keep them up to date. You might even want to contribute improvements to the central repository of the community.

If your company has a local repository of scripts, you may need to maintain a revision control system to synchronize changes to these scripts across multiple operators. If so, you need to be familiar with the following key operations:

■ **Get a local copy of a central repository:** git clone

■ **Add files to a local repository:** git add

- **Update the local repository:** git pull

- **Upload to the central repository:** git push

- **Execute a local commit:** git commit

The changes that you perform on the scripts daily are done on what is called a *workspace*. The local commits are saved in the local repository.

Figure 4-1 illustrates a very simplified view of Git operations.

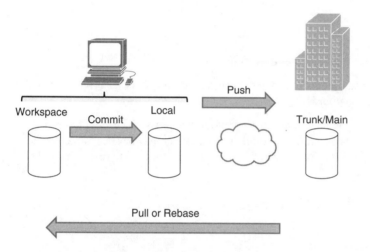

Figure 4-1 *Simplified View of Git Operations*

Installing/Setting Up Git

Git installation procedures vary depending on the platform. For instance, the installation command would be something like **yum install git** or **apt-get install git** depending on the OS distribution.

Configure your username and email address with **git config**, and this configuration information is stored in the ~/.gitconfig file.

Create a directory that you want to be the local repository on your computer by using the following configuration:

```
mkdir <directory name>
git init
```

Key Commands in Git

To get started, first clone a repository to your computer as shown in the following configuration:

```
git clone git+ssh://<username>@git.company.local:port/folder
```

As the command indicates, Git can use SSH to connect to the repository. Alternatively, it can use HTTP/HTTPS, as shown in the following configuration:

```
git clone https://github.com/datacenter/ACI
```

The **clone** command also adds a shortcut called *origin* to link to the main repository.

After you modify local files on your workspace, you save the changes in the local copy of the repository by "staging" the file with **git add** and saving it into the local repository with **git commit**, as shown in the following configuration:

```
git add <file name>
git commit
```

You also use **git add** to add new files to the repository.

The **git commit** command doesn't change the centralized repository (aka trunk or main-line). It saves changes on your local machine.

After several commits, you may want to upload your changes to the central repository. Before you do so, to avoid conflicts with other changes that may have occurred on the remote repository since you cloned or pulled it, rebase the local copy first, using either of these configurations:

```
git pull --rebase origin master
```

or

```
git fetch origin master
git rebase -i origin/master
```

where **origin** refers to the remote repository, **master** indicates that **git** is asking the local repository to appear as master, and the interactive **rebase** lets you fix the conflicts.

After you merge the changes from the remote repository and the local changes, use the following command to upload the changes to the remote repository:

```
git push origin master
```

Operations with the Cisco APIC

With Cisco ACI, administrators configure modern data center networks by using a mix of CLI commands, REST calls, and Python scripting, as illustrated by Figure 4-2.

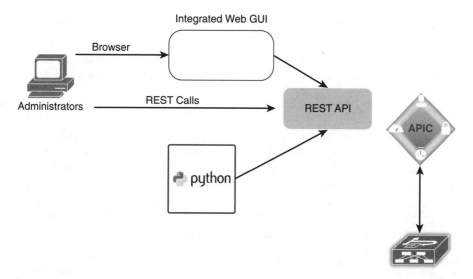

Figure 4-2 *Cisco APIC Northbound and Southbound Interfaces*

With Cisco ACI, the user defines configurations on the Cisco APIC controller in several ways:

■ Using REST calls with XML- or JSON-formatted payloads that are sent to the Cisco APIC. These can be sent in many ways, using tools such as Postman or Python scripts that send REST calls.

■ Using a custom-built graphical user interface that sends REST calls.

■ Using the CLI to navigate the object model from the Cisco APIC.

■ Using Python scripts that use the associated Cisco ACI libraries.

Each tool has its areas of strength and weakness, but the following is most likely how different teams use the tools:

■ **GUI:** Mainly used for infrastructure administration and for monitoring and trouble-shooting purposes. It is also used to generate templates.

■ **CLI on Cisco APIC:** Mainly used to create shell scripts and to troubleshoot.

■ **POSTMAN and other REST tools:** Mainly used for testing and to define configurations to be automated.

■ **Scripts based on XML, JSON, and REST calls:** Simple scripts for the operator to perform CLI-like operations without the need to really understand Python.

■ **Scripts based on the software development kit (SDK):** Simple scripts for the operator to perform feature functionalities without the need to wait for a software release to provide the automated results desired.

■ **PHP and web pages with embedded REST calls:** Mainly used to create simple user interfaces for operators or IT customers.

■ **Advanced orchestration tools such as Cisco Intelligent Automation for Cloud or UCS Director:** Used for end-to-end provisioning of compute and network.

Object Tree

Everything in the Cisco ACI infrastructure is represented as a class or a *managed object* (abbreviated "MO"). Each managed object is identified by a name and contains a set of typed values, or *properties*. For instance, a given tenant is an object of the same type and with a specific name, such as Example.com. A routing instance in the fabric is an object, as is a port on a switch. Objects can be concrete (labeled "C" in the Cisco APIC REST API User Guide) or abstract (labeled "A" in the Cisco APIC REST API User Guide); a tenant, for instance, is an abstract object, while a port is a concrete object.

All configurations in Cisco ACI consist of creating such objects, modifying their properties, deleting the objects, or querying the tree. For instance, to create or manipulate objects, you use REST calls with a URL of this type: https://<IP of the controller>/api/mo/uni/.xml. To perform an operation on a class, use a REST call with a URL of this type: https://<IP of the controller>/api/class/uni/.xml. You navigate the object data store (that is, the current tree saved in the distributed database) with a tool called *Visore*, which is accessible by pointing your browser to the APIC controller with the following URL: https://<hostname>/visore.html.

Visore is an object browser; as such, it lets you query the tree for classes or objects. For instance, you can enter the name of a class such as **tenant** and get the list of instances of this class (that is, the specific tenants that you instantiated). Or, if you can enter the distinguished name of a particular tenant object, you get the information about that specific tenant. An example of Visore is depicted in Figure 4-3.

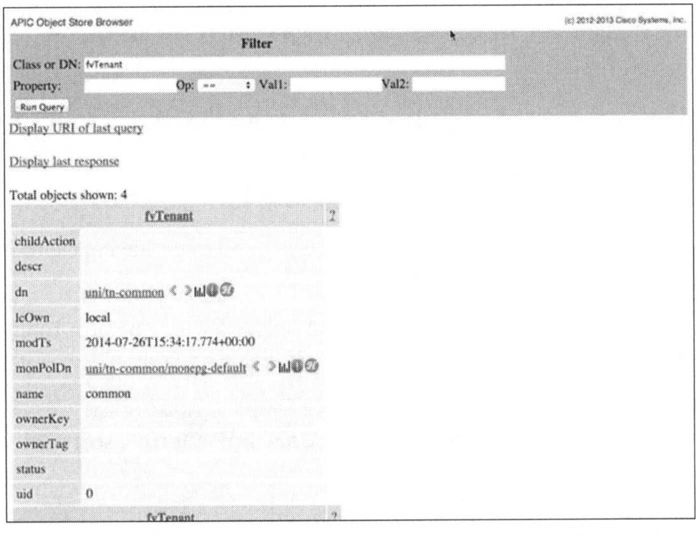

Figure 4-3   *Visore*

Classes, Objects, and Relations

Managed object instances can contain other instances, forming a parent-child relationship as part of a tree, known as the *Managed Information Tree* (MIT). Figure 4-4 provides a high-level view of the object tree organization. At the root is "the class universe." Next are the classes that belong to the infrastructure (that is, physical concepts such as ports, port channels, VLANs, etc.) and classes that belong to logical concepts (such as the tenant, networks within the tenant, etc.).

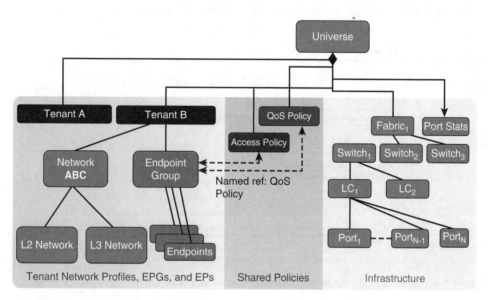

Figure 4-4 *Hierarchy of the Object Model*

To create or manipulate objects, you send REST calls that identify the resources by their distinguished name (DN) or by their relative name (RN). A DN identifies a managed object directly, while an RN identifies an object by reference to its parent object. A switch port is the child of a line card, which is the child of a switch, which is a child of the root class. As an example, the RN for a particular port is Port-7 and its DN is /Root/Switch-3/Linecard-1/Port-7.

Note You can find the list of packages and all the classes by exploring the APIC API Model Documentation on the APIC controller itself (this link provides the instructions: http://www.cisco.com/c/en/us/td/docs/switches/datacenter/aci/apic/sw/1-x/api/rest/ b_APIC_RESTful_API_User_Guide.html).

All classes are organized as members of packages. Cisco ACI defines, among others, the following packages:

- **Aaa:** user class for authentication, authorization, accounting

- **fv:** fabric virtualization

- **vz:** virtual zone

Figure 4-5 illustrates the list of classes that are part of the package fv.

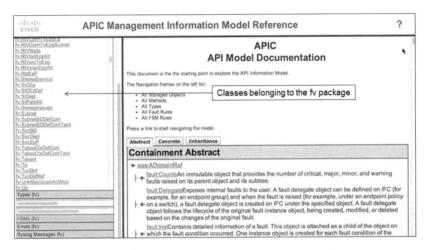

Figure 4-5   *The APIC Management Information Model Reference*

The class for tenant is named fv:Tenant, where fv indicates the package that the class belongs to. The distinguished name of a tenant is uni/tn-[name], where uni is the class universe and tn stands for target name. Figure 4-6 illustrates the information that you find for the class tenant in the API APIC Model Documentation, which shows the relationship of the class tenant with the other classes. The vrf/routing information (Ctx) is a child of the class tenant.

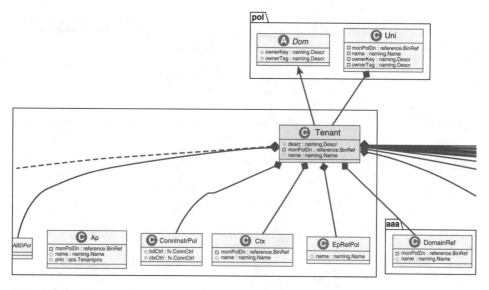

Figure 4-6 *Tenant Class*

You can explore the object data store for the class tenant by entering the string fvTenant (without a colon) in the search field (labeled "Class or DN") of Visore.

The relationship is expressed in XML format following a template that resembles Example 4-12.

Example 4-12 *XML Format*

```
<zzzObject property1 = "value1",
      property2 = "value2",
      property3 = "value3">
   <zzzChild1 childProperty1 = "childValue1",
        childProperty2 = "childValue1">
     </zzzChild1>
</zzzObject>
```

It is not possible to express all object relationships simply by using the parent-child relationship. Some objects are not related in terms of parent-child relationship but depend on each other. The dependency between two such objects is expressed in terms of a *relation*. All managed objects that express a relationship between classes or objects that is not a parent-child relationship are prefixed with Rs, which stands for relation source: {SOURCE MO PKG}::Rs{RELATION NAME}.

Figure 4-7 illustrates the model for the class infra from package infra.

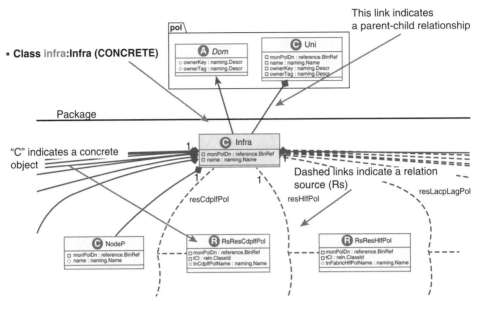

Figure 4-7   *The Infra Class*

Example 4-13 shows an object called the selector.

The configuration in Example 4-13 shows a selector for leaf 101 and a reference to a selection of ports on this leaf (port 1 and port 2). NodeP is a class that is a child of class infra (hence infraNodeP). The name of the object that selects leaf101 is "leaf101" (an arbitrary name chosen by the administrator). The object LeafS is a selector of switches that are children of the class NodeP. Furthermore, RsAccPortP defines a relation to the port selector that has been instantiated as "port1and2" (arbitrary name chosen by the admin).

Example 4-13   *Object NodeP in XML Format*

```
<infraInfra dn="uni/infra">
[...]
   <infraNodeP name="leaf101 ">
      <infraLeafS name="line1" type="range">
         <infraNodeBlk name="block0" from_="101" to_="101" />
      </infraLeafS>
      <infraRsAccPortP tDn="uni/infra/accportprof-port1and2 " />
   </infraNodeP>
[...]
</infraInfra>
```

Figure 4-8 illustrates the relationship between the classes. The solid line indicates a parent-child relationship and the dashed line indicates a relation.

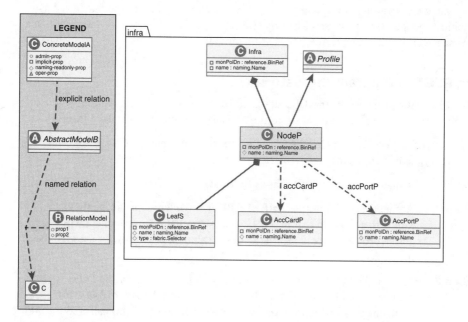

Figure 4-8 *NodeP Class*

Naming Conventions

Using the API APIC Model Documentation, you can find the exact naming rules. These are some of the common naming rules:

- **MO:** Managed Object (i.e., a class)

- **PKG:** Package (collection of classes)

- **vz:** virtual zone

- **Br:** Binary

- **CP:** Contract Profile

- **fv:** fabric virtualization

- **AEPg:** application endpoint group

- **Rs:** relation source

- **Cons:** consumer

Class names are expressed as package:class.

Object Store

The object store is a distributed database that runs on the APIC controller and stores key-value pairs with relational and tree capabilities. The object store can be viewed as multiple independent databases. The object store exposes all the state of the system in a formalized way according to the information model.

Using REST to Program the Network

The Cisco ACI management model is designed for automation. Every configurable element is part of the object tree known as the Management Information Tree (MIT).

The networking elements in Cisco ACI can be configured using the GUI, REST calls, or a CLI that operates on the managed objects.

The typical sequence of configuration is as follows:

Step 1.   Authenticate: Call **https://<IP of APIC controller>/api/mo/aaaLogin. xml** with a payload that in XML is **<aaaUser name='username' pwd= 'password'/>**. This call returns a cookie value that the browser uses for the next calls.

Step 2.   Send HTTP POST to apply the configuration: The URL of the POST message varies depending on the object; for example: **https://<IP of APIC controller>/ /api/mo/uni.xml**, where **api** indicates that this call is to the API, **mo** indicates that this call is to modify a managed object, **uni** (universe) refers to the root of the object tree, and **.xml** indicates that the payload is in XML format. If the end of URL were **.json**, that would mean that the payload is in JSON format.

Step 3.   Verify the HTTP status code: You want a response of 200 OK.

With REST calls, the configuration is defined in the XML or JSON payload. The XML or JSON syntax/format depends on the controller object model. You can find examples for the Cisco Nexus 9000 and ACI on Github.

The following configuration shows a REST call to create a "tenant" (or virtual data center) with APIC:

```
HTTP POST call to https://ipaddress/api/node/mo/uni.xml
XML payload: <fvTenant name='Tenant1' status='created,modified'></fvTenant>
```

You can also use REST calls to delete objects by using the HTTP method DELETE or by using **"status="deleted"** with a POST call, as shown in Example 4-14.

Example 4-14 *Deleting Objects with REST Calls*

```
method: POST
url: http://<APIC IP>/api/node/mo/uni/fabric/comm-foo2.json
payload {
                "commPol":{
                   "attributes":{
                      "dn":"uni/fabric/comm-foo2",
                      "status":"deleted"
                   },
                   "children":[]
                }
             }
```

Tools to Send REST Calls

A simple way to perform configurations via REST calls is by using the tool called *POSTMAN*. Figure 4-9 shows how to use POSTMAN with the Cisco APIC.

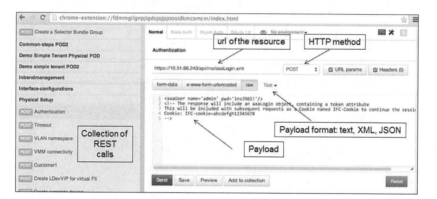

Figure 4-9 *Sending a REST Call with POSTMAN*

The first call you want to place is the Authentication call, with which you provide your username and password to the controller. Subsequent calls reuse the cookie token that you receive from the controller. Figure 4-9 also illustrates the configuration controls that POSTMAN offers. To place a call, you simply need to enter the URL of the resource as indicated, select the POST method, and fill the payload field with the XML- or JSON-formatted configuration.

Example 4-15 shows portions of a script, xml2REST.py, that takes as input the Domain Name System (DNS) name or IP address of the server and the name of a text file that includes the XML configuration settings.

Example 4-15   *Python Script to Send REST Calls*

```python
#!/usr/bin/python
[...]

def runConfig( status ):
            with open( xmlFile, 'r' ) as payload:
                if( status==200):
                    time.sleep(5)
                else:
                    raw_input( 'Hit return to process %s' % xmlFile )
                data = payload.read()
                url = 'http://%s/api/node/mo/.xml' % apic
                r = requests.post( url, cookies=cookies, data=data )
                result = xml.dom.minidom.parseString( r.text )
                status = r.status_code
try:
    xmlFile = sys.argv[1]
except Exception as e:
    print str(e)
    sys.exit(0)
apic = sys.argv[2]
auth = {
    'aaaUser': {
        'attributes': {
            'name':'admin',
            'pwd':'P@ssw0rd'
            }
        }
    }
status = 0
while( status != 200 ):
    url = 'http://%s/api/aaaLogin.json' % apic
    while(1):
        try:
            r = requests.post( url, data=json.dumps(auth), timeout=1 )
            break;
        except Exception as e:
            print "timeout"
    status = r.status_code
    print r.text
    cookies = r.cookies
    time.sleep(1)
runConfig( status )
```

Alternatively, if you want to perform a CLI-based configuration from your desktop to the controller, you can also use cURL or wget, as shown in Example 4-16, where the first REST call is used to provide a token cookie, which is saved in a text file and then reused in later calls.

Example 4-16 *Using cURL to Send REST Calls*

```
curl -X POST http://<APIC-IP>/api/aaaLogin.xml -d '<aaaUser name="admin"
  pwd="password" />' - cookie.txt


curl -b cookie.txt -X POST http://<APIC-IP>/api/mo/uni/tn-finance.xml -d
  '<fvTenant />'
```

REST Syntax in Cisco ACI

The format for the URL to place REST calls in Cisco ACI is as follows:

http://host[:port]/api/{mo|class}/{dn|className}.{json/xml}[?options]

The following list explains the meaning of each field in the URL:

- **/api/:** Specifies that the message is directed to the API.

- **mo | class:** Specifies whether the target of the operation is a managed object (MO) or an object class.

- **dn:** Specifies the distinguished name (DN) of the targeted MO.

- **className:** Specifies the name of the targeted class. This name is a concatenation of the package name of the object queried and the name of the class queried in the context of the corresponding package. For example, the class aaa:User results in a className of aaaUser in the URI.

- **json/xml:** Specifies whether the encoding format of the command or response HTML body is JSON or XML.

Simple operations are performed as shown in the following configuration to create a tenant (fvTenant):

```
POST to http://apic1/api/mo/uni.xml
<fvTenant name='Tenant1' status='created,modified'>
</fvTenant>
```

Example 4-17 shows how to create an application network profile (fvAp).

Example 4-17   *REST Call to Create an Application Network Profile*

```
POST to http://apic1/api/mo/uni.xml
<fvTenant name='Tenant1' status='created,modified'>
   <fvAp name='WebApp'>
   </fvAp>
</fvTenant>
```

Example 4-18 shows how to add an endpoint group (fvAEPg).

Example 4-18   *REST Call to Add an EPG*

```
POST to http://apic1/api/mo/uni.xml
<fvTenant name='Tenant1' status='created,modified'>
<fvAp name='WebApp'>
   <fvAEPg name="WEB" status="created,modified"/>
</fvAp>
</fvTenant>
```

The syntax for class-level queries is different in that, instead of using the distinguished name, you enter the concatenation of the package name and the class name:

<system>/api/*<component>*/class/**<pkgName><ClassName>**.[*xml*|*json*]**?**{*options*}

The following list explains the meaning of each field in the URL:

- **pkgName:** Represents the package name of the object queried.

- **className:** Represents the name of the class queried in the context of the corresponding package.

- **RN:** Collection of relative names forming a full DN identifying the path to the managed object on the MIT.

The following options can be used for queries:

- **query-target=[_self|children|subtree]:** Specifies whether to retrieve the object itself, children of the object, or a subtree

- **target-subtree-class=[mo-class*]:** Specifies the object classes to be retrieved if **query-target** is other than **self**

- **query-target-filter=[FILTER]:** Specifies object filters to be retrieved if **query-target** is other than **self**

- **rsp-subtree=[no|children|full]:** For objects returned, indicates whether subtree information should be included

- **rsp-prop-include=[all|naming-only|config-explicit|config-all|oper]:** Specifies what type of properties to include in the result

The format of the filter is as follows:

```
FILTER = OPERATOR(parameter|(FILTER)[/parameter|(FILTER)|value[,parameter|
(FILTER)|value]...])
```

The supported operators are

- **eq:** Equality

- **ne:** Inequality

- **lt:** Less than

- **gt:** Greater than

- **le:** Less or equal

- **ge:** Greater or equal

- **bw:** Between

- **Logical operators:** Not, and, or, xor, true, false

- **Anybit:** True if at least one bit is set

- **Allbits:** True if all bits are set

- **Wcard:** Wildcard

- **Pholder:** Property holder

- **Passive:** Passive holder

As an example, this is a query to show all fabric ports that failed in the given data range:

```
query-target-filter = "and(eq(faultevent:type,failed),eq(faultevent:object,
fabric_port), bw(faultevent:timestamp,06-14-12,06-30-12))"
```

Modeling Tenants in XML

This section shows how to create a tenant with the necessary bridging domain and routing instance. Example 4-19 shows how the tenant provides connectivity to servers through subnets 10.0.0.1/24 and 20.0.0.1/24. The default gateway can be either 10.0.0.1 or 20.0.0.1. Servers can connect to EPG VLAN10 or EPG VLAN20.

The EPG is also created as a port group in a VMware vSphere Distributed Switch (vDS) on VMware ESX. The virtual machine manager and Cisco APIC negotiate to determine which VLAN or VxLAN to use for the communication in this port group.

In Example 4-19, the meaning of the fields is as follows:

- **fvCtx:** Indicates the routing instance

- **fvBD:** The bridge domain

- **fvRsCtx:** The pointer from the bridge domain to the routing instance

- **fvSubnet:** The list of subnets and default gateways for the bridge domain

- **fvRsDomAtt:** The reference to the virtual machine mobility domain

Example 4-19   *Complete Tenant Configuration*

```
POST to http://apic1/api/mo/uni.xml
<polUni>
    <fvTenant dn="uni/tn-Customer1" name="Customer1">
    <fvCtx name="customer1-router"/>
    <fvBD name="BD1">
        <fvRsCtx tnFvCtxName="customer1-router" />
        <fvSubnet ip="10.0.0.1/24" scope="public"/>
        <fvSubnet ip="20.0.0.1/24" scope="public"/>
    </fvBD>
  <fvAp name="web-and-ordering">
    <fvAEPg name="VLAN10">
      <fvRsBd tnFvBDName="BD1"/>
      <fvRsDomAtt tDn="uni/vmmp-VMware/dom-Datacenter"/>
    </fvAEPg>
    <fvAEPg name="VLAN20">
      <fvRsBd tnFvBDName="BD1"/>
      <fvRsDomAtt tDn="uni/vmmp-VMware/dom-Datacenter"/>
    </fvAEPg>
</fvTenant>
</polUni>
```

Defining the Relationship Among EPGs (Providers and Consumers)

The communication path between EPGs is managed using the concept of contracts. Contracts define the protocols and Layer 4 ports that are used for the communication path between two EPGs.

Example 4-20 shows how a contract defines a permit all filter, where:

- **vzBrCP:** Indicates the name of the contract.

- **vzSubj:** Refers to the subject and is the name of the container of filters, which are similar to an ACL but more powerful in that they allow for separate inbound and outbound filtering

- **vzRsSubfiltAtt:** Refers to a filter; the default filter is permit any any

Example 4-20 *Definition of a Contract*

```
<vzBrCP name="A-to-B">
    <vzSubj name="any">
        <vzRsSubjFiltAtt tnVzFilterName="default"/>
    </vzSubj>
</vzBrCP>
```

The relationship between contracts is defined according to which EPG provides the contract and which EPG consumes the contract. Example 4-21 illustrates how EPG-A is made to talk to EPG-B, where:

■ **fvRsProv:** Indicates the name of the contract that EPG-A provides

■ **fvRsCons:** Indicates the name of the contract that EPG-B consumes

Example 4-21 *Definition of an EPG*

```
<fvAp name="web-and-ordering">
  <fvAEPg name="EPG-A">
    <fvRsProv tnVzBrCPName="A-to-B" />
  </fvAEPg>
  <fvAEPg name="EPG-B">
    <fvRsCons tnVzBrCPName="A-to-B"/>
  </fvAEPg>
</fvAp>
```

A Simple Any-to-Any Policy

The configuration described in the previous section instantiates a bridge domain for use by the tenant and a routing instance and default gateway. Servers can then be associated with EPGs VLAN10 and VLAN20. If the servers are in the same EPG, they can talk without any further configuration, but if they are part of different EPGs, the administrator has to configure explicit contracts and define which EPG can talk with which EPG.

Example 4-22 completes the previous configuration and enables any-to-any communication among EPGs just as a conventional routing and switching infrastructure would provide.

Example 4-22 *Definition of an Any-to-Any Policy*

```
POST to http://apic1/api/mo/uni.xml
<polUni>
    <fvTenant dn="uni/tn-Customer1" name="Customer1">
    <vzBrCP name="ALL">
      <vzSubj name="any">
```

```
            <vzRsSubjFiltAtt tnVzFilterName="default"/>
        </vzSubj>
    </vzBrCP>
    <fvAp name="web-and-ordering">
      <fvAEPg name="VLAN10">
        <fvRsCons tnVzBrCPName="ALL"/>
        <fvRsProv tnVzBrCPName="ALL" />
      </fvAEPg>
      <fvAEPg name="VLAN20">
        <fvRsCons tnVzBrCPName="ALL"/>
        <fvRsProv tnVzBrCPName="ALL" />
      </fvAEPg>
    </fvAp>
  </fvTenant>
</polUni>
```

ACI SDK

The main reason to use Python instead of sending plain-vanilla REST calls is that Python enables you to parse command-line options and configurations. You could use Python with simple scripts that turn XML into REST calls, but this approach requires formatting the XML configuration files according to the ACI object model. As a result, if you create such a script and you want to share it with other administrators/operators, they would have to understand the ACI object model. Ideally, you want to create scripts with configuration files and command-line options that anybody skilled in networking could use without having to learn the ACI object model. For this you need a Python SDK for ACI.

The ACI SDK provides modules that enable you to perform all the operations that the Cisco ACI fabric offers with the following advantages compared to the approach of just using REST calls and XML configurations:

- You can use Python to parse configuration files in whichever format you prefer.

- The SDK APIs can be identical over time, while the specific format of the XML object model may change.

- You can perform more sophisticated conditional operations, string manipulation, and so on.

ACI Python Egg

To use the functionalities provided by the SDK, you need to install the SDK egg files as shown in the following configuration. The filename of the egg looks like this: acicobra-1.0.0_457a-py2.7.egg. To install this package, use setup tools and pip as previously described.

```
sudo python setup.py easy_install ../acicobra-1.0.0_457a-py2.7.egg
```

Depending on where the ACI files have been installed, you may need to indicate the path in the Python code with the following call:

```
sys.path.append('your sdk path')
```

A good practice is to use **virtualenv** to create multiple Python environments with potentially different sets of libraries installed. To do this, you need to start with the **virtualenv** installation as shown in Example 4-23.

Example 4-23 *Creating a Virtual Environment for Cobra*

```
prompt# sudo pip install virtualenv
prompt# virtualenv cobra1
prompt# cd cobra1
prompt# source bin/activate
(cobra1)prompt# pip install requests
(cobra1)prompt# easy_install -Z acicobra-1.0.0_457a-py2.7.egg
```

Now run Python scripts from any directory on the host.

How to Develop Python Scripts for ACI

Python scripts must log in to the controller, get a token, and keep using this token to perform the whole configuration. Example 4-24 shows the initial calls for logging in to the fabric.

Example 4-24 *Logging In to the Fabric with the SDK*

```
import cobra.mit.access
import cobra.mit.session

ls = cobra.mit.session.LoginSession(apicurl, args.user, args.password)
md = cobra.mit.access.MoDirectory(ls)
md.login()
```

After logging in, look up objects by DN or classes as shown in the following configuration:

```
topMo=md.lookupByDn('uni')
topMp=md.lookupByClass('polUni')
```

A previous configuration illustrated how to create objects that perform operations related to fabric discovery of leafs. This is not going to modify anything on the object store of the controller until someone sends a configuration request as shown in Example 4-25.

Example 4-25   *Fabric Discovery*

```
import cobra.model.fabric


# login as in the previous Example
#
topMo = md.lookupByDn(str(md.lookupByClass('fabricNodeIdentPol')[0].dn)
leaf1IdentP = cobra.model.fabric.NodeIdentP(topMo, serial='ABC', nodeId='101',
name="leaf1")
leaf2IdentP = cobra.model.fabric.NodeIdentyP(topMo, serial='DEF', nodeId='102',
name="leaf2")
[...]
c = cobra.mit.request.ConfigRequest()
c.addMo(topMo)
md.commit(c)
```

Query the object tree for a particular class or object as described in Example 4-26. The advantage of doing this is that the DN is not hard-coded.

Example 4-26   *Querying with Cobra*

```
from cobra.mit.request import DnQuery, ClassQuery
# After logging in, get a Dn of the Tenant
cokeQuery = ClassQuery('fvTenant')
cokeQuery.propFilter = 'eq(fvTenant.name, "tenantname")'
cokeDn = str(md.query(cokeQuery)[0].dn)
```

Where to Find Python Scripts for ACI

At the time of writing, Python scripts are posted on github at the following URL: https://github.com/datacenter/ACI

For Additional Information

RFC 3535: http://tools.ietf.org/html/rfc3535

ACI Management Information Model:

http://www.cisco.com/c/en/us/support/cloud-systems-management/application-policy-infrastructure-controller-apic/products-technical-reference-list.html

http://www.cisco.com/c/en/us/support/cloud-systems-management/application-policy-infrastructure-controller-apic/tsd-products-support-configure.html

Github: https://github.com/

Python: https://www.python.org/

Summary

This chapter described the new skills that administrators and operators need to have to use Application Centric Infrastructure to configure network properties. These include the ability to configure REST calls and the ability to use and potentially create Python scripts. This chapter also introduced the key concepts of Python and the key formats that are used for REST calls and for configuration files. Finally, this chapter explained how to get started with REST configurations and the ACI SDK, and provided examples to illustrate the concepts.

Chapter 5

Data Center Design with Hypervisors

The goal of this chapter is to describe the networking requirements and design considerations when using hypervisors in the data center.

Managing virtualized data centers poses several challenges to the network administrator, such as:

- Because every server includes a networking component, the number of networking components is proportional to the number of servers.

- There is little visibility of the traffic originated by virtual machines (VM) because often the switching is performed within the server itself.

- Network configurations need to be deployed across a large number of servers while ensuring that they fit with the mobility requirements of VMs.

Cisco provides several technologies that address the networking needs for these environments. There are at least four different approaches to integrate VM switching in the data center:

- **Using virtual switches:** Involves switching traffic with a software switch within the server (for instance, based on the Cisco Nexus 1000V Series Switches)

- **Port extension:** Entails modeling the virtual ports on a "controlling bridge" (Virtual Networking TAG, VNTAG also found as VN-TAG)

- **Endpoint group extension:** Involves extending the Cisco ACI endpoint groups into the virtualized server

- **Building an overlay from the server:** consists of creating an overlay network from the virtual switch level.

Cisco ACI is designed to provide a multi-hypervisor solution, so the network administrator must be familiar with a variety of hypervisors. This chapter illustrates the key characteristics and naming conventions of the most popular hypervisors, including Linux Kernel-based Virtual Machine (KVM), Microsoft Hyper-V, and VMware ESX/ESXi, Citrix XenServer.

The approach that ACI takes with regard to switching VM traffic consists of having virtualized servers send traffic out to the leaf of the ACI fabric for data-forwarding purposes. This approach has the following advantages:

■ The network infrastructure can be tested independently of the software, which allows validation with known traffic-generation tools to automatically validate the traffic forwarding for virtualized servers.

■ This type of infrastructure offers predictable performance because traffic forwarding involves no compute processors.

Virtualized Server Networking

Virtualized server solutions are comparable in many ways and have similar goals. However, they use different naming conventions to reference components. This section sheds light on the role and naming of each component.

Typical components of a given virtualized server environment consist of the following:

■ **Hypervisor:** The software that provides virtualization of a physical host

■ **Virtual machine manager:** The element that manages virtual machines across multiple virtualized hosts

■ **Virtual software switch:** The software that provides switching for virtual network adapters

■ **Endpoint group:** The segmentation of a virtual switch into multiple security zones

■ **Cloud orchestration:** The element that provides the ability to order and instantiate virtualized workloads and their connectivity

Table 5-1 offers a mapping between these components and the most widely used virtualization solutions on the market.

Table 5-1 *Virtualized Server Solution Concepts in Different Vendor Implementations*

	KVM	Microsoft	VMware	XEN
Hypervisor	KVM	Hyper-V	ESX/ESXi	XenServer
Virtual Machine Manager	virt-manager	System Center Virtual Machine Manager	vCenter	XenCenter

	KVM	Microsoft	VMware	XEN
Software Switch	Open vSwitch	Hyper-V Virtual Switch	VMware standard vSwitch, VMware vSphere Distributed Switch/ Distributed Virtual Switch	Virtual switch, option to use Open vSwitch or XEN bridge
Endpoint Group	Bridge (br0, br1, etc.)	Virtual Subnet Identifier	Port group	Virtual Network, or Bridge if using Open vSwitch (br0, br1, etc.)
Cloud Orchestration	OpenStack	Azure	vCloud Director	
Virtual Network Adapter	Guest NIC, tap0 if using Open vSwitch	Virtual Network Adapter	vNIC	VIF (virtual interface), tap0 if using Open vSwitch
Virtual Machine Hot Migration	KVM Live Migration	Microsoft Live Migration	vMotion	XenMotion
Physical NICs	Eth0, eth1, etc.		vmnic	Pif or eth0, eth1, etc.

Why Have a Software Switching Component on the Server?

Quoting from the "Transparent Bridging" section of Cisco DocWiki (http://docwiki.cisco.com/wiki/Transparent_Bridging):

> The bridge uses its [MAC address] table as the basis for traffic forwarding. When a frame is received on one of the bridge's interfaces, the bridge looks up the frame's destination address in its internal table. If the table contains an association between the destination address and any of the bridge's ports aside from the one on which the frame was received, the frame is forwarded out the indicated port. If no association is found, the frame is flooded to all ports except the inbound port.

Figure 5-1 represents a virtualized server with two VMs: VM1 and VM2. This server connects to an external Layer 2 switch via an Ethernet port (whether it is Gigabit Ethernet or 10-Gigabit Ethernet is immaterial). VM1's MAC address is MAC1, and VM2's MAC address is MAC2. The switch port connecting to the virtualized server is Ethernet1/1. The Layer 2 forwarding table (i.e., MAC address table) contains the MAC address of each VM and the port from which it has been learned. As an example, the switch forwards a frame whose destination MAC address is MAC1 to port Ethernet1/1; similarly, this switch forwards a frame whose destination MAC address is MAC2 out of port Ethernet1/1.

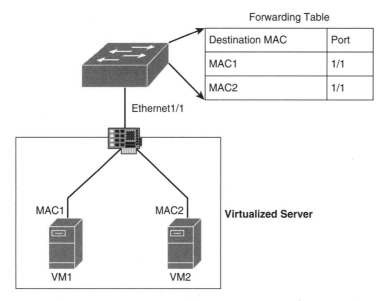

Figure 5-1   *Topology to Explain Why vSwitches Are Necessary*

Imagine now that a server needs to send traffic to VM1 as shown in Figure 5-2. The switch simply looks up the destination MAC address in the Layer 2 forwarding table and forwards the frame accordingly.

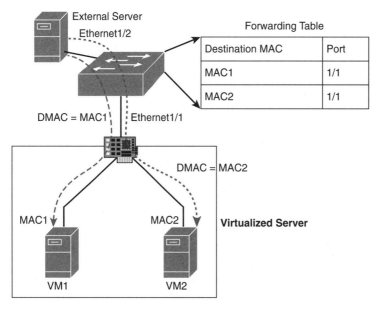

Figure 5-2   *Physical-to-Virtual Communication Path*

Now the VM1 sends a frame to VM2 (MAC2) as shown in Figure 5-3. The switch looks up the destination MAC address in the Layer 2 forwarding table and finds a match for MAC2 associated with Ethernet1/1. What do you expect to happen at this point?

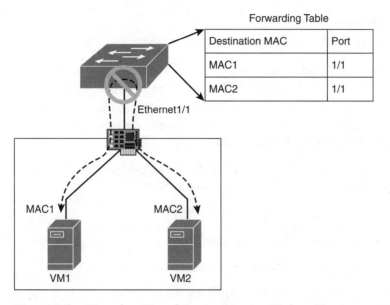

Figure 5-3 *Virtual-to-Virtual Communication Violates Transparent Bridging Rules*

Based on the rules of Layer 2 forwarding, a Layer 2 frame is never sent "back" to the same interface where it came in. This means that the communication between VM1 and VM2 is not possible.

Based on the previous paragraph, it should be clear that for two VMs that reside on the same server to be able to communicate at Layer 2, an external Layer 2 switch is not enough. In fact, an external switch is never able to switch traffic for two VMs that are sending frames on the same physical interface (or, in other words, for two VMs that reside on the same physical server).

The solutions to enable VM-to-VM communication are as follows:

- A virtual switch such as the Cisco Nexus 1000V or Open vSwitch

- A tag to preserve the semantics of transparent bridging and expose the virtual machines' virtual ports to an external bridge based, for instance, on the Cisco VN-TAG

The above are the reasons why virtual switching exists.

Overview of Networking Components

This section covers the networking concepts that are common on most hypervisors.

Virtual Network Adapters

Within a virtualized server, the term *network interface card* (NIC) has several meanings:

- The physical NICs of the server are the regular network adapters physically installed on the server, sometimes referred to as *pNICs* or physical interfaces (PIF).

- The virtual network adapters refer to the virtual machine NIC (called a *vNIC* in VMware nomenclature), which is a "software entity" within the guest operating system (although it can be hardware accelerated).

Some of the physical NICs that exist on a virtualized server are used for virtual machine access to the physical network. In VMware ESX terminology, these are referred to as *vmnic(s)*.

A virtual switch carries the traffic between a virtual network adapter and a physical NIC and switches traffic between virtual network adapters.

Figure 5-4 shows the physical and virtual network adapters.

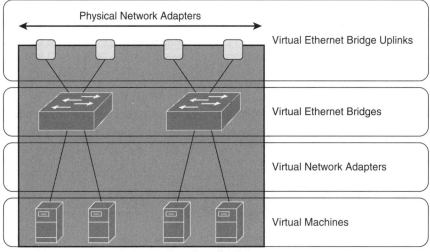

Figure 5-4 *Networking in a Virtualized Server*

In Figure 5-4, four physical NICs are present on the server platform. The virtualized server contains two virtual Ethernet bridges. Four VM are present, each configured with one single virtual network adapter.

Virtual Switching

The virtual Ethernet bridge links local VMs to each other and to the external enterprise network via a software construct named *virtual Ethernet bridge*. The virtual Ethernet bridge or virtual switch emulates a traditional physical Ethernet network switch to the extent that it forwards frames at the data link layer (Layer 2). The virtual switch doesn't run Spanning Tree Protocol (STP), yet it ensures loop-free connectivity and traffic load distribution from the virtual servers to the upstream links.

The vSwitch has a Layer 2 forwarding table that it uses to forward traffic based on the destination MAC address. The vSwitch forwarding table contains the MAC addresses for the VMs and their associated ports. When a frame is destined to a VM, the vSwitch sends the frame directly to the VM. When the destination MAC address does not exist in the VM, or it is multicast or broadcast, the vSwitch sends the traffic out to the physical network adapters. If multiple physical network adapters are present, virtual Ethernet bridges implement solutions to avoid introducing loops.

In summary, a regular Ethernet switch "learns" the forwarding table based on traffic that it sees on its ports. In a vSwitch, the forwarding table contains only the MAC addresses of the VMs. Everything that doesn't match the VM entries goes out to the server NICs, including broadcasts and multicast traffic.

Endpoint Groups

The concept of the endpoint group (EGP) introduced by Cisco Application Centric Infrastructure is similar to the concept of port profile used on the Cisco Nexus 1000V Switch and the concept of port group used in VMware ESX.

Virtual machines connect to virtual Ethernet bridges by means of virtual network adapters. The networking configuration on the virtualized server associates virtual network adapters with a "security zone" that is associated with a VLAN or a VXLAN.

Endpoint groups enable administrators to group virtual network adapters from multiple VMs and configure them simultaneously. The administrator can set specific QoS, security policies, and VLANs by changing the EPG configuration. Even if EPGs on the virtualized servers assign virtual network adapters to a VLAN, no one-to-one mapping exists between them and VLANs.

Distributed Switching

Distributed switching simplifies the provisioning of network properties across virtualized servers. With a distributed virtual switch, a user can define the switching properties for a cluster of several virtualized hosts simultaneously, instead of having to configure each host individually for networking. An example of such an implementation is the Cisco Nexus 1000V Switch or Open vSwitch or VMware vNetwork Distributed Switch.

Hot Migration of Virtual Machines

Hot migration is the method used by virtualized servers to migrate powered-on VMs from one physical host to another. For this migration to be possible, the originating virtualized host and the target virtualized host must provide Layer 2 connectivity on the production VLAN for the VM, because the moving VM must find the same exact end-point group on the target virtualized server, as shown in Figure 5-5.

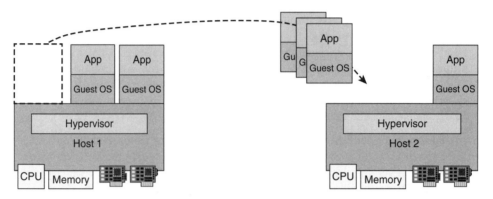

Figure 5-5 *Hot Migration of Virtual Machines*

Segmentation Options

One of the principal requirements of large-scale data centers is the capability to segment several *tenants*, each of which is a hosted enterprise or a department. This requires the capability to offer enough "labels" to distinguish traffic of different tenants. The traditional way to provide this segmentation consists of using VLANs, but more and more implementations are using VXLAN for scalability reasons.

VLANs

The current VLAN space is expressed over 12 bits (802.1Q tag), which limits the maximum number of Layer 2 segments in a data center to 4096 VLANs. This often becomes a scalability limit quickly, considering that every tenant may need at least a couple of security zones also called segments. In recent years, most software switch implementations have introduced support for VXLAN. The Cisco Nexus 1000V provides this service.

VXLANs

VXLAN offers the same service to an end system as a VLAN but with a much larger addressing space. VXLAN is an overlay that encapsulates a Layer 2 frame into a User Datagram Protocol (UDP) header. Within this header, the 24-bit VXLAN identifier provides 16 million logical networks that are mapped to bridge domains locally. Figure 5-6 illustrates this approach with the Cisco Nexus 1000V. Two virtualized servers are enabled with the Cisco Nexus 1000V Virtual Ethernet Module (VEM). Virtual machines on either server have the illusion of being connected on adjacent Layer 2 segments, while in reality their traffic is encapsulated in VXLAN and carried across a routed network.

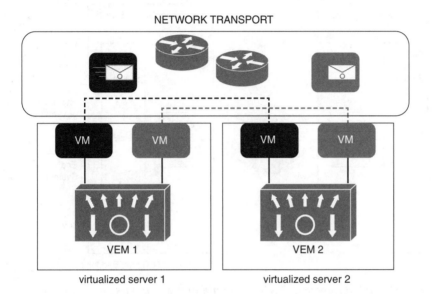

Figure 5-6 *Solving VLAN Scalability Problems with Overlays*

VXLAN Packet Format

Figure 5-7 shows the packet format of a VXLAN packet. VXLAN is an Ethernet packet encapsulated in UDP.

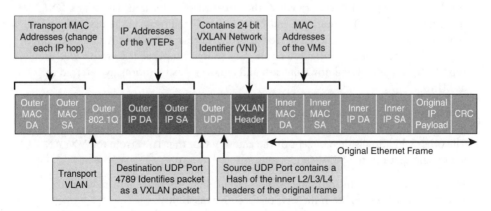

Figure 5-7 *VXLAN Packet Format*

VXLAN Packet Forwarding

Figure 5-8 illustrates the key architectural elements of a VXLAN transport. Two entities, which can be physical or virtual, communicate over a routed infrastructure. Each entity provides a bridge domain locally and encapsulates the traffic in the overlay to send it to the destination end host (or switch).

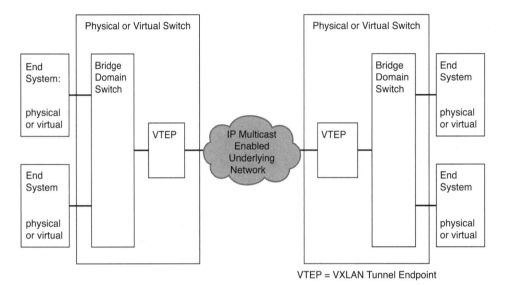

Figure 5-8   *VXLAN Architecture with VXLAN Termination Endpoints*

When a host (physical or virtual) needs to communicate to another host (physical or virtual) whose MAC-to-VTEP association is known, the packet is encapsulated by the local VTEP with the destination IP address of the destination VTEP. In this case the traffic is unicast.

When the MAC-to-VTEP association is unknown, the packet must be flooded in order for the originating VTEP to learn where the target MAC is located. Therefore, VXLAN implementations today require the capability to run IP multicast in the data center core to create multicast distribution trees for unknown unicast traffic and for broadcast traffic. The IP core must be configured for IP Any Source Multicast (*,G) to provide the support for broadcast, unknown unicast, and multicast traffic (normally referred to as BUM).

The constraint with this approach is that even if the number of unique labels has increased, the scalability limits on the control plane related to flooding are not removed. The other limitation is the concept of the gateway that translates from the VXLAN addressing space to the VLAN addressing space.

In summary, these are the advantages of using full VXLAN tunnels from virtualized server to virtualized server in the case of Cisco Nexus 1000V:

- No need to configure trunking of VLANs on all server NICs

- Larger segmentation space

- Alleviates the load on STP in the network

These are the main disadvantages of using VXLAN tunnels from virtualized servers:

- Multicast still required to provide the MAC learning functionalities, so VXLAN per se doesn't remove flooding

- Lack of visibility for proper traffic prioritization

- Gateway from VXLAN to VLANs (also known as VXLAN Tunnel Endpoint, or VTEP) is a bottleneck

VXLANs Without Multicast

Most software switching implementations, such as Cisco Nexus 1000V, have found ways to remove the need for multicast. A centralized management element (which in the case of Cisco Nexus 1000V is called *Virtual Supervisor Module* [VSM]) maintains a database of which segments are configured on a particular virtualized host and which MACs are on which host. The first information enables the replication of multicast and broadcast frames only to the hosts where the bridge domain exists.

The mapping database of MAC to VTEP (or VEM) association enables the traffic forwarding from a VEM directly to another VEM as follows:

- A VEM detects the MAC address of a VM (by the port attached or by looking at the source MAC address in the data traffic).

- The information about the learned MAC address, along with segment information, is published by the VEM to the VSM.

- The VSM creates the segment and MAC address to VTEP association.

- The VSM distributes the associations to all other VEMs (can be localized based on segment locations).

- VEMs populate the MAC addresses learned in the Layer 2 table for forwarding.

Microsoft Hyper-V Networking

Hyper-V Hyper-V was introduced as a role as part of Windows Server 2008 and it has become available as a standalone version called Microsoft Hyper-V server.

Among other things, using Windows core OS means that there is no graphical user interface and the configurations are performed via Windows PowerShell.

The feature set of Hyper-V is similar to the features of VMware ESX. For instance, instead of vMotion migration, Hyper-V has Live Migration. Instead of a vNetwork Distributed Switch (vDS), Hyper-V has a logical switch. Instead of the concept of the data center, Hyper-V has a folder.

The suite of products that manages Hyper-V is called *System Center*. The following list provides the key components and terminology that you need to understand to use Hyper-V:

- **System Center Virtual Machine Manager (SCVMM):** Runs on a centralized server and manages virtualized hosts, VMs, storage, and virtual networks. Equivalent to vCenter.

- **SCVMM Server Console:** A console process to interface with SCVMM server that provides the PowerShell API for scripting and automation.

- **Virtual Machine Management Service (VMMS):** A process running in the parent partition of each virtualized server that uses the WMI interface. It manages Hyper-V and VMs on the host.

- **Hyper-V Switch:** The extensible virtual switch in the hypervisor.

- **Windows Management Instrumentation (WMI):** Used by SCVMM to interface with VMMS on the host.

- **Windows Network Virtualization (WNV):** A module that adds network virtualization generic routing encapsulation (NVGRE) capabilities to build overlays.

- **Virtual Subnet Identifier (VSID) or Tenant ID:** Used in NVGRE

- **Windows Azure Pack:** It is a set of technologies that integrates with SCVMM and Windows server to provide a self-service portal

Figure 5-9 displays the Hyper-V architecture and interaction with the key components just defined.

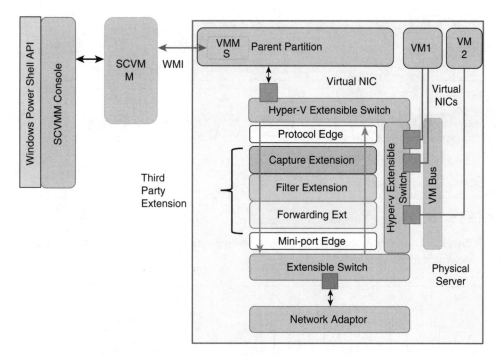

Figure 5-9 *Hyper-V Architecture*

Another key concept in Microsoft Hyper-V is the *forwarding extension*, which allows the insertion of third-party processing in the data path from the guest to the network adapters. A forwarding extension can accomplish the following in the two directions of the data path:

- Filter packets

- Inject new packets or modified packets into the data path

- Deliver packets to one of the extensible switch ports

Figure 5-10 shows a topology with multiple host groups.

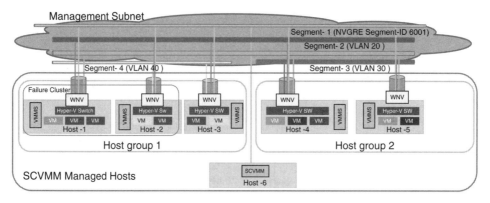

Figure 5-10 *Hyper-V Topology*

Figure 5-11 illustrates some of the key networking concepts introduced by Hyper-V and described in detail next.

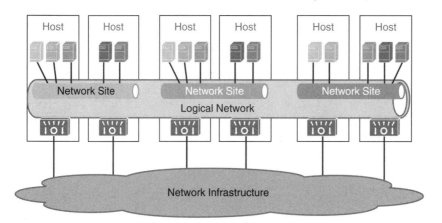

Figure 5-11 *Networking Concepts in Hyper-V*

Microsoft uses the following terminology for the networking components of Hyper-V:

■ **Logical switch:** Represents a distributed virtual switch. One instance of it is deployed in each Hyper-V host. Each uplink NIC (or a NIC team) can have only one logical switch. This is the equivalent of a VMware vDS.

■ **Logical Network:** A placeholder for all networking constructs such as subnets, VLANs, network virtualization, and VM networks.

■ **Logical Network Definition (LND) or network site:** An isolation construct in SCVMM. This building block contains one or more VLANs with IP subnets.

■ **VM Network:** A virtual machine networking construct. It enables connectivity from VMs to logical networks, VLANs, and subnets.

A logical network represents a network with a certain type of connectivity characteristic. A logical network is not a one-to-one mapping with a specific classic network concept. An instantiation of a logical network on a set of host groups is called a *network site*. As Figure 5-12 illustrates, it is possible to have a single logical network but three different network sites for the same logical network. Furthermore, you can divide the network site into multiple VM networks and associate VMs with the VM network.

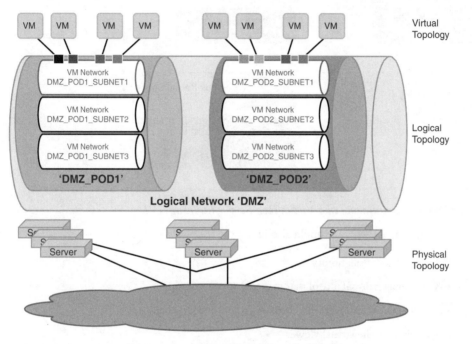

Figure 5-12 *Networking Concepts Hierarchy in Hyper-V*

Linux KVM and Networking

Linux Kernel-based Virtual Machine (KVM) is part of the kernel but it doesn't perform hardware emulation—a user-space element provides this. The management of virtual machines in Linux is achieved by using two elements:

- **libvirt:** A toolkit that enables the interaction with the virtualization features of Linux. Virt-viewer, virt-manager, and virsh (shell to manage virtual machines) rely on libvirt.

- **qemu:** A hardware-emulation component that runs in user space in KVM.

Figure 5-13 illustrates the relationship between these components.

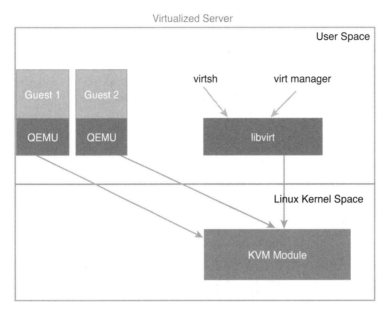

Figure 5-13   *Components in a Virtualized Server Running KVM*

When running KVM, you should also install the following packages:

- **libvirt:** The virtual library

- **virt-manager:** A GUI tool that manages KVM guests

- **virt-install:** A command-line tool to install virtual machines

- **virt-viewer:** The virtual viewer

The libvirt daemon service must be started at bootup of the KVM server. It is responsible for, among other things, the association of guest VM network adapters with Linux bridges and Open vSwitch (OVS) bridges.

Linux Bridging

Several configurations related to networking in a virtualized Linux host rely on the bridging capabilities offered by Linux. You should be familiar with the command **brctl**, with which you can

- Add a bridge: **brctl addbr <bridge name>**

- Add a physical interface to a Linux bridge: **brctl addif <bridge name> <device>**

- List the bridges: **brctl show**

- List the MAC addresses that have been learned: **brctl showmac <bridge name>**

The **brctl** command can also be used to control virtual bridges that are created via libvirt.

Note   To discover how to configure networking in a virtualized Linux host, refer to the libvirt documentation at http://wiki.libvirt.org/page/VirtualNetworking.

By default, a virtualized Linux host that is running the libvirt daemon has a virtual bridge running, called *virbr0*. Use the commands **ifconfig virbr0** to see its characteristics. If you need to add network adapters to a virtual bridge, use the **brctl** command as follows: **brctl addif <name of the bridge> <name of the interface>**.

Note   To attach a guest VM network adapter to a virtual bridge, refer to the instructions at http://wiki.libvirt.org/page/Networking#Guest_configuration.

Using virt-manager simplifies the configuration tasks.

Open vSwitch

Open vSwitch (OVS) is a software switch with many networking features, such as:

- IEEE 802.1Q support
- NetFlow
- Mirroring

Note   You can find the complete list of features of Open vSwitch at http://openvswitch. org/features/.

Open vSwitch works on hypervisors such as KVM, XenServer, and VirtualBox. Open vSwitch can run as a standalone virtual switch, where every virtual switch is managed independently, or it can run in a "distributed" manner with a centralized controller by exposing these two configuration elements:

- Flow-based forwarding state, which can be remotely programmed via OpenFlow
- Switch port state, which can be remotely programmed via the Open vSwitch Database (OVSDB) management protocol

Open vSwitch also supports the ability to create GRE- or VXLAN-based tunnels.

OVS Architecture

One of the key characteristics of Open vSwitch is that it has a flow-based forwarding architecture. This is similar to the concept of a control plane and data plane separation in many Cisco architectures where the supervisor provides the control plane function and the data plane handles the packet-forwarding capabilities. This particular aspect of OVS allows it to run in a distributed manner in OpenFlow architectures.

OVS has three main components:

- A kernel component implementing the fast path
- A user space component implementing the OpenFlow protocol
- A user space database server

Figure 5-14 illustrates the architectural components of OVS.

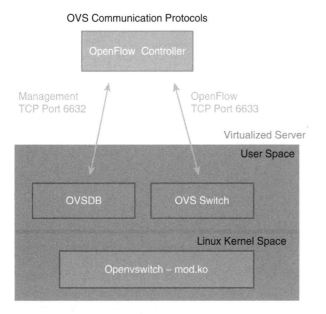

Figure 5-14   *OVS Architecture*

OVS has a user-space control plane and a kernel-space data plane component. The control plane has two elements:

- **vswitchd:** Manages the individual instances of Open vSwitch(es) on the server
- **ovsdb-server:** The configuration database

The OVS database stores switch configurations in JSON format, and in fact it can be programmed via JSON RPCs.

The virtual switch can be divided in multiple bridges for segmentation purposes.

Traffic forwarding is performed after parsing packets via a classifier and a flow lookup. If a flow entry exists in kernel space, the packet is forwarded according to this entry, including in the case where the packet must be tunneled over VXLAN or GRE. Otherwise it is sent to user space for further processing.

The flow lookup includes matching the following fields:

- Input port
- VLAN ID
- Source MAC address
- Destination MAC address
- IP Source
- IP Destination
- TCP/UDP/... Source Port
- TCP/UDP/... Destination Port

Note The main performance challenge in Open vSwitch is related to the connection setup rate, because the lookup is performed in user space.

Note For additional information regarding OVS code and architecture, visit https://github.com/openvswitch/ovs.

Example Topology

Figure 5-15 illustrates a simple topology for an OVS deployment. Each virtualized server has an OVS instance with a bridge (br0). The virtual machines' NICs (tap0 and tap1) are connected to the bridge.

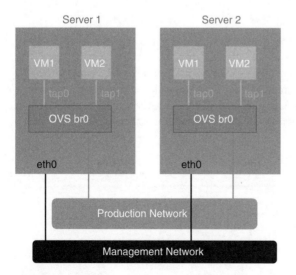

Figure 5-15 *OVS Deployment Topology*

ovs–vsctl is the utility for querying and configuring ovs–vswitchd. Example 5-1 shows the configuration for the topology depicted in Figure 5-15. The configuration parameter tag specifies which VLAN tap0 or tap1 connects to by means of the configuration parameter called *tag*. The physical NIC that is used as the uplink is configured by adding eth0 or eth1 to the bridge instance (br0 in Example 5-1).

Example 5-1   *Configuring an OVS Switch*

```
ovs-vsctl add-br0
ovs-vsctl add-port br0 tap0 tag=1
ovs-vsctl add-br0 eth1
ovs-vsctl list-br
```

Note   To see more examples of OVS configuration:

http://openvswitch.org/support/config-cookbooks/vlan-configuration-cookbook/

https://raw.githubusercontent.com/openvswitch/ovs/master/FAQ

The following configuration shows how to install OVS and design OVS to communicate with an OpenFlow controller that is not running on the same server as OVS itself (hence "out-of-band" as the mode). This design also configures OVS to run with local forwarding if the connectivity to the controller is lost.

```
ovs-vsctl set-controller br0 tcp:<IP of the controller>:6633
ovs-vsctl set-controller br0 connection-mode=out-of-band
ovs-vsctl set-fail-mode br0 standalone
```

Open vSwitch with OpenStack

When Open vSwitch is used with OpenStack, the mapping between Linux bridges, tap interfaces, and the Open vSwitch elements can implement more complex topologies in order to be consistent with the semantics of OpenStack. As shown in Figure 5-16, each VM has a tap interface connected to a Linux bridge, which connects via a virtual Ethernet interface called veth to an Open vSwitch (br-int). VLAN tagging is also used to create multi-tenancy. This topology also allows the integration of iptables.

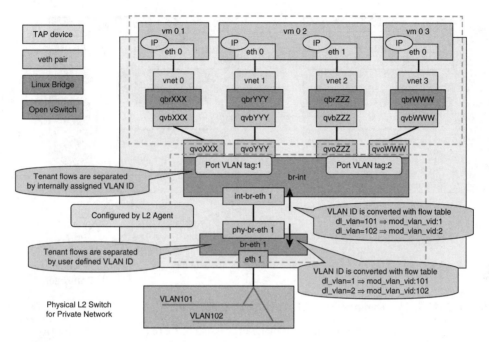

Figure 5-16 *OpenStack with Open vSwitch*

OpenFlow

OpenFlow is a specification developed by the Open Networking Foundation (OFM) that defines a flow-based forwarding infrastructure and a standardized application programming interface (API) that allows a controller to direct the functions of a switch through a secure channel.

> **Note**   For more information about OpenFlow, visit http://pomi.stanford.edu/content.php?page=research&subpage=openflow.

OVS can potentially be deployed with an OpenFlow controller. The centralized controller could be NOX, for instance (www.noxrepo.org). The topology looks like the one depicted in Figure 5-17.

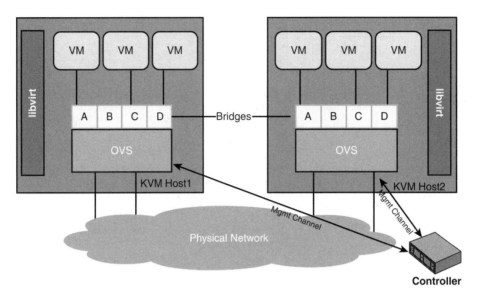

Figure 5-17   *OVS Deployment with OpenFlow Controller*

This architecture enables the control plane processing to be redirected to the controller. The flow tables in the OVS switches store flow information, a set of action rules, and counters. The action rules can be any of the following:

- Forward packet to a port

- Encapsulate and forward to controller

- Drop the packet

- Send to normal processing pipeline

OpenFlow features and capabilities evolve with newer versions. This is a list of the versions currently available:

- OpenFlow 1.0, which is the basic OpenFlow implementation

- OpenFlow 1.1, which includes, among other things, the ability to model "virtual ports" (complex network configurations such as link aggregation) and the ability to implement multiple flow tables

- OpenFlow 1.2, which includes IPv6 and extensible flow match support

- OpenFlow 1.3, which includes per-flow meters and on-demand flow counters

- OpenFlow 1.4, which includes more extensible protocols and flow monitoring

Note   For more information, refer to the latest OpenFlow specifications.

The following snippet shows how to set the OpenFlow versions allowed:

```
ovs-vsctl set bridge switch protocols=OpenFlow10,OpenFlow12,OpenFlow13
```

Open vSwitch Database (OVSDB) management protocol is a management interface that allows a controller to configure tunnels, QoS, and configurations that cannot be achieved by simply storing flows.

> **Note**   For more details regarding OVSDB, visit http://tools.ietf.org/html/rfc7047.

The following is a list of the functions that OVSDB provides:

- Creation, modification, and deletion of OpenFlow data paths (bridges)
- Configuration of the controllers to which an OpenFlow data path should connect
- Configuration of the managers to which the OVSDB server should connect
- Creation, modification, and deletion of ports on OpenFlow data paths
- Creation, modification, and deletion of tunnel interfaces on OpenFlow data paths
- Creation, modification, and deletion of queues
- Configuration of QoS policies, and attachment of those policies to queues
- Collection of statistics

VMware ESX/ESXi Networking

Describing the details of VMware ESX/ESXi is beyond the scope of this chapter. However, the following list includes some key terminology and concepts that you must be familiar with to configure ESX/ESXi in the data center:

- **vSphere ESXi:** The hypervisor.
- **vCenter:** Enables the administrator to manage a group of ESX hosts and the associated data storage.
- **vNetwork Distributed Switch (aka Distributed Virtual Switch):** A single vSwitch running across all hosts on a data center within a vCenter. This simplifies the task of maintaining a consistent network configuration across multiple hosts.
- **dvPort group:** A port group associated with a vNetwork Distributed Switch.
- **vShield Manager:** The equivalent of a firewall running on each ESX host. vShield Manager works in association with a vCenter Server.
- **vCloud Director:** Cloud orchestration software that enables customers to build multi-tenant hybrid clouds. It does so by managing vCenter and vShield instances.

■ **vApp:** A collection of VMs managed as a single entity by vCloud Director. The VMs are connected by multiple segments, some of which are specific to the vApp itself.

In a data center fabric, the element that requires physical network connectivity is the ESXi server.

An ESX server, in its basic configuration, includes interfaces used for management (the Service Console), production traffic (traffic going to VMs), and what is called the *VM Kernel*. The most notable examples of why the VM Kernel needs network access include iSCSI access to storage (when configured as VM File System) and ESX-to-ESX server communication for the purpose of "migrating" VM from one server to another (vMotion technology).

The elements in the topology that require virtual network connectivity are the VMs that are part of a vApp.

VMware vSwitch and Distributed Virtual Switch

VMware ESX provides support for switching via either the standard vSwitch or a distributed virtual switch. Distributed switching can be configured either with the native VMware implementation, the VMware vNetwork Distributed Switch (vDS), or the Cisco Nexus 1000V distributed virtual switch (DVS).

The vSwitch operates like a regular Layer 2 Ethernet switch. The vSwitch forwards traffic among VMs and between VMs and the LAN switching infrastructure. The ESX server NICs (vmnic(s)) are the vSwitch uplinks.

The vSwitch has a Layer 2 forwarding table that it uses to forward traffic based on the destination MAC address. The vSwitch forwarding table contains the MAC address for the VMs and their associated virtual ports. When a frame is destined to a VM, the vSwitch sends the frame directly to the VM. When the destination MAC address does not exist in the VM, or it is multicast or broadcast, it sends the traffic out to the vmnic(s) (that is, to the server NIC ports).

The configuration of redundant vSwitch uplinks is called *NIC teaming*. vSwitches do not run Spanning Tree Protocol, so the vSwitch implements other loop-prevention mechanisms. These loop-prevention mechanisms include dropping inbound traffic for possible "returning" frames, and distance vectors which are logics where, a frame for example ingressing from one NIC (uplink) is not going to go out (egress) of the ESX/ESXi server from a different NIC (which would otherwise be the case for, say, broadcasts).

With a vSwitch, you can create segmentation to isolate groups of VMs by using the concept of port groups. Each port group can be associated with a particular VLAN. The vNICs of the VM are assigned to a port group that is associated with a specific VLAN, in this case VLANs A and B. The virtual switch defines the Vmnic(s) as ports supporting all of the VLANs within the switch; that is, as trunks.

Figure 5-18 illustrates the concept.

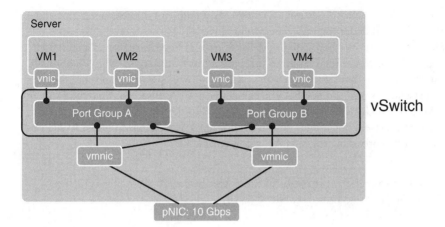

Figure 5-18 *Port Group and VLANs*

> **Note** For more information, visit http://www.vmware.com/files/pdf/virtual_networking_concepts.pdf.

VMware ESXi Server Traffic Requirements

The three most relevant traffic types to consider when deploying virtualized servers are as follows:

- **Virtual machine data traffic:** You need to consider data traffic transmitted or received by virtual machines.

- **VMware ESX management traffic:** VMware vCenter Server requires access to the VMware ESX management interface to monitor and configure the VMware ESX host.

- **VMware VMKernel traffic:** VMware vMotion uses the VMware VMKernel path to copy the memory from the originating host to the destination VMware ESX host.

VMware vMotion traffic requires a constant high level of bandwidth only when VMware vMotion is initiated. It usually generates a burst of data over a period of 10 to 60 seconds. The duration of the virtual machine migration is extended based on the amount of bandwidth available. Because VMware vMotion processing is mainly a memory operation, it can easily take advantage of connectivity that exceeds Gigabit Ethernet bandwidth.

VXLAN Tagging with vShield

vShield Manager creates networks by using VXLANs. A VXLAN network is allocated a unique VNID by vShield Manager from a pool of VNIDs assigned by the user. vShield is configured with a VXLAN Segment ID range and a multicast address pool. This configuration is located under the Datacenter field in vShield Manager on the Network Virtualization tab. This is where you can define a pool of Segment-IDs and a multicast address range. You would then assign to this pool a "network scope," which is normally one or more clusters. Then, you can create VXLAN networks with a name, and they appear in vCenter as port groups that you can connect a VM vNIC to. Next, add vShield Edge VM to the VXLAN network so that it connects to the regular VLAN-based network. To do this, select the "Edge" option from vShield Manager and choose which host or physical port is providing the VXLAN gateway function.

Note   For more information about vShield Edge, visit http://www.vmware.com/files/pdf/techpaper/vShield-Edge-Design-Guide-WP.pdf.

vCloud Director and vApps

VMware vCloud Director is a cloud orchestration product that has the capability to build secure multi-tenant clouds. vCloud Director provides resources management and enables you to create the following:

- A virtual data center (vDC) for each tenant organization

- A catalog and a self-service portal for the end user to start and decommission a virtual application (vApp) on-the-fly

vCloud organizes resources in a hierarchy, as follows:

- **Provider vDC:** A collection of vCenter resources that constitutes a "provider," such as the IT department of an enterprise

- **Organization vDC:** A segment of the provider vDC, such as a business unit within an enterprise.

- **vApp:** A collection of VMs that is powered on or off as a single building block

To orchestrate resources, vCloud Director relies on vCenter, vShield Manager, and vShield Edge, as depicted in Figure 5-19.

As Figure 5-19 illustrates, vShield Manager manages the networking component of vCloud Director. vShield Edge is the element that runs in each ESXi host, and it is provisioned automatically by vShield Manager.

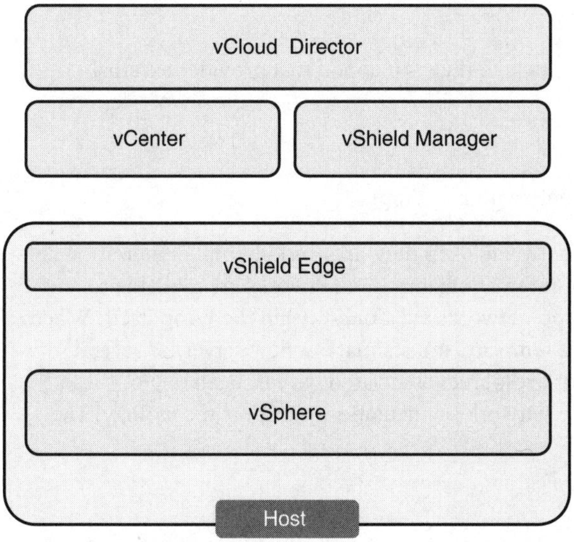

Figure 5-19 *Building Blocks of vCloud Director*

vCloud Networks

vCloud Director introduces a new hierarchy of networking constructs:

- **External (provider) network:** The "real" network that connects to the external world. Organizations (tenants) connect to this network to exit the cloud.

- **Organization vDC network:** It can be "external" (i.e., the network that is then plugged into the external network) or internal. The external one can use Network Address Translation (NAT).

- **vApp network:** vApp networks are created by vCloud consumers and connect multiple virtual machines in a vApp. vApp networks separate vApp virtual machines from the workloads in the organization virtual datacenter network. The effect is similar to placing a router in front of a group of systems (vApp) to shield the systems from the rest of the corporate network. vApp networks are instantiated from a network pool and consume vSphere resources while the vApp is running.

From a vSphere point of view, these are all VM networks.

The unit of defining networks in vCloud is called *organizations*. Each organization uses external organization vDC network (which is a traditional port group) and some internal organization networks (which can be vDCNI). Within each organization there are several vDCs, which are basically resource pools with networks as one of the types of resources. There is a one-to-one mapping between network pools and organization vDC network. vApps belong to some vDC within this organization and take network resources from the pools defined in the vDC.

Each vApp can use the following:

■ External organization network (which then is mapped to a provider external network)

■ Internal organization network

■ vApp networks (which exist only within a vApp)

There's no substantial difference between vApp networks and internal organization networks. The main difference is that internal organization networks are available to any vApp in an organization, while vApp networks exist only within the vApp itself. When the end user selects a vApp from a template, it instantiates a new server, or several servers interconnected, and the network resources associated with it. Each one of these networks must be backed by some network segmentation/transport technology. The backing type can be

■ VLAN backed

■ Cloud Director Network Isolated (vCNI) backed (which is Mac-in-Mac mechanism as defined in IEEE 802.1ah-2008)

■ Port group backed (only preprovisioned)

■ VXLAN backed

Figure 5-20 illustrates the concept of a vApp as part of an organization.

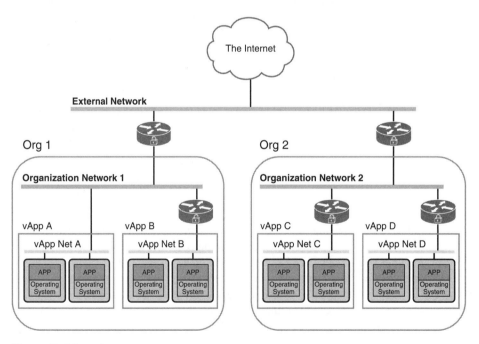

Figure 5-20   *vApp*

Cisco Nexus 1000V

Cisco Nexus 1000V is a feature-rich software switch that runs on multiple hypervisors. Cisco Nexus 1000V provides functions such as:

- ACL filtering on individual VM ports

- Switched Port Analyzer (SPAN), or Remote SPAN, features of individual VMs

- NetFlow statistics of the local traffic

- Capability to shut down VM ports individually

The Cisco Nexus 1000V is a distributed software switch. It consists of two main components: the Virtual Supervisor Module (VSM, the control-plane component) and the Virtual Ethernet Module (VEM, the data-plane component). Together these components provide the abstraction of a physical switch, whose supervisor is the VSM and whose line cards are the VEMs that run within each VMware ESX host.

All configurations are performed on the VSM and propagated to the VEMs that are associated with it. A VSM can be a virtual machine and run redundantly just like a redundant supervisor. It is possible to add a VMware ESX host to the Cisco Nexus 1000V vDS from VMware vCenter to make a VMware ESX host become part of a Cisco Nexus 1000V domain, and as a result run a VEM. A VSM running as a virtual machine provides the abstraction of a CLI managing a large modular switch. The user employs Secure Shell (SSH) Protocol at the management interface of the VSM, or simply uses the console—the virtual machine console screen—to configure the network characteristics of the VMware deployment. The VSM forwards the configurations (VLANs, QoS, private VLANs, etc.) to all the VEMs that are part of the same domain or, in other words, that are under the same Cisco Nexus 1000V.

The following are the most important traffic types that make the VEMs and the VSM operate like a single entity:

- **Control traffic:** This traffic is generated by the Cisco Nexus 1000V and exchanged between the primary and secondary VSMs as well as the VSMs and VEMs. It requires very little bandwidth (less than 10 KBps) but demands absolute priority. Control traffic should be considered the most important traffic in a Cisco Nexus 1000V network.

- **Packet traffic:** Packet traffic is used to transport selected packets to the VSM for processing. The bandwidth required for the packet interface is extremely low, and its use is intermittent. If Cisco Discovery Protocol (CDP) and Interior Gateway Management Protocol (IGMP) features are turned off, there is no packet traffic at all.

Control and packet VLANs are carried on the uplink from the VMware ESX server to the switch. For this reason, the initial communication between the VSM and the VEM is aided by VMware vCenter to remove any dependency on the success of the

VSM-to-VEM communication. This is so that communication can begin even if the network configuration on the uplinks is not yet functioning.

The communication between VSM and VMware vCenter uses the management interface (mgmt0) on the VSM. The protocol runs on HTTPS. The key information is provided to VMware vCenter by pointing the browser to the VSM IP address and downloading the extension key, extension.xml, which is added to VMware vCenter as a plug-in.

As a first approximation, port profiles are the equivalent of a distributed virtual port group on a VMware vNetwork Distributed Switch. Port profiles are used to configure interfaces. A port profile can be assigned to multiple interfaces, giving them all the same configuration. Changes to the port profile can be propagated automatically to the configuration of any interface assigned to it.

In the VMware vCenter Server, a port profile is represented as a distributed virtual port group. The virtual Ethernet and Ethernet interfaces are assigned in VMware vCenter Server to a port profile for the following reasons:

- To define port configuration by policy

- To apply a single policy across a large number of ports

- To support both virtual Ethernet and Ethernet ports

Port profiles that are configured as capability uplinks can be assigned by the server administrator to physical ports (vmnic(s)).

An uplink port profile can also be a system port profile. An uplink port profile is a system port profile when it carries the system VLANs used for the communication between the VSM and the VEM.

A typical configuration of an uplink port profile that is also a system port profile looks like the configuration shown in Example 5-2.

Example 5-2 *Uplink Port Profile in Nexus 1000V*

```
port-profile system-uplink
  capability uplink
  vmware port-group fabric_uplinks
  switchport mode trunk
  switchport trunk allowed vlan 23-24
  <channel-group configuration>
  no shutdown
  system vlan 23-24
state enabled
```

Some parameters in this configuration are of special interest:

- **capability uplink:** Indicates that this port profile is to be used on the physical NICs.

- **system vlan:** Makes this particular uplink port profile also a system port profile. The most common use of **system vlan** is to add the packet and control VLANs to this port profile. These VLANs still need to be configured under **switchport trunk** for them to be forwarding.

Every VMware ESX host must have at least one physical interface associated with a system port profile. Without this port profile, the Cisco Nexus 1000V associations with the VMware ESX host can still happen, but the VEMs will not appear as line cards or modules on the VSM.

The system VLANs have a special meaning because they are granted network communication in a preferential way over the regular VLANs. So even if the PortChannel configuration on the uplink port profile is not fully functional, the VSM can still configure the VEM.

In the absence of the system VLAN definition, the VEM connectivity is dependent on a successful PortChannel configuration on the VSM. But this configuration requires a preexistent functioning PortChannel configuration to help ensure VSM-to-VEM connectivity. The system VLAN configuration removes this dependency, allowing the VSM to configure the VEM even if the PortChannel setup has not yet been completed for the virtual machine production VLANs.

Users can assign vmnic(s) to an uplink port profile when they add a VMware ESX host to the Cisco Nexus 1000V from VMware vCenter and select the distributed virtual uplink port profile. After the VEMs are associated with the VSM, the network adapters of the VMware ESX hosts appear as an Ethernet module.

Regular port profiles are assigned to virtual machine virtual adapters. In Cisco Nexus 1000V terminology, these virtual adapters are referred to as *virtual Ethernet* (vEth) interfaces. A regular port profile is defined as shown in Example 5-3.

Example 5-3 *Port Profile in Cisco Nexus 1000V*

```
port-profile vm-connectivity
  vmware port-group connectivity-via-quad-gige
  switchport mode access
  switchport access vlan 50
  no shutdown
  state enabled
```

Virtual machines attach to port profiles through the choice of the distributed virtual port group from the VMware vCenter configuration. The association between the port profile and a VLAN defines the way the traffic flows from the virtual machine to the outside network.

It is possible to have multiple uplink port profiles for each VMware ESX host, but they cannot have overlapping VLANs, which would break the uniqueness of the association.

The ability to define the associated VLAN on a particular port profile and uplink port profile allows the user to control which path the virtual machines take to communicate to the rest of the network.

Port Extension with VN-TAG

Port extension refers to the capability to index a remote port as if it were directly attached to a switch (Controlling Bridge). The remote entity where the port is located is called a *port extender*. A port extender can aggregate physical ports or virtual ports, so this concept has several areas of applicability: for instance, virtualized servers and blade servers, or even satellite switches.

In the case of virtualized servers, the Controlling Bridge is a physical switch, and the network adapter within the virtualized servers provides the port extender functionality. With this arrangement, each virtual NIC defined on the server appears as a physical NIC directly connected to the Controlling Bridge. For this to occur, the port extender needs to tag the traffic that is generated by the VMs with information about the source interface (a virtual interface) and forward the traffic to the Controlling Bridge.

The Controlling Bridge performs the lookup in the Layer 2 table to identify the destination interface (which may be a virtual interface). Before sending the frame to a virtualized server, the Controlling Bridge attaches the TAG containing information about the destination virtual interface. Compare the port extender functionality to that of a line card and the Controlling Bridge to that of a supervisor/fabric device in a large modular system ("Extended Bridge"). At the time of this writing, Cisco offers technology that is based on the VN-TAG. Cisco and other vendors are currently working on the definition of the IEEE 802.1Qbh standard, which defines a very similar tag for the same purpose.

Note A summary of the current status of the standards for port extension and how they map to Cisco technology can be found at:

http://www.cisco.com/en/US/prod/collateral/switches/ps9441/ps9902/
whitepaper_c11-620065_ps10277_Products_White_Paper.html

The VN-TAG is a special tag added to a Layer 2 frame that allows for an external switch to forward frames that "belong" to the same physical port. Quoting the proposal by Joe Pelissier (Cisco Systems), "For frames from the bridge to the VNIC, the tag should provide a simple indication of the path through the IV(s) to the final VNIC. For frames from the VNIC to the bridge, the tag should provide a simple indication of the source VNIC." (See http://www.ieee802.org/1/files/public/docs2008/new-dcb-pelissier-NIV-Proposal-1108.pdf.)

Note   IV stands for "interface virtualizer," the component that adds the VNTAG to the traffic coming in from the virtual interfaces (downlinks) going to the bridge (uplinks).

The tag referred to in the previous quotation is the VNTAG that is prepended to the Layer 2 frame as depicted in Figure 5-21.

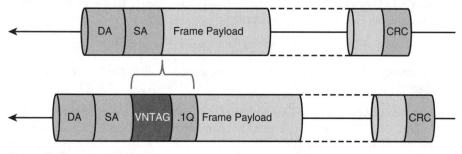

Figure 5-21   *VNTAG*

The VN-TAG allows association of a MAC not only with the Ethernet port of the upstream switch but also with the "virtual" Ethernet port (the virtual interface, or VIF) internal to the server, thus preserving the Ethernet switching semantics. As depicted in Figure 5-22, VM1 is "attached" to VIF1, and VM2 is "attached" to VIF2. The forwarding table of a VNTAG-capable switch contains the information about the destination MAC address and the virtual interface that the MAC is associated with.

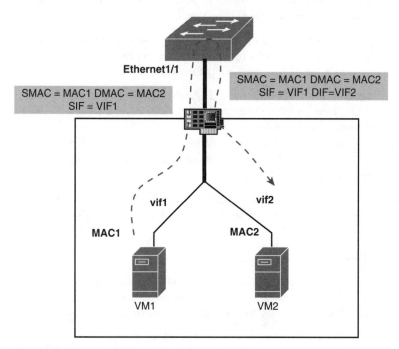

Figure 5-22   *Traffic Forwarding with VNTAG*

VM1 sends out a frame that the network adapter modifies to include the virtual interface information as follows:

SMAC=MAC1 DMAC=MAC2 Source Interface=VIF1 Destination Interface=0

The upstream switch looks up the Layer 2 forwarding table to match the destination MAC (DMAC), which in the example is MAC2. The lookup returns VIF2 as the result, thus the VNTAG-capable switch adds the destination interface (DIF) information to the Layer 2 frame, which in this example is VIF2:

SMAC=MAC1 DMAC=MAC2 Source Interface=VIF1 Destination Interface=VIF2

By performing this operation, Layer 2 forwarding can be extended to VM-to-VM switching.

As this section makes clear, VN-TAG is an enabler of virtualization insofar as that without VNTAG, two VMs would not be able to communicate (if it weren't for some software running on the server itself).

Additionally, VN-TAG can identify the configuration of the vNIC port of a given VM independently of which ESX server the VM resides on.

Cisco ACI Modeling of Virtual Server Connectivity

Cisco ACI is the latest technology introduced by Cisco to address the need for connectivity of both virtual and physical workloads. Cisco ACI complements and integrates with existing technologies described so far in the chapter.

Applications are a collection of virtual and physical workloads interconnected by virtual and physical networks. ACI provides a way to define the relationships between these workloads and to instantiate their connectivity in the network fabric.

ACI defines the concept of the endpoint group (EPG), which is a collection of physical or virtual endpoints. EPGs are correlated to a bridge domain or Layer 2 namespace, and each Layer 2 bridge domain can be enabled with or without flooding semantics. Bridge domains are part of a single Layer 3. The Layer 3 offers the subnet connectivity to the workloads connected to the EPGs. Think of this almost as an SVI with corresponding IP primary addresses or IP secondary addresses.

The entire definition of the EPG with their associated network protocols, as well as networking constructs, together is part of a folder such as a self-contained tenant.

Overlay Normalization

Cisco ACI provides overlay independence and bridges frames to and from VXLAN, NVGRE, VLAN, and IEEE 802.1Q encapsulation. This approach provides flexibility for heterogeneous environments, which may have services residing on disparate overlays.

ACI also enables dynamic workload mobility, management automation, and programmatic policy. As workloads move within the virtual environment, the policies attached to
the workloads are enforced seamlessly and consistently within the infrastructure.

Figure 5-23 illustrates the interaction between the APIC and the hypervisors in the
data center.

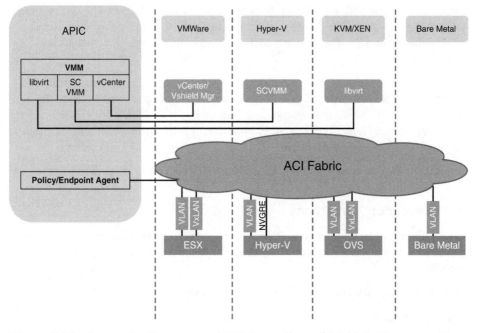

Figure 5-23   *Interaction Between the APIC Controller and Multiple Hypervisor Types*

VMM Domain

ACI uses the concept of a Virtual Machine Manager (VMM) domain. Examples of
VMMs include VMware vCenter and Microsoft SCVMM. ACI associates some attributes with a VMM domain such as the VMM IP addresses and credentials. A VMM
domain is also a VM mobility domain. VMM domain mobility is only achieved within
the VMM domain, not across different VMM domains. The other information that is
part of a VMM domain is the namespace, which can be either a VLAN namespace or a
VXLAN namespace. You can reuse namespaces across different VMM domains.

When implementing a VXLAN namespace, there is no need to reuse the namespace.
Sixteen million tags should be more than enough even for a data center with a large
number of security zones.

In ACI, VLANs or VXLAN at the leaf have local significance on the leaf itself or even at
the port level. This is because ACI remaps them to a fabric-wide unique VXLAN number. At the time of this writing, using VLANs for segmentation is advantageous because
it is very efficient in terms of performance on the server (less overhead). Hence, given

that the VLAN space is limited to 4096 tags, by using the VMM domain concept you can create multiple pockets of 4096 VLANs (4096 EPGs) where VMs can move without constraints.

Endpoint Discovery

ACI uses three methods to discover the presence of virtual endpoints. The first method of learning is control plane learning, which is achieved through an out-of-band hand-shake. vCenter or SCVMM can run a control protocol that is used to communicate with APIC.

The in-band mechanism to discover endpoints is a protocol called *OpFlex*. OpFlex is a southbound policy protocol that is used not only to relegate policy information but also to propagate information such as endpoint reachability. If OpFlex is not available, ACI also uses CDP and Link Layer Discovery Protocol (LLDP) to map which port a given vir-tualized server is connected to.

In addition to control protocol–based discovery, ACI also uses data path learning.

Policy Resolution Immediacy

ACI defines connectivity between EPGs with policies. To prevent consuming hardware resources unnecessarily, ACI tries to optimize the distribution and instantiation of policies.

ACI defines two types of policy deployment and resolution:

- Immediate
- On-demand

The policy resolution immediacy controls whether policies are distributed to the leaf Data Management Engine (deployment) immediately or upon discovery of endpoints (on-demand). Similarly, the resolution configuration controls whether the application of the policy in hardware is based on the discovery of the endpoint (on-demand) or immediate.

If the policy is on-demand, ACI pushes the policies down to leaf nodes only when an actual vNIC is attached.

Cisco ACI Integration with Hyper-V

ACI integrates with Hyper-V via SCVMM APIs or through the Windows Azure Pack API. The Windows Azure Pack is a new cloud portal offering from Microsoft. In this case, an administrator creates different types of options for tenants and provides them with certain privileges, such as access and the ability to create networks. There's a plug-in that allows populating the information such as: ACI networks, EPGs, contracts, and so forth.

There is a specific tab underneath the tenant space in the Azure Pack where the administrator can post in the XML representation of an EPG contract or application network protocol. The XML representation is then transferred into the APIC controller. That pushes the actual network configurations to the APIC, and then the APIC allocates the specific VLAN to be used for each of the EPGs.

As Figure 5-24 illustrates, the APIC creates a logical switch in Hyper-V and each EPG becomes a VM network.

After this, the tenant can instantiate the VMs that are on Windows Server 2012 and can attach endpoints through the leaf nodes. At that point, because OpFlex is running on the actual hypervisor, ACI knows where the VM is, so ACI can download the policies where necessary.

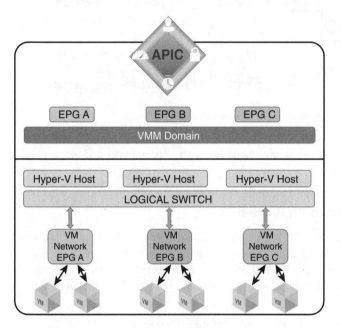

Figure 5-24 *Cisco ACI Concepts Equivalent in Hyper-V*

Cisco ACI Integration with KVM

The integration of ACI with KVM is mediated by the use of OpenStack, which is covered in Chapter 6. This section simply illustrates the communication pattern among the components, as shown in Figure 5-25.

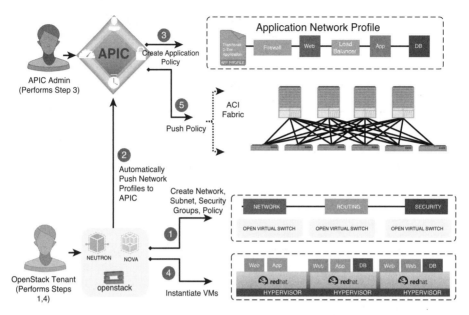

Figure 5-25   *Cisco ACI Interaction with OpenStack and KVM*

In the case of KVM and OpenStack, the plug-in in OpenStack communicates with the APIC and with KVM to synchronize the allocation of VLANs and VXLANs to ensure they match the EPG definition.

Cisco ACI Integration with VMware ESX

The APIC controller integrates with VMware vCenter to extend the ACI policy framework to vSphere workloads. ACI integrates with vShield Manager for the provisioning of VXLANs between virtualized hosts and ACI leafs. Endpoint groups in ACI are automatically extended to virtualized hosts via the automatic creation of a vDS switch that represents ACI.

Figure 5-26 illustrates how ACI interacts with VMware vCenter.

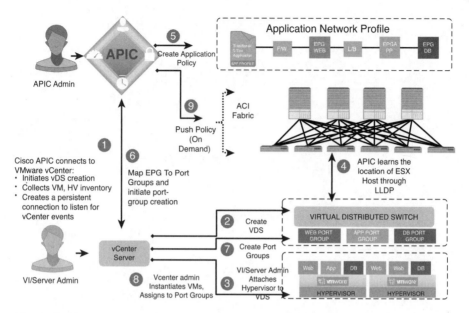

Figure 5-26 *Interaction Between the APIC Controller and vCenter*

Associate APIC and vCenter by setting up a VMM domain. This creates a new VMware distributed virtual switch on vCenter. Next, attach each particular hypervisor to the DVS itself by associating the DV uplinks on the newly created vSwitch to the EXS host.

The ACI fabric learns the location of the DVS via LLDP. From this moment on, the APIC administrator runs the APIC and then creates application network profiles. These get pushed out through the respective VMM domain as a port group. Each of the EPGs that the administrator creates, such as EPG web, EPG app, EPG database, and equivalent port groups, is also created under the DVS. The virtual administrator then associates these port groups to the relevant VM.

Summary

This chapter described the requirements to connect virtual machines to each other and the rest of the network. It explained why virtual switches and other technologies like VN-TAG have been developed. This chapter also illustrated the differences in the implementation of virtual switching in different hypervisors. The last part of the chapter explained how ACI provides multi-hypervisor connectivity and how it interfaces with each hypervisor.

Chapter 6

OpenStack

This chapter explains the benefits of combining OpenStack with Cisco ACI. It examines the Cisco ACI APIC OpenStack architecture along with the possible operations of this combination. The goal of this chapter is to present the OpenStack concepts and allow you to use it together with Cisco ACI.

What Is OpenStack?

OpenStack (http://www.openstack.org/) is an open source software platform for orchestration and automation in data center environments. It is typically used for private and public clouds. OpenStack is designed to automate, supervise, and manage compute, network, storage, and security in virtualized environments. The goal of the OpenStack project is to deliver solutions for all types of clouds by being simple to implement, feature rich, scalable, and easy to deploy and operate. OpenStack consists of several different projects that deliver components of the OpenStack solution.

Historically, OpenStack was founded by Rackspace and NASA and grew into a community of collaborating developers working on open projects.

OpenStack has different components. The software suite is available for download online and can operate on multiple Linux distributions. The current main components of OpenStack are

- Compute (Nova)
- Networking (Neutron)
- Storage (Cinder and Swift)
- Dashboard GUI (Horizon)
- Identity (Keystone)
- Image service (Glance)

The major components are illustrated in Figure 6-1.

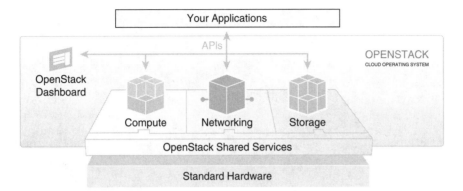

Figure 6-1   *OpenStack Main Components and High-Level Interaction*

Newer components are being created, such as:

- Physical compute provisioning (Ironic)
- Automation (Heat)

Each element uses the following design guidelines:

- **Component-based architecture:** Provides the capability to quickly add new functions

- **Highly available:** Provides scale for workloads

- **Fault-tolerant:** Isolates the processes to avoid cascading failures

- **Recoverable:** Failures should be easy to recover and debug

- **Open standards:** Provide a reference implementation for community APIs and compatibility with other popular cloud systems such as, for example, Amazon EC2.

Nova

Nova is the project for OpenStack Compute, a cloud computing fabric controller. It is the main component of an Infrastructure as a Service (IaaS) system. Its role is to host, provision, and manage virtual machines. This includes controlling the server, the operating system image management, and the dashboard for compute. The server resources are CPU, memory, disk, and interfaces. The image management consists of the storage, import, and sharing of virtual machine ISO files. Other functionalities in OpenStack include, but are not limited to, role-based access control (RBAC), allocation of pooled resources across compute elements, and the dashboard. Nova spans computes not only across KVM, but across other types of hypervisors such as Hyper-V, VMware ESX, and

Citrix XenServer. This allows OpenStack to orchestrate various hypervisors at the same time via APIs. With this compute element, you can create, configure, delete, and move VMs across hypervisors.

Neutron

The network element Neutron (previously called Quantum) offers a Networking as a Service interface to OpenStack. Whereas Nova provides an API to dynamically request and configure virtual servers for various hypervisors, Neutron provides an API to dynamically request and configure virtual networks. These networks connect interfaces from other OpenStack services such as the vNICs (virtual NICs) from Nova virtual machines. Although the core Neutron API is focused on Layer 2, it contains several extensions to provide additional services. Neutron is based on a plug-in model that enables various network solutions to implement the platform's virtual network constructs. Two popular open source virtual switching solutions are Linux Bridge and Open vSwitch (OVS, introduced in Chapter 5).

The type of functionality provided by OVS is comparable at a high level to the Cisco Nexus 1000V or the VMware vDS (virtual Distributed Switch). With Linux Bridge, it's possible to create bridge interfaces, interconnect virtual network interfaces with each other, and bridge the virtual network interfaces to the uplink interface. OVS uses a database model, called OVSDB, which can receive via CLI or API instructions for virtual networking configuration and store the configuration in a local database. This is different from Linux network environments, where you make network changes without saving the configuration files (for example, in /etc/network/interfaces), which is not persistent across a reboot. With OVSDB, all the changes are stored in a database. OVSDB communicates with the OVS process that sends instructions to the kernel.

Neutron provides a messaging bus, currently called Modular Layer 2 (ML2), which operates as a Layer 2 messaging bus. ML2 is an architecture employed to reuse plug-ins across different segments of the network. ML2 breaks the elements into "type" and "mechanism" drivers.

Cisco has multiple ML2 plug-ins for the Nexus 9000 as well:

- A Nexus plug-in that supports standalone mode
- AN ML2 version of the Nexus plug-in that supports Nexus 3000, 5000, 7000, and 9000
- An ML2 APIC plug-in (available starting from the Juno release)

The Neutron Core API structure has three core components:

- **Network:** An isolated Layer 2 segment, similar to a VLAN in the physical world. The network can be shared among tenants, and there is an admin-controlled network state.

■ **Subnet:** A block of IPv4 or IPv6 addresses that can be associated with a network. The allocation block is customizable, and it's possible to disable the default DHCP service of Neutron for the given subnet.

■ **Port:** A connection point for attaching a single device such as a NIC of a virtual server to a virtual network. It's possible to preassign MAC and/or IP addresses to a port.

Example 6-1 shows the options offered by the Neutron Network API, and Example 6-2 shows the subnet options.

Example 6-1   *Neutron Network API Options*

```
stack@control-server:/home/localadmin/devstack$ neutron net-create -help
usage: neutron net-create [-h] [-f {shell,table,value}] [-c COLUMN]
                          [--max-width <integer>] [--variable VARIABLE]
                          [--prefix PREFIX] [--request-format {json,xml}]
                          [--tenant-id TENANT_ID] [--admin-state-down]
                          [--shared]
                          NAME
Create a network for a given tenant.
Positional arguments
NAME
Name of network to create.
Optional arguments
-h, --help
show this help message and exit
--request-format {json,xml}
The XML or JSON request format.
--tenant-id TENANT_ID
The owner tenant ID.
--admin-state-down
Set admin state up to false.
--shared
Set the network as shared.
```

Example 6-2   *Neutron Subnet API Options*

```
stack@control-server:/home/localadmin/devstack$ neutron subnet-create --help
usage: neutron subnet-create [-h] [-f {shell,table,value}] [-c COLUMN]
                             [--max-width <integer>] [--variable VARIABLE]
                             [--prefix PREFIX] [--request-format {json,xml}]
                             [--tenant-id TENANT_ID] [--name NAME]
                             [--gateway GATEWAY_IP] [--no-gateway]
                             [--allocation-pool start=IP_ADDR,end=IP_ADDR]
```

```
                                [--host-route destination=CIDR,nexthop=IP_ADDR]
                                [--dns-nameserver DNS_NAMESERVER]
                                [--disable-dhcp] [--enable-dhcp]
                                [--ipv6-ra-mode {dhcpv6-stateful,dhcpv6-
    stateless,slaac}]
                                [--ipv6-address-mode {dhcpv6-stateful,dhcpv6-
    stateless,slaac}]
                                [--ip-version {4,6}]
                                NETWORK CIDR
```

Create a subnet for a given tenant.

Positional arguments

NETWORK

Network ID or name this subnet belongs to.

CIDR

CIDR of subnet to create.

Optional arguments

-h, --help

show this help message and exit

--request-format {json,xml}

The XML or JSON request format.

--tenant-id TENANT_ID

The owner tenant ID.

--name NAME

Name of this subnet.

--gateway GATEWAY_IP

Gateway IP of this subnet.

--no-gateway

No distribution of gateway.

--allocation-pool

start=IP_ADDR,end=IP_ADDR Allocation pool IP addresses for this subnet (This option
  can be repeated).

--host-route

destination=CIDR,nexthop=IP_ADDR Additional route (This option can be repeated).

--dns-nameserver DNS_NAMESERVER

DNS name server for this subnet (This option can be repeated).

--disable-dhcp

Disable DHCP for this subnet.

--enable-dhcp

Enable DHCP for this subnet.

--ipv6-ra-mode {dhcpv6-stateful,dhcpv6-stateless,slaac}

IPv6 RA (Router Advertisement) mode.

--ipv6-address-mode {dhcpv6-stateful,dhcpv6-stateless,slaac}

IPv6 address mode.

--ip-version {4,6} IP

version to use, default is 4.

Note   For information about all Neutron commands, visit the reference guide:
http://docs.openstack.org/cli-reference/content/neutronclient_commands.html

Neutron provides the capability of advanced services via service plug-ins. Here are the
four most common Neutron services used:

- **Layer 3:** This service enables the creation of a router for connecting and attaching
  Layer 2 tenant networks that require Layer 3 connectivity. It requires the creation of
  a floating IP for associating a VM private IP address to a public IP address. It allows
  the configuration of an external gateway for forwarding traffic outside of tenant
  networks.

- **LoadBalancer:** This service requires the creation of a load-balancer pool with members for a tenant. It enables the creation of a virtual IP (VIP) that, when accessed
  through the LoadBalancer, directs the request to one of the pool members. It allows
  the configuration of Health Monitor Checks for the pool members.

- **VPN:** This service is specific to a tenant and a router. The VPN connection represents the IPsec tunnel established between two sites for the tenant. It requires the
  creation of a the following elements: VPN, IKE, IPsec, and Connection.

- **Firewall:** This service provides perimeter firewall functionalities on a Neutron logical router for a tenant. It requires the creation of Firewall, Policy, and Rules.

When deploying Neutron, in addition to the neutron-server service, several agents are
needed depending on the configuration: L3 agent, DHCP, and Plugin. The agents can
be deployed on the controller node or on a separate network node, as depicted in
Figure 6-2.

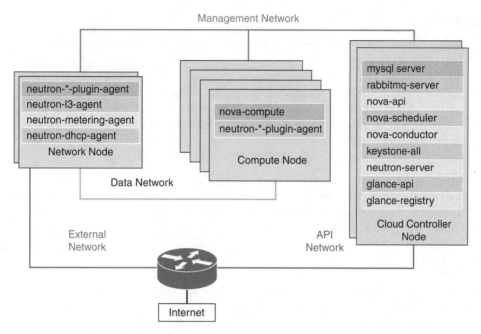

Figure 6-2 *Neutron Agents*

Swift

The storage element of OpenStack is provided by Swift and Cinder. Swift is a distributed object storage system designed to scale from a single machine to thousands of servers. It's optimized for multi-tenancy and high concurrency. It is useful for backups, and unstructured data capable to grow without bounds. Swift provides a REST-based API.

Cinder

Cinder is the storage project for block storage. It provides the capability to create and centrally manage a service that provisions storage in the form of block devices known as *cinder volumes*. The most common scenario is to provide persistent storage to virtual machines. Cinder allows, for example, virtual machine mobility, snapshot, and cloning. These functions can be enhanced by the vendor-specific, third-party driver plug-ins added to Cinder. The physical storage attached behind Cinder can be centralized or distributed using various protocols: iSCSI, NFS, and Fibre Channel.

Horizon

The GUI element Horizon is the OpenStack dashboard project. This presents a web-based GUI to access, provision, and automate the OpenStack resources such as Neutron, Nova, Swift, and Cinder. Its design facilitates the integration with third-party products and services such as billing, monitoring, and alarms. Horizon started as a single application to manage the OpenStack Nova project. Originally, the requirements consisted only of a set of views, templates, and API calls. It then expanded to support multiple OpenStack projects and APIs that became arranged into a dashboard and system panel group. Horizon currently has two central dashboards: project and user.

These dashboards cover the core OpenStack applications. There is a set of API abstractions for the core OpenStack project to provide a consistent, reusable set of methods for development and interaction. With these API abstractions, developers don't need to be familiar with the API of each OpenStack project.

Heat

Heat is the OpenStack orchestration program. It creates a human- and machine-accessible service for managing the entire lifecycle of infrastructure and applications within OpenStack clouds. Heat has an orchestration engine used to launch multiple composite cloud applications based on templates in the form of text files that can be treated like code. A native Heat template format is evolving, but Heat also provides compatibility with the AWS CloudFormation template format, allowing the many existing CloudFormation templates to be launched on OpenStack. Heat offers both an OpenStack-native REST API and a CloudFormation-compatible Query API.

Ironic

Ironic is the OpenStack project that provides Bare Metal Services. It enables users to manage and provision physical machines. Ironic includes the following components, as displayed in Figure 6-3:

- **Ironic API:** A RESTful API that processes application requests by sending them to the ironic-conductor over RPC.

- **Ironic Conductor:** Adds, edits, and deletes nodes; powers on/off nodes with IPMI or SSH; provisions, deploys, and decommissions bare-metal nodes.

- **Ironic client:** A CLI for interacting with the Bare Metal Service.

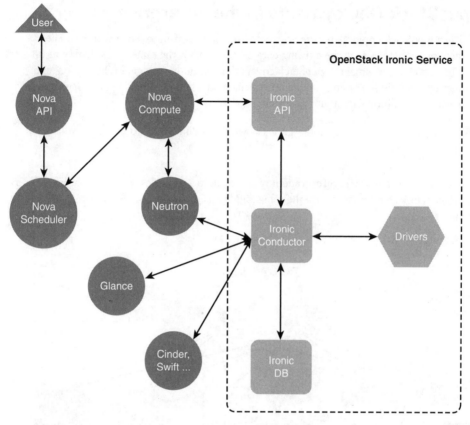

Figure 6-3 *Ironic Logical Architecture*

Additionally, the Ironic Bare Metal Service has certain external dependencies, which are very similar to other OpenStack services:

■ **A database to store hardware information and state:** You can set the database back-end type and location. Use the same database back end as the Compute Service. Employ a separate database back end to further isolate bare-metal resources (and associated metadata) from users.

■ **A queue:** A central hub for passing messages.

Triple0 is another project, meant to run OpenStack on OpenStack. It brings up bare-metal servers that can be set up to use OpenStack.

OpenStack Deployments in the Enterprise

The OpenStack components are connected to the top-of-rack (ToR) switches. The network architecture in the existing data center remains the same when deploying an OpenStack environment. OpenStack covers the compute, storage, orchestration, and management tiers. The apps are mainly unchanged when deployed in an OpenStack environment. Additional compute nodes are added for

- OpenStack controller nodes (at least two for redundancy, could be active/active)

- OpenStack support nodes

Note that certain users prefer to deploy these additional nodes as virtual machines for a homogenous deployment with the remaining hosts of the infrastructure which are virtual as well.

A typical ToR topology is depicted in Figure 6-4.

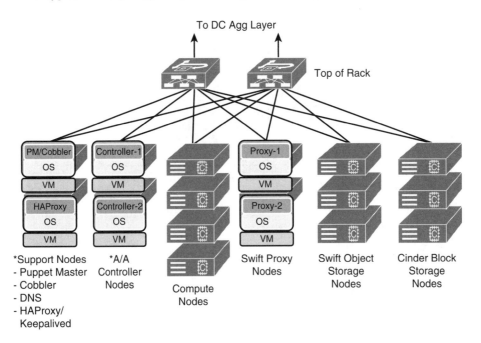

Figure 6-4   *OpenStack Deployment Typical Design*

A typical deployment often consists of a 200-node deployment with a Canonical or Red Hat operating system distribution. The deployment is configured either manually or fully automated with Puppet, Juju, or Turnkey.

When planning an OpenStack deployment, high-level considerations include

- Whether OpenStack deployment will be in an existing pod or a new one.

- Performing hardware inventory: all rack servers, all blade servers, hardware, and VMs.

- Which app(s) to run in the new deployment.

- Whether or not to use multi-tenancy. This is a functional and business topic as much as a technical one—always deploy with multi-tenancy in mind.

- IP address planning: NAT inside OpenStack? No NAT? Overlapping IPs?

- Automation choices.

- Whether to use a "pure" OpenStack (only OpenStack projects) deployment or a hybrid deployment where you use some of what OpenStack offers and leverage third-party application, management, and monitoring services.

- Knowing the limitations of current high-availability/disaster-recovery (HA/DR) models with OpenStack.

Regarding the network considerations, there are a few choices, such as:

- Private networks with per-tenant routers

- Provider routers

- Provider network extensions with VLANs (no NAT)

Most enterprises use the VLAN model when there is no need for NAT within the OpenStack system. Most of the NAT takes place on the edge, such as via the firewall, server load balancing (SLB), proxy, or routers. However, large enterprise deployments run into VLAN numbering limitations when the system is deployed in a brownfield design (sharing VLANs with other pods).

Benefits of Cisco ACI and OpenStack

The data center infrastructure is quickly transitioning from an environment that supports relatively static workloads confined to specific infrastructure silos to a highly dynamic cloud environment in which any workload can be provisioned anywhere and can scale on demand according to application needs. This transition places new requirements on the computing, storage, and network infrastructure.

Cisco ACI and OpenStack were both designed to help IT administrators navigate the transition to a cloud architecture. Cisco ACI offers a new approach to managing infrastructure designed to increase flexibility, scalability, and performance through a centralized policy-based framework. For example, normalizing at the leaf (no gateways on servers), improves the scalability. The solution was designed to span both physical and virtual infrastructure while still providing deep visibility and real-time telemetry.

Additionally, Cisco ACI was built for open APIs to allow integration with both new and existing infrastructure components.

Cisco has developed an open source plug-in for OpenStack Neutron that allows OpenStack tenants to transparently configure and manage a network based on Cisco ACI. This plug-in for the Cisco APIC automatically translates OpenStack Neutron API commands for networks, subnets, routers, and so on into an application network profile.

The Cisco APIC plug-in is available as an open source project component and supports major distributions of OpenStack from the Ice House release, including Canonical, Red Hat, and Mirantis distributions.

The Cisco ACI network fabric used in correlation with an OpenStack environment offers various benefits. Some of them are depicted in Figure 6-5.

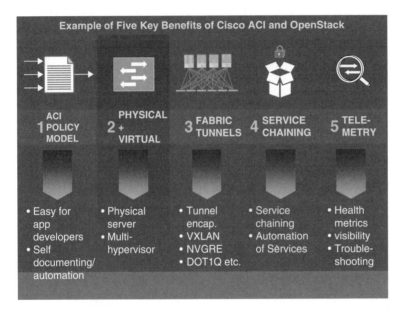

Figure 6-5 *Five Key Benefits of Cisco ACI and OpenStack*

Cisco ACI Policy Model

In a Cisco ACI network fabric, the applications running on the network are coupled with a policy that defines communication between application components and the outside world. This workflow is achieved through an abstract application-centric policy language, which can be translated into concrete network requirements such as VLANs, subnets, and access control lists (ACL). By introducing this concept of policy, Cisco ACI enables application developers to describe their network requirements, with these requirements transparently mapped to network hardware. This process enables both network and application developers to use a common requirements language and ultimately accelerate application deployment.

Physical and Virtual Integration

Cisco ACI was designed to bring together physical and virtual networking to offer an end-to-end solution. For example, Cisco ACI provides transparent support for a mission-critical physical database workload working in conjunction with virtualized web servers and applications. This feature allows operators to support multiple hypervisors, including Citrix Xen, Linux Kernel-based Virtual Machine (KVM), VMware hypervisors, and Microsoft Hyper-V, and connect physical servers on the same Cisco ACI network fabric. As open projects such as OpenStack Ironic continue to evolve, the capability to span these different environments will become an essential element of any cloud. The Cisco ACI network fabric allows OpenStack Neutron networks to transparently span physical and multi-hypervisor virtual environments.

Fabric Tunnels

Cisco ACI was also designed to offer a hardware-based tunneling environment that does not need to be configured device by device. Tunnels are automatically established within the network fabric, and any form of encapsulation (VXLAN, network virtualization generic routing encapsulation [NVGRE], or VLAN) can be passed in as input. The Cisco ACI network fabric is a normalization gateway capable of understanding the different overlay encapsulations and establishing communication between them. The result is very simple administration without the need to compromise performance, scalability, or flexibility.

Service Chaining

The Cisco ACI fabric offers a native service-chaining capability that allows a user to transparently insert or remove services between two endpoints. Furthermore, the Cisco ACI fabric can be configured in real time using the API of the service layer appliance, such as a firewall, load balancer, application delivery controller (ADC), and so forth. This capability allows both tenants and administrators to deploy complex applications and security policies in a fully automated manner across best-in-class infrastructure. This capability is available through the Cisco APIC and accessible through OpenStack API extensions currently in development. Because the Cisco ACI fabric is designed to span physical and virtual infrastructure, the service-chaining function can be applied to physical network service devices as well as virtualized devices running on any supported hypervisor.

Telemetry

Cisco ACI is designed to offer a combination of software and hardware that can provide real-time hop-by-hop visibility and telemetry. The Cisco APIC presents detailed information about the performance of individual endpoint groups and tenants in the network. This data includes details about latency, packet drops, and traffic paths and is available to see at the group or tenant level. Telemetry information is useful for a wide range of troubleshooting and debugging tasks, allowing an operator to quickly identify the source of a tenant problem across physical and virtual infrastructure.

OpenStack APIC Driver Architecture and Operations

The Cisco OpenStack plug-in is based on the OpenStack Neutron multivendor framework Modular Layer 2 (ML2) plug-in. ML2 allows an administrator to specify a set of drivers to manage portions of the network. Type drivers specify a particular type of tagging or encapsulation, and mechanism drivers are designed to interact with specific devices within the network. In particular, Cisco created a Cisco APIC driver that communicates using the open REST APIs exposed by Cisco APIC, as shown in Figure 6-6.

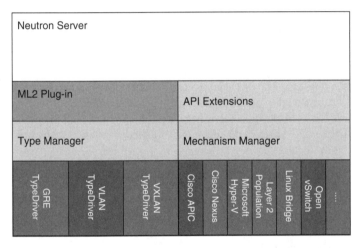

Figure 6-6   *Modular Layer 2 Plug-in Components Used by Cisco ACI (in Red)*

This integration is supported initially on OpenStack Icehouse distributions from a number of vendors, including Red Hat, Canonical, and Mirantis. Additionally, Cisco is working closely with a number of other partners such as Big Switch Networks, IBM, Juniper, Midokura, Nuage, One Convergence, and Red Hat to drive the Group Policy API project within the OpenStack community.

How Integration Works

OpenStack integration uses two separate ML2 drivers to integrate with different portions of the network, as shown in Figure 6-7:

- **Open vSwitch (OVS) driver:** Cisco ACI integration is performed on an unmodified version of the OVS driver and supports the OVS driver that ships with most major OpenStack distributions. An OVS driver in Neutron here is used to select a VLAN tag for a network and configure it on an OVS port on a hypervisor as different virtual machines are instantiated. This tag serves as an identifier for the Cisco ACI fabric. Cisco ACI does not require modifications to either the OVS driver or the OVS itself for this integration.

■ **Cisco APIC driver:** The Cisco APIC driver is a new component created by Cisco. It transparently maps Neutron resources to the application network profile configuration in the Cisco APIC. The specific mappings are described in Table 6-1. The driver also dynamically adds endpoint group (EPG) mappings as each virtual machine is instantiated on a network.

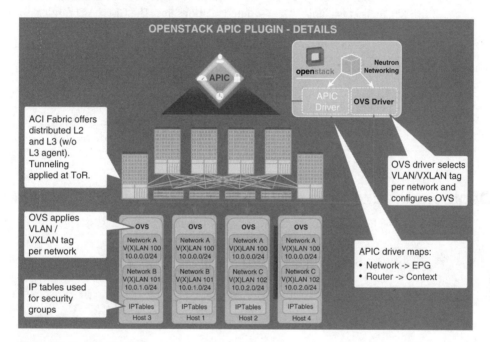

Figure 6-7 *Architecture*

Table 6-1 *Plug-in Mappings*

Neutron Object	APIC Mapping	Description
Project	Tenant (fvTenant)	The project is directly mapped to a Cisco APIC tenant.
Network	EPG (fvAEPg) Bridge domain (fvBD)	Network creation or deletion triggers both EPG and bridge domain configurations. The Cisco ACI fabric acts as a distributed Layer 2 fabric, allowing networks to be present anywhere.
Subnet	Subnet (fvSubnet)	The subnet is a one-to-one mapping.

Neutron Object	APIC Mapping	Description
Security group and rule	–	Security groups are fully supported as part of the solution. However, these resources are not mapped to the Cisco APIC, but are enforced through IP tables as they are in traditional OpenStack deployments.
Router	Contract (vzBrCP) Subject (vzSubj) Filter (vzFilter)	Contracts are used to connect EPGs and define routed relationships. The Cisco ACI fabric also acts as a default gateway. The Layer 3 agent is *not* used.
Network: external	Outside	An outside EPG, including the router configuration, is used.
Port	Static path binding (fvRsPathAtt)	When a virtual machine is attached, a static EPG mapping is used to connect a specific port and VLAN combination on the ToR.

Deployment Example

This section provides an example of how to deploy OpenStack and the Cisco plug-in.

Note   The OpenStack documentation contains instructions and guidelines for deploying OpenStack:

http://docs.openstack.org/trunk/install-guide/install/apt/content/index.html

A typical OpenStack deployment contains the following three types of nodes, as shown in Figure 6-8:

■ **Controller node:** Runs core OpenStack services for computing and networking. It may be run redundantly for high-availability purposes depending on your OpenStack configuration.

■ **Network node:** Runs the Domain Host Configuration Protocol (DHCP) agent and other networking services. Note that for the Cisco APIC driver, the Layer 3 agent is not used. You can run the network node and the controller node on the same physical server.

■ **Compute node:** Runs hypervisors and tenant virtual machines. Each compute node contains an Open vSwitch as well.

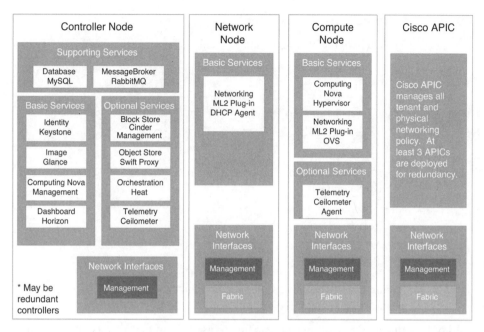

Figure 6-8 *Typical OpenStack Deployment Contains Three Types of Nodes*

OpenStack must be deployed behind a leaf-spine topology built from Cisco Nexus 9000 Series Switches configured to run in Cisco ACI mode. The Cisco APIC and OpenStack controller and network nodes are deployed redundantly behind leaf switches (using either in-band or out-of-band management). In many common deployments, the network node is located on the same server as the controller node. Additionally, computing nodes running virtual machines must be deployed behind leaf switches as well and will scale with the needs of the cloud deployment.

Installation of Icehouse

The Cisco APIC driver can be installed on top of OpenStack Neutron.

Note Although deployment options vary depending on the tools used, one of the best guides for deployment can be found at http://docs.openstack.org/icehouse/install-guide/install/apt/content.

The instructions in the following steps are intended as a guide for installing the Cisco APIC driver on top of an existing ML2 plug-in deployment in Neutron. They assume that the controller and network node run on the same physical server.

Step 1.   Set up apt-get and get packages:

- On both the Neutron controller and Nova computing nodes

- On the Neutron controller, there are more packages to install

Note   More detailed installation information can be found at http://www.cisco.com/go/aci.

Step 2.   Create the configuration for Cisco APIC in /etc/neutron/plugins/ml2/ml2_conf_cisco.ini:

```
[ml2_cisco_apic]
apic_hosts=192.168.1.3
apic_username=admin
apic_password=secret
```

Be sure that the Neutron server initialization includes this configuration file as one of the --config-file options.

Step 3.   Update the Neutron configuration to use ML2 as the core plug-in. Also configure the Cisco APIC to provide routing services by updating /etc/neutron/neutron.conf to include:

- service_plugins:

```
neutron.services.l3_router.l3_apic.ApicL3ServicePlugin
```

- core_plugin:

```
neutron.plugins.ml2.plugin.Ml2Plugin
```

Also, update the ML2 mechanism driver list to include the following two drivers (for example, if you are using /etc/neutron/plugins/ml2/ml2_conf.ini for the ML2 configuration, update it):

- mechanism_drivers:

```
openvswitch,cisco_apic
```

Step 4.   Update ML2 for the VLAN segments. For instance, if you are using VLANs 100 to 200 on physnet1, configure ML2 as follows:

```
tenant_network_types = vlan
type_drivers = local,flat,vlan,gre,vxlan
mechanism_drivers = openvswitch,cisco_apic

[ml2_type_vlan]
```

```
network_vlan_ranges = physnet1:100:200

[ovs]
bridge_mappings = physnet1:br-eth1
```

Configuration of the Cisco APIC Driver

To activate the Cisco APIC driver, it must be placed in the ML2 directory used by Neutron. This placement occurs automatically during any supported installation process through an OpenStack distribution. If you experience problems, verify that you have all the files for the Cisco APIC driver, listed in Table 6-2.

Table 6-2 *Cisco APIC Driver Files*

Filename	Common Location	Description
apic_client.py apic_model.py apic_manager.py mechanism_apic.py ...	<neutron>/plugins/ml2/ drivers/cisco/apic	ML2 driver for Cisco APIC
l3_apic.py	<neutron>/services/l3_router/	Layer 3 extensions for Cisco APIC
*_cisco_apic_driver.py *_cisco_apic_driver_update.py *_add_router_id_*_apic.py	<neutron>/db/migration/ alembic_migrations/versions	Database migration files
neutron.conf	/etc/neutron	Global configuration file for Neutron
cisco-apic.filters	/etc/neutron/rootwrap.d	Allows Link Layer Discovery Protocol (LLDP) services to run as root
ml2_conf.ini	/etc/neutron/plugins/ml2	ML2 configuration file created by Neutron
ml2_conf_cisco.ini	/etc/neutron/plugins/ml2	ML2 configuration file specific to Cisco APIC

In Table 6-2, <neutron> is the neutron base directory, as shown in this configuration:

```
/usr/lib/python2.7/dist-packages/neutron
```

Neutron.conf File

Enable the ML2 plug-in in your neutron.conf file and specify the Cisco APIC Layer 3 service plug-in:

- service_plugins:

  ```
  neutron.services.l3_router.l3_apic.ApicL3ServicePlugin
  ```

- core_plugin:

  ```
  neutron.plugins.ml2.plugin.Ml2Plugin
  ```

ML2_conf.ini File

Your ml2.conf file should activate the two appropriate mechanism drivers for the OVS and the Cisco APIC. It also must specify a VLAN range to be used between the servers and the fabric leaf switches as well as the mapping between the Linux interface and OVS bridge. It should resemble Example 6-3. The ML2_conf.ini file parameters are explained in the upcoming "Configuration Parameters" section.

Example 6-3 *ML2_conf.ini Parameters to Configure*

```
tenant_network_types = vlan
type_drivers = local,flat,vlan,gre,vxlan
mechanism_drivers = openvswitch,cisco_apic

[ml2_type_vlan]
network_vlan_ranges = physnet1:100:200

[ovs]
bridge_mappings = physnet1:br-eth1
```

ML2_cisco_conf.ini File

You must include an additional configuration file for the Cisco APIC driver in the same directory. It should resemble Example 6-4.

Example 6-4 *ML2_cisco_conf.ini Parameters to Configure*

```
[DEFAULT]
apic_system_id=openstack

[ml2_cisco_apic]
apic_hosts=10.1.1.10
apic_username=admin
apic_password=password
```

```
apic_name_mapping=use_name
apic_vpc_pairs=201:202,203:204


[apic_external_network:ext]
switch=203
port=1/34
cidr_exposed=192.168.0.2/24
gateway_ip=192.168.0.1


#note: optional and needed only for manual configuration
[apic_switch:201]
compute11,compute21=1/10
compute12=1/11


[apic_switch:202]
compute11,compute21=1/20
compute12=1/21
```

Configuration Parameters

Table 6-3 lists the configuration parameters you can specify in the ML2_conf.ini file.

Table 6-3 *Configuration Parameters*

Parameter	Required	Description
apic_hosts	Yes	List of Cisco APIC IP addresses (comma separated).
apic_username	Yes	Username for the Cisco APIC; usually admin is used to allow configuration of multiple tenants.
apic_password	Yes	Password for the Cisco APIC user identified by the username.
apic_name_mapping	No	The Cisco APIC driver has two modes. It can create objects using the same names configured in OpenStack, or it can use universal user IDs (UUID) selected by OpenStack. Because OpenStack does not require unique names, network creation commands will fail on the Cisco APIC if duplicate names are used. The options are use_name and use_uuid.
apic_system_id	No	Name for the VLAN or VXLAN namespace in the Cisco APIC fabric (apic_phys_dom); this name is used if multiple OpenStack instances are run on the same fabric.

Host-Port Connectivity

The Cisco APIC driver must understand which ports are connected to each hypervisor. This is accomplished through two mechanisms. By default, the plug-in uses LLDP to automatically discover neighbor information, so this section is optional. This feature provides automatic discovery of the computing nodes on the switch port and allows physical port mobility across leaf switches in the Cisco ACI fabric. The other mechanism is to manually define what ports are connected to which hypervisor.

However, for troubleshooting purposes, a user may want to override this behavior or configure it manually to rule out an LLDP issue. This configuration also is required if, for instance, you are using dual-homed servers connected through PortChannels. In this case, add configuration blocks for each computing node in the OpenStack environment. The format is as follows:

```
[apic_switch:node-id]
compute-host1,compute-host2=module-id.node-id
```

External Networks

Connections to external Layer 3 networks are configured automatically through the plug-in. To activate this feature, provide the information listed in Table 6-4.

Table 6-4   *Connecting to External Networks*

Configuration	Required	Description
switch	Yes	Switch ID from Cisco APIC
Port	Yes	Switch port to which the external router is connected
Encap	No	Encapsulation used
Cidr_exposed	Yes	Classless interdomain routing (CIDR) exposed to the external router
gateway_way	Yes	IP address of the external gateway

PortChannel Configuration

For redundancy, it is common to configure multiple uplinks from a host to a switch. This feature is supported by the Cisco APIC plug-in and can be configured by enumerating virtual PortChannel (vPC) pairs:

```
apic_vpc_pairs=switch-a-id:switch-b-id,switch-c-id:switch-d-id
```

Troubleshooting

If you believe the plug-in is properly installed, but it is not functioning properly, begin troubleshooting by verifying the proxy settings and physical host interface:

■ **Proxy settings:** Many lab environments require proxy settings to reach external IP addresses. Note that OpenStack also relies on internal communications, so local HTTP/HTTPS traffic must not be sent through the same proxy. For example, on Ubuntu, the proxy settings might look like the following in /etc/environment:

```
http_proxy="http://1.2.3.4:80/"
https_proxy="http://1.2.3.4:8080/"
HTTP_PROXY="http://proxy.yourco.com:80/"
HTTPS_PROXY="http://proxy.yourco.com:8080/"
FTP_PROXY="http://proxy.yourco.com:80/"
NO_PROXY="localhost,127.0.0.1,172.21.128.131,10.29.198.17,172.21.128.98,local
address,.localdomain.com" [->
The IP addresses listed here are the IP addresses of the NIC of the server
for OpenStack computing and controller nodes, so they don't go to proxy when
they try to reach each other.]
no_proxy="localhost,127.0.0.1,172.21.128.131,10.29.198.17,172.21.128.98,local
address,.localdomain.com"
```

■ **Host interface:** Verify that the physical host interface attached to the leaf switch is up and attached to the OVS bridge. This interface is typically configured as part of the OVS installation process. To verify that an interface (for example, eth1) is present on an OVS bridge, run this command:

```
$> sudo ovs-vctl show

abd0fa05-6c95-4581-a906-46634db74d91
    Bridge "br-eth1"
        Port "phy-br-eth1"
            Interface "phy-br-eth1"
        Port "br-eth1"
            Interface "br-eth1"
                type: internal
        Port "eth1"
            Interface "eth1"
    Bridge br-int
        Port "int-br-eth1"
            Interface "int-br-eth1"
        Port br-int
            Interface br-int
                type: internal
    ovs_version: "1.4.6
```

Note The installation, configuration, and troubleshooting methods might change from release to release of OpenStack. Please refer to the latest documentation on http://www.cisco.com/go/aci for the OpenStack installation guide.

The Group Based Policy Project at OpenStack

Group Based Policy is an OpenStack community project available from Juno OpenStack release onwards. Group Based Policy runs on top of existing OpenStack and can work with existing Neutron or vendor drivers. The idea of Group Based Policy is to enable Neutron to be configured in a policy fashion with EPGs, contracts, and so on. This simplifies the current Neutron method of configuration and enables easier application-oriented interfaces than with the current Neutron API model. The goal of the Group Based Policy API extensions is to allow easier consumption of the networking resources by separate organizations and management systems.

Group Based Policy is a generic API designed to be used with a broad range of network back ends. It is backward compatible with the existing Neutron plug-ins but also can be used natively with Cisco ACI to expose a policy API. The architecture of Group Based Policy is depicted in Figure 6-9.

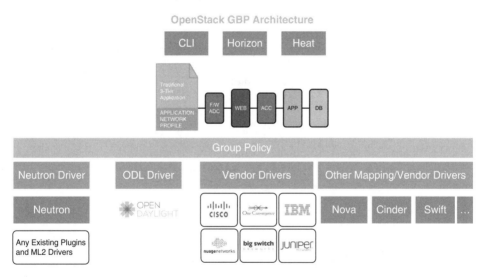

Figure 6-9   *Group Based Policy Architecture.*

Group Based Policy benefits from the same approach as the concepts elaborated in Chapter 3, "The Policy Data Center." The combination of the OpenStack workflow along with the ACI workflow is detailed in Figure 6-10.

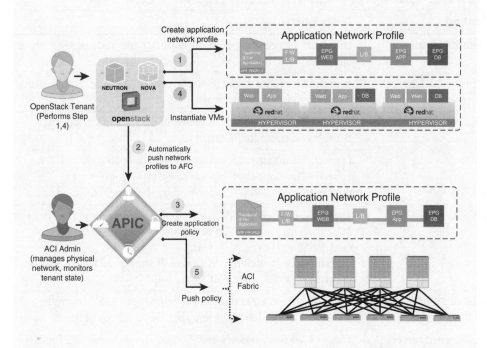

Figure 6-10 *Group Based Policy Workflow*

With Group Based Policy, ACI can be used in conjunction, making the configuration the same on both ends. It is also possible to use Group Based Policy without ACI, with other network devices that are compatible with Neutron ML2 extensions.

Note   For additional information, visit:

https://blueprints.launchpad.net/group-based-policy/+spec/group-based-policy-abstraction

https://wiki.openstack.org/wiki/GroupBasedPolicy

Summary

This chapter detailed OpenStack and its relation to Cisco ACI. ACI learns any changes made on OpenStack and configures the whole fabric to be able to service the new workloads and networks created in OpenStack. Table 6-5 summarizes the features and capabilities of the OpenStack ML2 APIC driver for OpenStack Neutron. Group Based Policy is a new project within the OpenStack community with the goal to bring the policy data center networking abstraction to OpenStack.

Table 6-5 *Summary of OpenStack APIC Driver Features and Capabilities*

Feature	Description
Neutron L2 support	Distributed Layer 2 support allowing flexible placement of virtual machines.
Neutron L3 support	Support for multiple routers implemented in the ACI fabric using distributed hardware gateways.
Security group	Security group support as implemented by OpenStack (using IPTables on compute nodes).
Scale	Layer 2: The number of supported Neutron networks is 4000. Layer 3: The number of supported Neutron routers is the same as the number of contracts supported by the attached ACI fabric.
OVS compatibility	The APIC driver is compatible with the OVS driver in the Neutron ML2 framework. The OVS driver automatically handles server configuration for the ACI fabric. OVS interaction with the ACI fabric is supported for VLAN and, in future versions, over VXLAN as well.
Multiple APIC support	The APIC driver communicates with multiple APIC controllers and is resilient to failure of any specific APIC controller.
Dual-homed servers	The APIC driver supports dual-homed servers using vPC functionality of the ACI fabric's ToR switches.
Automatic hypervisor discovery	The APIC driver automatically discovers hypervisor physical connectivity to top of rack using LLDP and dynamically provisions the ACI fabric. This allows physical topology changes without any reconfiguration.
Licensing	The APIC driver is open source and available without additional licensing on the APIC or ACI fabric. The latest code for Icehouse is available at: https://github.com/noironetworks/neutron/tree/cisco-apic-icehouse/neutron/plugins/ml2/drivers/cisco/apic
Supported versions	The APIC driver is currently supported on OpenStack Icehouse and will be supported on future versions of OpenStack as well.

Chapter 7

ACI Fabric Design Methodology

The goal of this chapter is to explain the Cisco ACI fabric design methodology. Cisco ACI fabric consists of discrete components that operate as routers and switches but are provisioned and monitored as a single entity. Thus, the fabric operates like a single switch and router that provides the following advanced traffic optimization features:

- Security

- Telemetry functions

- Stitching together of virtual and physical workloads

The main benefits of using a Cisco ACI fabric are

- Single point of provisioning, either via GUI or via REST API

- Connectivity for physical and virtual workloads with complete visibility of virtual and physical machine traffic

- Hypervisor compatibility and integration without the need to add software to the hypervisor

- Simplicity of automation

- Multitenancy (network slicing)

- Hardware-based security

- Elimination of flooding from the fabric

- Ease of mapping application architectures into the networking configuration

- Capability to insert and automate firewalls, load balancers, and other Layer 4 through 7 services

Summary of ACI Fabric Key Functionalities

This section describes the key functionalities of the ACI fabric so that you can better understand how to design and configure the ACI fabric.

ACI Forwarding Behavior

The forwarding in ACI changes the existing network forwarding paradigm by introducing new key concepts such as the following:

- Classification of workloads independent of the transport VLAN, VXLAN, or subnet. The classification is based on security zones, called *endpoint groups* (EPG), and it is not a one-to-one mapping with subnets or VLANs as in traditional networking.

- Although both Layer 2 and Layer 3 networks are fully supported, packets are transported across the fabric using Layer 3 routing.

- Flooding in bridge domains is not necessary.

- Traffic forwarding is similar to host-based routing; within the fabric the IP is an endpoint or a tunnel endpoint identifier.

If you are familiar with the concepts of Cisco TrustSec, and in particular with the Security Group Tag (SGT), you may find the concept of the EPG to be similar to that of the SGT. If you are acquainted with Cisco Locator/ID Separation Protocol (LISP), you may find similarities in terms of the use of the IP as an identifier of the host. With Cisco FabricPath, you will find similarities in the way that the fabric handles multicast, with the capability to do equal-cost multipathing for Layer 2 traffic. In other words, ACI forwarding is a superset of all these existing technologies, and more.

Prescriptive Topology

With Cisco ACI the topology is prescriptive and automatically enforced with auto-discovery, zero-touch provisioning, and a built-in cable plan. The Cisco ACI topology consists of a set of leaf devices connected to a set of spine devices in a full bipartite graph, or Clos architecture using 40-Gigabit Ethernet links.

All leaf devices are connected to all spine devices, all spine devices are connected to all leaf devices, and links between spines devices or between leaf devices are disabled if present.

Leaf devices can connect to any network device or host and are the place at which policies are enforced. Leaf devices also provide the capability to route and bridge to external network infrastructures such as:

- Campus

- WAN

- Multiprotocol Label Switching (MPLS)

- Virtual private network (VPN) cloud

In this case they are sometimes referred to as *border leaf devices*. At the time of writing, the ACI fabric does not implement VPN or MPLS, so an external device for this purpose needs to be connected to the fabric, such as a Cisco ASR 9000.

The following endpoints can be connected to leaf devices:

- Virtualized servers

- Bare-metal servers

- Mainframes

- Layer 4 through 7 services nodes

- IP storage devices

- Switches

- Routers

Spine devices constitute the backbone of the fabric and provide the mapping database function.

Figure 7-1 describes how to implement an ACI fabric.

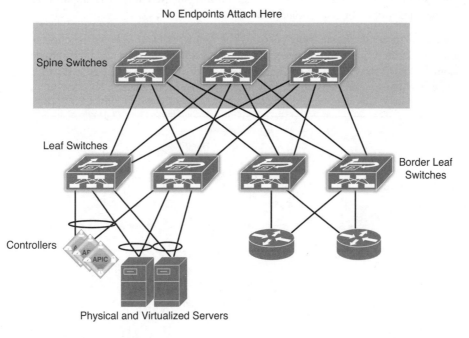

Figure 7-1 *Cisco ACI Fabric*

Overlay Frame Format

Existing data center networks suffer from a shortage of VLAN segments. ACI addresses this problem by using Virtual Extensible LAN (VXLAN), a Layer 2 overlay scheme over a Layer 3 network. A 24-bit VXLAN Segment ID or VXLAN Network Identifier (VNI) is included in the encapsulation to provide up to 16 million VXLAN segments for traffic isolation and segmentation, in contrast to the 4000 segments achievable with VLANs. Each of these segments represents a unique Layer 2 broadcast domain or a Layer 3 context depending on whether bridging or routing is used, and can be administered in such a way to uniquely identify a given tenant's address space or subnet. VXLAN encapsulates Ethernet frames in an IP packet using UDP as the encapsulating protocol.

ACI forwarding is based on the VXLAN encapsulation, with some differences from the original VXLAN protocol. Regular VXLAN leverages multicast in the transport network to simulate flooding behavior for broadcast, unknown unicast, and multicast in the Layer 2 segment. Unlike traditional VXLAN networks, the ACI preferred mode of operations does not rely on multicast for learning and discovery but on a mapping database that is populated upon discovery of endpoints in a way that is more similar to LISP. It does rely on multicast for multicast and broadcast if they need to be supported.

An ACI VXLAN (VXLAN) header provides a tagging mechanism to identify properties associated with frames forwarded through an ACI-capable fabric. It is an extension of the Layer 2 LISP protocol (draft-smith-lisp-layer2-01) with the addition of a policy group, load and path metrics, counter and ingress ports, and encapsulation information. The VXLAN header is not associated with a specific Layer 2 segment or Layer 3 domain but instead provides a multifunction tagging mechanism used in the ACI application-defined networking (ADN) enabled fabric.

Figure 7-2 shows the frame format used by the ACI fabric. Part a shows the original Ethernet frame as generated by an endpoint, part b shows the original frame encapsulated into UDP via VXLAN, part c shows the format of VXLAN headers, and part d shows the mapping of the ACI VXLAN packet format onto regular VXLAN.

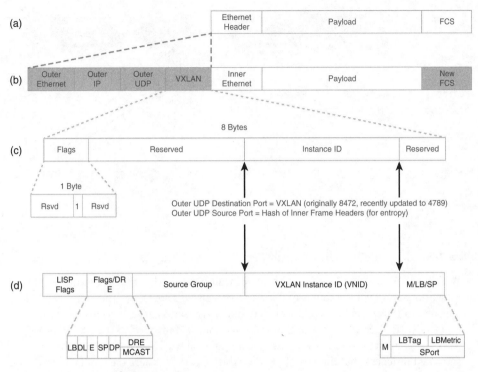

Figure 7-2 *Cisco ACI VXLAN Frame Format*

VXLAN Forwarding

The ACI fabric decouples the tenant endpoint address, its "identifier," from the location of that endpoint, which is defined by its "locator" or VXLAN tunnel endpoint (VTEP) address. As illustrated in Figure 7-3, forwarding within the fabric is between VTEPs and leverages an extended VXLAN header format referred to as the *ACI VXLAN policy header*. The mapping of the internal tenant MAC or IP address to location is performed by the VTEP using a distributed mapping database.

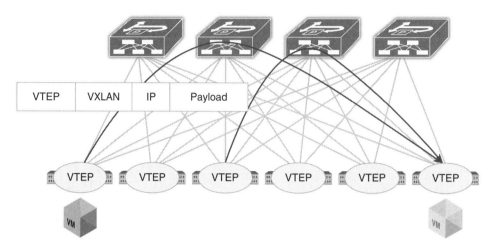

Figure 7-3 *Cisco ACI VXLAN Forwarding*

With Cisco ACI, all workloads are equal, regardless of whether they are virtual or physical workloads. Traffic from physical servers, virtualized servers, or other network devices
attached to leaves can be tagged with network virtualization generic routing encapsulation (NVGRE), VXLAN, or VLAN headers and then is remapped to the ACI VXLAN.
Also, the communication between virtual and physical workloads doesn't go through a
gateway bottleneck, but directly along the shortest path to where the workload is. Figure
7-4 displays the VLANs and VXLANs being normalized at the leaf switch layer.

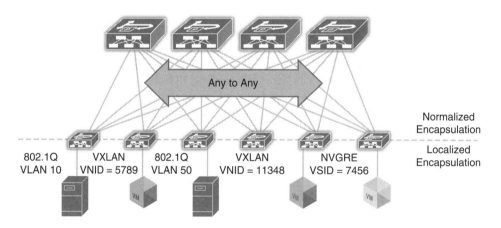

Figure 7-4 *VLAN and VXLANs Are Normalized at the Edge*

Pervasive Gateway

With ACI you don't have to configure Hot Standby Router Protocol (HSRP) or Virtual
Router Redundancy Protocol (VRRP) addresses. The ACI fabric uses the concept of a
pervasive gateway, which is an anycast gateway. The subnet default gateway addresses

are programmed in all leaves with endpoints present for the specific tenant subnet. The benefit is a simple communication where each top-of-rack device takes the role of a default gateway, instead of sending this traffic all across the fabric to a specific default gateway.

Outside Versus Inside

ACI distinguishes between workloads and networks that are connected directly to the fabric and workloads and networks that are external to the fabric. "External" connectivity refers to connecting the fabric to a WAN router, or simply to the rest of the campus network. Leaves that provide this connectivity are often referred to as *border leaves*, even if they are not dedicated to this role. Any ACI leaf can be a border leaf. There is no limitation in terms of number of leaves that can be used for the border leaf role. The border leaf can also be used to connect to compute, IP storage, and service appliances.

In ACI, inside networks are associated with a particular bridge domain of a tenant network. In other words, all workloads that have been discovered in a given tenant belong to an inside network. Outside networks are learned via a border leaf. An exception is made for Layer 2 extension. L2 extension maps to a bridge domain but is "external." All devices that are not connected via Layer 2 or Layer 3 extension are "internal."

At the time of writing, the fabric can learn about external network connectivity in the following way:

- Static routing with or without VRF-lite (Virtual Routing and Forwarding lite is the simplest form of VRF implementation. In this implementation, each router within the network participates in the virtual routing environment in a peer-based fashion.)

- Open Shortest Path First (OSPF)

- Internal Border Gateway Protocol (iBGP)

- Layer 2 connectivity by extending the bridge domain

ACI uses multiprotocol BGP (MP-BGP) between leaf and spine switches to propagate external routes. The BGP route reflector technology is deployed to support a large number of leaf switches within a single fabric. All the leaf and spine switches are in a single BGP autonomous system (AS). After a border leaf learns the external routes, it then redistributes the external routes of a given VRF instance to MP-BGP address family VPNv4 (or VPNv6 when using IPv6) to the other leaf switches. With address VPNv4, MP-BGP maintains a separate BGP routing table for each VRF instance.

Within MP-BGP, the border leaf advertises routes to a spine switch, which is a BGP route reflector. The routes are then propagated to all the leaves where the VRFs (or Private Networks in APIC GUI terminology) are instantiated. Figure 7-5 shows the concept.

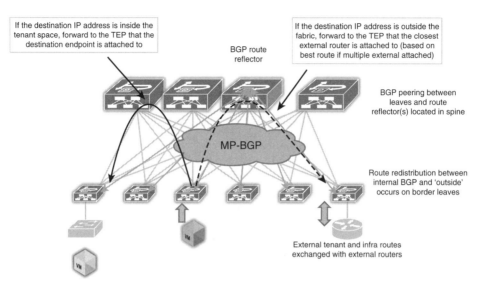

Figure 7-5 *Outside Networks Are Advertised via MP-BGP*

The subnet configuration within each bridge domain allows you to control which subnets from the fabric should be advertised to the outside.

From a policy perspective, external traffic is classified into an EPG just like an inside network. Policies are then defined between internal and external EPGs. Figure 7-6 illustrates the concept. There can be multiple outside EPGs for each external network.

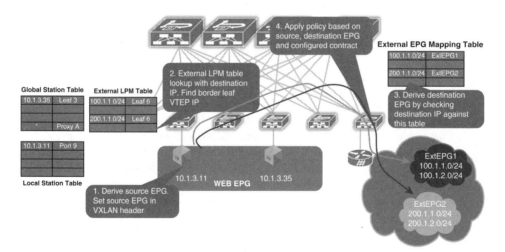

Figure 7-6 *Applying Policies from Internal to External EPGs*

Packet Walk

Forwarding within the fabric is between VTEPs and uses some additional bits in the existing VXLAN header to carry policy information. The mapping of the internal tenant MAC or IP address to a location is performed by the VTEP using a distributed mapping database. Cisco ACI supports full Layer 2 and Layer 3 forwarding semantics; no changes are required to applications or endpoint IP stacks. The default gateway for each bridge domain is a pervasive switch virtual interface (SVI) configured on top-of-rack (ToR) switches wherever the bridge domain of a tenant is present. The pervasive SVI has an anycast gateway per subnet, which is global across the fabric.

Figure 7-7 illustrates the forwarding of unicast frames in ACI from one hypervisor to another.

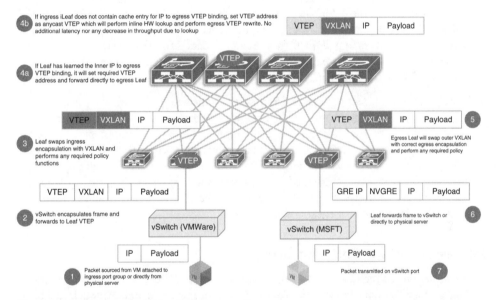

Figure 7-7   *Packet Walk for ACI Forwarding*

As Figure 7-7 illustrates, the default gateway for the virtual machine is the pervasive gateway on the leaf. The leaf normalizes the encapsulation and it performs a lookup on the destination IP. If it does not find the endpoint address it is looking for, it encapsulates the packet to the proxy function residing in the spine switch and forwards it as unicast. The spine switch, upon receiving a packet addressed to its proxy function, looks up the destination identifier address in its forwarding tables, which contain the entire mapping database. On the basis of the result, the spine switch encapsulates the packet using the correct destination locator while retaining the original ingress source locator address in the VXLAN encapsulation. This packet is in turn forwarded as a unicast packet to the intended destination. Address Resolution Protocol (ARP) flooding is eliminated by using this same mechanism. But instead of encapsulating and forwarding based on the Layer 2 destination broadcast address of the ARP packet, the target IP address in the payload of the ARP packet is used. The described mechanism is then employed. If the target IP address is not found in the forwarding table of the leaf, the packet is unicast encapsulated and sent to the proxy. If the target IP address is found in the forwarding table of the leaf, the packet is forwarded accordingly.

The fabric routes if the destination MAC address is a router MAC address; otherwise, it bridges. Classical bridging semantics are preserved for bridged traffic (with exceptions, as described shortly)—no time-to-live (TTL) decrement, no MAC address header rewrite, and so forth—and routing semantics are preserved for routed traffic. Non-IP packets are always forwarded using the MAC address, while IP packets are either bridged or routed depending upon whether or not they are addressed to the default gateway at Layer 2. The fabric learns the MAC address for non-IP packets and learns the MAC and IP addresses for all other packets.

For bridged traffic, the default behavior is to use the spine proxy function for unknown unicast packets, to eliminate Layer 2 flooding. This enhances network behavior to avoid sending these packets to endpoints they are not intended for. However, you can disable this default behavior and use classical flooding, if required. Our recommendation is to leave the default behavior unchanged.

When the packet is sent to anycast VTEP on the spine and there is no entry present (traffic miss) for that destination in the mapping database in the spine, the packet is handled differently for bridged versus routed traffic. For bridged traffic miss, the packet is dropped. For routed traffic miss, the spine communicates with the leaves to initiate an ARP request for the destination address. The ARP request is initiated by all the leaves that have the destination subnet. After the destination host responds to the ARP request, the local database in the leaf and the mapping database in the spine are updated. This mechanism is required for silent hosts.

Segmentation with Endpoint Groups

You can think of the Cisco ACI fabric logically as a distributed switch/router that also indicates application connectivity relationships according to the policy model. ACI provides the following layers of segmentation:

- Segmentation using bridge domains

- Segmentation among different tenants of the same fabric

- Segmentation among endpoints of the same tenant

Segmentation is achieved by leveraging the VNID field of the VXLAN header and the ACI extensions for the EPG. Traditionally, segmentation was performed with VLANs that incidentally were also broadcast and flooding domains. With Cisco ACI the two concepts are decoupled. Bridge domains are the elements that provide a flooding and broadcast domain when required. When flooding is not required, bridge domains simply act as a container for one or more subnets. Also, when routing is turned off on a bridge domain, the bridge domain also provides segmentation just like a classical VLAN. EPGs, which are like port groups or port profiles, provide segmentation among workloads. EPGs contain one or more virtual and physical servers that require similar policy and connectivity. Examples of this are application tiers, development stages, or security zones.

The Cisco ACI fabric allows you to define the communication path among EPGs, just as you do by stitching virtual lines between VLANs using IP routing and access control lists (ACL). Segmentation extends from the fabric to the virtualized servers so that the Cisco ACI fabric provides meaningful services (such as traffic load balancing, segmentation, filtering, traffic insertion, and monitoring) to workloads.

Figure 7-8 shows that the fabric provides a distributed policy consisting of two EPGs connected by a firewall.

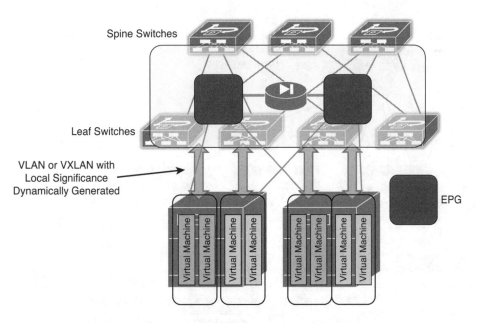

Figure 7-8 *Cisco ACI Fabric Provides Distributed Policy*

Each EPG in Figure 7-8 can belong to one or more subnets. Virtual workloads are connected into port groups that are synchronized with the EPGs and send traffic tagged with VLAN IDs or VXLAN VNIDs to the leaf devices. VLANs and VXLANs are dynamically generated and are not maintained by the user. They have local significance to the leaf switch and VMM domain, and they serve the purpose of segmenting traffic on the link between the server and the leaf. They are also used to signal the EPG membership of the source traffic. (The VMM domain is covered later in the chapter in the section "Virtual Machine Mobility Domains.")

The policy enforcement consists of inserting workloads into the correct EPG and into binding sources to the appropriate EPGs and also destinations into their appropriate EPGs, security, QoS, logging, and so on. The policy enforcement is performed at the leaf. The policy is then enforced on the combination of source and destination EPG and information from the packet.

Management Model

Among its many innovations, Cisco ACI is changing network management from a traditional feature-by-feature, link-by-link approach to a declarative model, in which the controller relies on each node to render the declared desired end state. The user configures policies on the Cisco APIC and it propagates the policy configuration through the OpFlex protocol to all the leaf devices in the fabric, as shown in Figure 7-9.

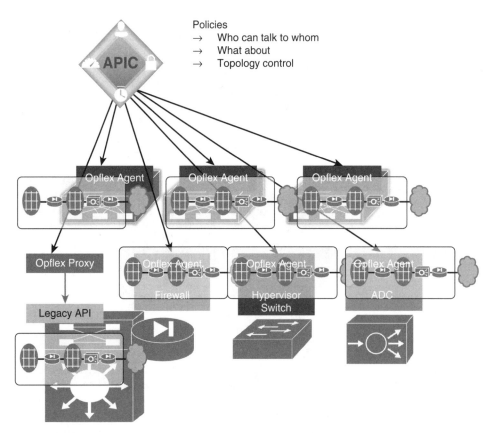

Figure 7-9 *Cisco ACI Propagates Policies to All the Leaf Devices in the Fabric*

If the server and the software switching on the server support OpFlex, the policy can also be applied within the server. Each networking element (physical or virtual) then renders the policies according to the local capabilities, as shown in Figure 7-10.

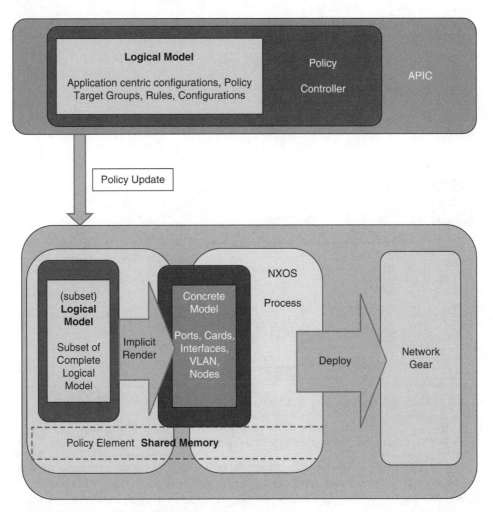

Figure 7-10 *Each Networking Element Renders Policies According to Local Capabilities*

You can define configurations on the Cisco APIC controller in several ways, as described next and displayed in Figure 7-11:

- Using the easy-to-use GUI running on the same appliance that provides the controller function

- Using Representational state transfer (REST) calls with intuitive XML- or JSON-formatted payloads that are sent to the Cisco APIC; these can be sent in many ways, using tools such as Google's POSTMAN or Python scripts that send REST calls

- Using a custom-built GUI that sends REST calls

- Using the command-line interface (CLI) to navigate the object model from the Cisco APIC

- Using Python scripts that use the associated Cisco ACI libraries

- Via integration with third-party orchestration such as OpenStack

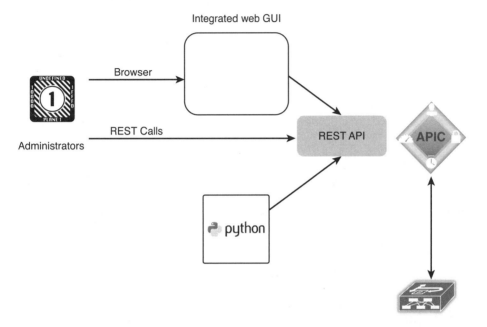

Figure 7-11   *Users Can Define Configurations on the Cisco APIC in Several Ways*

Even if spine and leaf devices are receiving the policy configurations from the controller, you can still connect to each device through the console or the management (mgmt0) port and use the well-known Cisco Nexus Software CLI to monitor how policies are rendered. However, when connecting directly to a leaf or spine, only read operations are allowed to prevent state synchronization issues with the APIC controller.

Each tool has its areas of strength and weaknesses. This is how different teams will most likely use the tools:

- **GUI:** Mostly for the infrastructure administration and for monitoring and trouble-shooting purposes. It is also used to generate templates.

- **CLI on Cisco APIC:** Mainly to create shell scripts and for troubleshooting

- **POSTMAN and other REST tools:** Mostly to test and define configurations to be automated. The scripts are based on XML, JSON, or REST calls with simple scripts for the operator. A scripting language can be used, such as Python, or it can be directly done via POSTMAN.

- **Python scripts:** Mainly to create comprehensive provisioning. The SDK provided with Cisco ACI performs this.

- **PHP and web pages with embedded REST calls:** Mostly to create simple user interfaces for operators or IT customers.

- **Advanced orchestration tools like OpenStack or Cisco Intelligent Automation for Cloud (IAC) or Cisco UCS Director:** Mainly for end-to-end provisioning of compute and network

Hardware and Software

The topologies described in this chapter are based on the following components:

- **Spine switches:** The spine provides the mapping database function and connectivity among leaf switches. At the time of this writing, spine switches are either the Cisco Nexus N9K-C9508 switch equipped with N9K-X9736PQ line cards or fixed form-factor switches such as the Cisco Nexus N9K-C9336PQ ACI spine switch. Spine switches provide high-density 40-Gigabit Ethernet connectivity between leaf switches. The Cisco Nexus 9336PQ form factor is well suited for smaller deployments because it provides 36 ports of 40-Gigabit Ethernet. The Cisco Nexus 9508 provides 288 40-Gigabit Ethernet ports.

- **Leaf switches:** The leaf provides physical server connectivity, virtual server connectivity, and policy enforcement. At the time of this writing, leaf switches are fixed form-factor switches with either SFP+, 10GBASE-T, or QSFP+ front-panel ports such as the Cisco Nexus N9K-9372-PX, N9K-9372TX, N9K-9332PQ, N9K-C9396PX, N9K-C9396TX, and N9K-C93128TX switches. The choice of leaf switches provides the option to use 10GBASE-T or Enhanced Small Form-Factor Pluggable (SFP+) connectivity to the servers. Leaf switches are used in two modes: as standalone Cisco Nexus devices, or as devices that are part of the Cisco ACI fabric (with an ACI version of the Nexus software).

- **Cisco APIC:** The controller is the point of configuration of policies and the place where statistics are archived and processed to provide visibility, telemetry, application health information, and overall management of the fabric. The Cisco APIC is a physical server appliance like a UCS C220 M3 rack server with two 10-Gigabit Ethernet interfaces that are meant to be connected to the leaf switches and with Gigabit Ethernet interfaces for out-of-band management. Two controller models are available: Cisco APIC-M and APIC-L.

■ **40-Gigabit Ethernet cabling:** Leaf and spine switches can connect at 40 Gbps with multimode fiber by using the new Cisco 40-Gbps short-reach (SR) bidirectional (BiDi) Quad SFP (QSFP) optics modules, which do not require new cabling. With these optics modules, you can connect equipment at distances up to 100 meters on OM3 cabling and up to 125 meters or more on OM4 cabling. Other QSFP options are also available for 40-Gbps links.

Note   For more information about 40-Gbps cabling options, visit: http://www.cisco.com/c/dam/en/us/products/collateral/switches/nexus-9000-series-switches/white-paper-c11-729384.pdf

or: http://www.cisco.com/c/en/us/td/docs/interfaces_modules/transceiver_modules/compatibility/matrix/OL_24900.html

■ **Classic 10-Gigabit Ethernet cabling:** Cabling to the server with 10-Gigabit Ethernet is implemented with SFP+ fiber or copper or with 10GBASE-T technology.

Cisco Nexus 9000 series switches can be deployed in two modes:

■ **Standalone mode:** The switch provides functionalities that are similar to those of the other Cisco Nexus switches with the addition of programmability, Linux containers, Python shell, and so on. This chapter is not based on the use of standalone mode.

■ **Fabric mode:** The switch operates as part of a fabric. This chapter is based on the use of the Nexus 9000 series switches in ACI mode.

Note   The Cisco NX-OS software that you use for ACI mode deployments is not the same image that you load on Cisco Nexus 9000 Series switches used in standalone mode. If you have an existing Cisco Nexus 9300 platform deployed as a regular Layer 3 switch, you need to install the Cisco NX-OS software for ACI mode operations.

Physical Topology

Cisco ACI uses a spine-and-leaf topology. All leaf nodes connect to all spine nodes, but a full mesh is not required. Spine nodes don't connect to each other, and leaf nodes don't connect to each other. As Figure 7-12 shows, a simple topology can consist of a pair of spine switches (such as the Cisco Nexus 9336PQ switches) with leaf devices dual-connected at 40-Gigabit Ethernet to each spine device. Servers can be connected to two leaf devices, potentially in a PortChannel or virtual PortChannel (vPC). Any leaf switch can also be a border leaf switch for outside connectivity from each tenant. All devices can be connected through the mgmt0 port to an out-of-band management network. You can connect the out-of-band management network to the mgmt0 port of the switches as well as the REST API of the APIC.

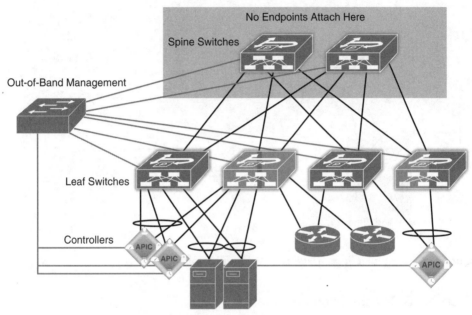

Figure 7-12 *Simple Physical Topology*

The cabling can be fully meshed between spine and leaf devices, but this is not mandatory. You can also have a setup in which some leaf devices are in the transit path between two separated physical areas, in which case the spine devices in one area likely won't be attached to all of the leaf devices in the other room, as shown in Figure 7-13. Topology such as this is suboptimal but it might be convenient for a fabric split between different rooms or nearby buildings.

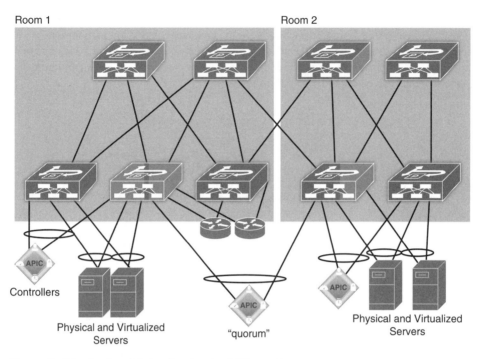

Figure 7-13 *Leaf and Spine Devices in Different Rooms*

Cisco APIC Design Considerations

Cisco APIC contains the database for the policies that govern the fabric. The controller automatically archives the following data:

■ Policies (are also replicated)

■ Statistics

■ Endpoint database (which is also replicated)

Because of this design, the Cisco APIC database is based on these principles:

■ High-performance computing (HPC)-type clustering with all active nodes

■ High availability (three controllers are recommended, although the fabric can be managed with just one)

■ Low latency

■ Incremental scalability

■ Consistency

■ Partition tolerance

The fabric continues to forward traffic even in the absence of the controller. New servers or VMs can be added and VMs can move in the fabric in the absence of the controller. The only thing that cannot be done in the absence of the controller is change the policy.

The Cisco APIC controller should be dual-attached to two leaf devices. No configuration is required to build the NIC teaming interface; the 10-Gigabit Ethernet ports of the Cisco APIC appliance are preconfigured for NIC teaming.

The fabric needs at least one Cisco APIC server to provide switch bootup, policy management, and fault and statistics correlation. Three controllers are recommended for redundancy, although you can still provision and configure policies for the fabric with a single controller. Three controllers provide optimal redundancy and support both Cisco APIC software upgrades and failure scenarios. More than three controllers can be used for geographical redundancy and in cases in which you need additional transactional scale (high transaction rate for the API for policy creation or monitoring of the network).

The members of the Cisco APIC cluster do not need to form a full cluster prior to switch node bootstrapping. The controller cluster is designed to operate in split-brain mode, which occurs on bootup and during a partitioning network failure (large-scale failure).

Connectivity between Cisco APIC cluster members takes place through the management port and infrastructure VRF, so an out-of-band management network is not needed for the cluster to form. But the cluster does not have to form before each individual node can initiate the fabric and switch.

When you define the Cisco APIC cluster, you are asked how many members you want to be present at steady state. This number tells the cluster how many other nodes to expect so that each node can track bootup scenarios (only the first node has been attached), partitioned fabrics, and other cases in which only a subset of the total target number of Cisco APIC nodes is active.

When all nodes are active, the distributed management information tree (DMIT) for the Cisco APIC cluster has the database shards (containers for the managed objects representing the system and policy) replicated across the servers and assigns one of the shard copies as the primary, with transactions performed against that copy. If three servers are defined in a cluster, when all three are active, each supports transactions against one-third of the DMIT. If only two servers are active, each has half of the shards marked as primary, and the system load is shared across the two active Cisco APIC nodes.

Spine Design Considerations

The main function of the spine is to provide the mapping database in case a leaf hasn't learned yet about the mapping of an endpoint and to forward traffic among leaf switches.

The mapping database is maintained by the fabric that contains the mapping for each endpoint attached to the network (identifier) and the address of the tunnel endpoint that it sits behind (locator). The endpoint address is both the MAC address and the IP address of the endpoint plus the logical network that it resides in (VRF or bridge domain instance). The mapping database in the spine is replicated for redundancy and is synchronized across all spines. The entries in the mapping database don't expire (age out) by themselves. They only expire after they have expired from the leaf first. Once a mapping entry has expired on a leaf, the leaf instructs the spine to remove its entry.

The mapping database is stored in a redundant fashion within each spine. It is replicated among spine switches so that if a spine disappears, traffic forwarding continues.

Modular spine switches have greater mapping database storage capacity than fixed form-factor spines. In fact, the mapping database is sharded across fabric cards, so the more fabric cards, the more endpoint mappings that can be stored. The use of added fabric cards also depends on the forwarding capacity that you want to give to line cards.

Each entry in the mapping database is stored in at least two fabric cards for redundancy. The two fabric cards are programmed in such a way that there is no hotspot for a heavy destination. In case of a fabric card failure, the traffic is sent to the next spine. This feature is called *spine chaining*. Essentially, a chain of spines is configured internally, where one spine acts as the backup for the other spine. The chain is managed internally by Cisco APIC. No direct link is allowed or required between the spine switches.

Leaf Design Considerations

Leaf switches provide physical and virtual server connectivity. They terminate VLANs and VXLANs and encapsulate the traffic in a normalized VXLAN header, and they are the enforcement point for policies. The Cisco ACI fabric decouples the tenant endpoint address, its identifier, from the location of that endpoint, which is defined by its locator, or VXLAN termination endpoint address. Typically, you want to look at leaf switches in pairs, because of the likelihood that you are going to connect servers with PortChannels in vPC mode to the leaf switches. Cisco ACI leaf switches support vPC interfaces similar to the Cisco Nexus family of switches (IEEE 802.3ad PortChannels with links split across two devices). However, with Cisco ACI a peer link is not necessary to connect the leaf switches. It's easy to define pairs of leaf switches using switch profiles.

Leaf switches can be the attachment point simultaneously for workloads and for the border leaf to provide connectivity to the WAN connecting to an external router with IP.

For policy propagation to the leaf, choose among these three modes, depending on the trade-off you want to make between scalability and immediacy:

- **Policy preconfiguration:** Cisco APIC pushes all policies to all leaf switches in a VMM domain, and policies are immediately programmed into the hardware or software data path. (VMM domains are defined in the section "Virtual Machine Mobility Domains" later in the chapter.)

- **No policy prepopulation:** Policy is requested from Cisco APIC when a notification is received or data-path detection occurs for a new endpoint. Packets are dropped until the policy programming is complete.

- **Policy prepopulation with on-demand configuration (default):** Cisco APIC pushes all policies to all leaf switches in a VMM domain. The policy is programmed when the VMM is notified or the data plane learns of a new endpoint. During the configuration stage, the packets are forwarded and the policy is applied on the egress leaf.

Unknown Unicast and Broadcast

Traffic forwarding in Cisco ACI operates as follows:

- Cisco ACI routes traffic destined for the router MAC address.

- Cisco ACI bridges traffic that is not destined for the router MAC address.

In both cases, the traffic traverses the fabric encapsulated in VXLAN to the VTEP destination IP address of the endpoint.

Cisco ACI doesn't use flooding by default, but this behavior is configurable. The mode of operation whereby ACI discovers endpoints and populates the mapping database is called *hardware proxy*. With this mode of operation, unknown unicast packets are never flooded. Furthermore, ACI offers the ability to transform ARP requests into unicast. All these options are configurable, as shown in Figure 7-14. Notice that the bridge domain must be associated with a router instance for the subnets to be instantiated. The other fields control the way in which unknown unicast traffic and multicast traffic are forwarded.

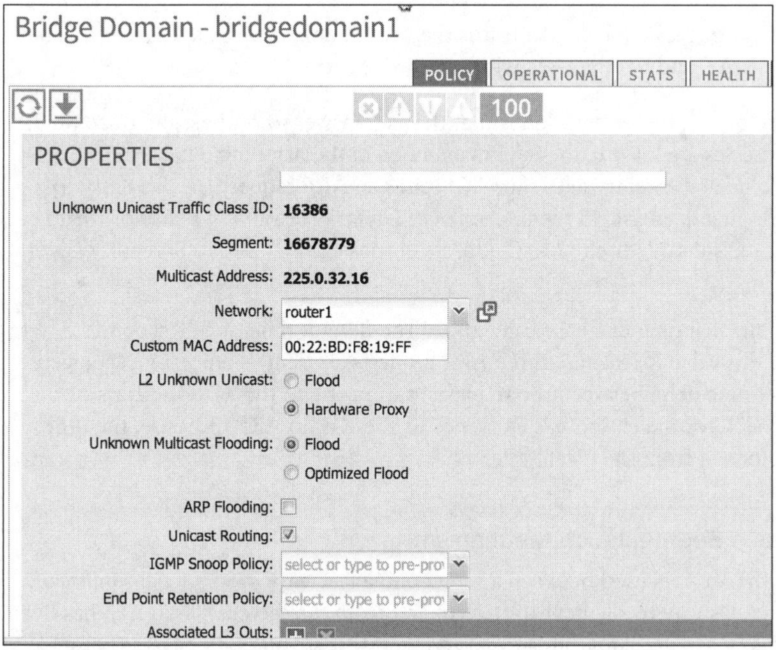

Figure 7-14 *Forwarding Options*

These are the options for Layer 2 unknown unicast frames:

■ **Flood:** If the flood option is enabled in a bridge domain, the packet is flooded in the bridge domain by using a multicast tree rooted in the spine that is scoped to the bridge domain.

■ **No-flood (default):** The packet is looked up in the spine, and if it is not found in the spine, it is dropped. This mode of operation is called hardware proxy.

These are the options for unknown multicast frames (frames destined to a group for which the fabric didn't receive an IGMP join):

■ **Flood (default):** Flood in the bridge domain.

■ **Optimized Flood:** Send the frame only to the router ports.

These are the forwarding options for ARP:

■ **Flood:** Use traditional ARP flooding.

■ **Unicast forwarding based on target IP (default):** Send ARP to the destination endpoint using unicast mechanisms.

The Unicast Routing field controls whether this is a pure Layer 2 bridge domain or provides a pervasive default gateway:

■ If unicast routing is disabled, ACI only learns MAC addresses.

■ If unicast routing is enabled, ACI learns the MAC address with Layer 2 traffic and learns the MAC and IP addresses with Layer 3 traffic.

With hardware proxy, the assumption is that devices answer to probes, and once the IP and MAC addresses are known, they are maintained in the mapping database. If unicast routing is enabled and an entry ages out, ACI sends an ARP request for this entry to update the mapping database. In the case of pure Layer 2 forwarding behavior (that is, if unicast routing is disabled), the MAC address entries expire just like in regular Layer 2 switching.

The entries in the mapping database can expire. The default timer is 900 seconds. After 75 percent of this value is reached, three ARP requests are sent as unicast in a staggered fashion (with a time delta between the requests) as a probe to the MAC address of the endpoint to check for the endpoint's existence. If there is no ARP response, then the endpoint is removed from the local table.

Use of VLANs as a Segmentation Mechanism

In Cisco ACI the VLANs used between a server and a leaf have switch local significance and are used exclusively to segment traffic coming from the servers. Cisco ACI has been designed so that when you are using virtualized workloads, you don't have to enter

VLAN numbers manually per each endpoint group. Whenever possible, leverage the dynamic negotiation of VLANs between the virtualized server and the Cisco ACI fabric.

Figure 7-15 shows how a virtualized server tags traffic with a VLAN or a VXLAN and sends it to the leaf. The tenant configuration defines the VLAN or VXLAN that belongs to the EPG.

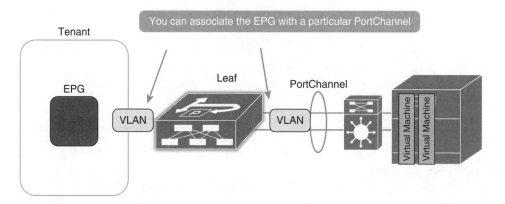

Figure 7-15 *Use of VLANs for Segmentation*

In the case of physical workloads, use VLANs to map traffic coming from a trunk into the correct EPG.

EPG configurations are performed within a tenant space. ACI distinguishes between administrator roles as either tenant administrators or infrastructure administrators. This provides a way for the infrastructure administrator to limit what each individual tenant can do, and scope for instance which VLAN can be used on which ports. A tenant administrator can associate an EPG to a leaf, port, and VLAN. This configuration becomes active only if the infrastructure administrator associates the leaf and port with a VLAN namespace (via physical domain via attach entity profile (AEP)) that the VLAN is part of.

VLANs and VXLANs Namespaces

A single fabric may have multiple virtualized server domains, each consuming 4000 VLANs (EPGs), so sometimes you may want to reuse a VLAN range multiple times. The same pool of VLANs can be reused as long as it is associated with a different set of leaf switches and a different VMM domain. Alternatively, if you use VXLANs between the virtualized server and the Cisco ACI network, there is less need for reuse because the addressing space is larger.

In spanning-tree networks, you specify which VLANs belong to which ports by using the **switchport trunk allowed vlan** command. In Cisco ACI, you specify a domain (physical or virtual), and associate the domain with a range of ports. Unlike traditional Cisco standalone operations, in Cisco ACI the VLANs used for port groups on virtualized servers are dynamically negotiated, as shown in Figure 7-16.

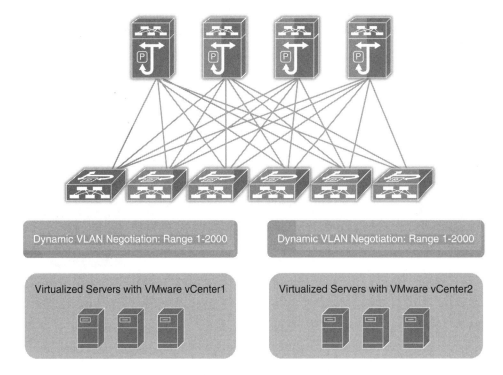

Figure 7-16   *Reusing VLANs with Dynamic Negotiation*

There are two types of pools of VLANs:

- **Static VLAN pools:** These are used for *static binding*, static association of an EPG with a particular port and VLAN.

- **Dynamic VLAN pools:** VLANs from these pools are allocated dynamically between the fabric and the Virtual Machine Manager.

Concept of Domain

Depending on whether you connect physical servers or virtual servers to the Cisco ACI fabric, you define either a physical domain or a virtual domain. Virtual domains reference a particular virtual machine manager (for example, VMware vCenter 1 or data center ABC) and a particular pool of VLANs or VXLANs to be used. A physical domain is similar to a virtual domain except that there's no virtual machine manager associated with it.

The person who administers the VLAN or VXLAN space is the infrastructure administrator. The person who consumes the domain is the tenant administrator. The infrastructure administrator associates domains with a set of ports that are entitled or expected to be connected to virtualized servers or physical servers through an attach entity profile (AEP). You don't need to understand the details of the AEP except that it encapsulates the domain. The AEP can include boot policies for the virtualized server to boot from the network, and you can include multiple domains under the same AEP and authorize virtualized servers of different kinds. Example 7-1 shows an AEP that specifies that Cisco ACI should expect a VMware ESX server managed by VMware vCenter 1 on port 1/3 on leaf 101. Normally you would specify a greater range of ports (for example, the VMware vMotion domain).

Example 7-1 *Mapping Virtualized Servers Mobility Domain to the Fabric*

```
<infraInfra dn="uni/infra">
<!-- attachable entity, i.e. Domain information  -->
   <infraAttEntityP name="Entity_vCenter1_Domain">
      <infraRsDomP tDn="uni/vmmp-VMware/dom-vCenter1" />
   </infraAttEntityP>
<!-- Policy Group, i.e. a bunch of configuration bundled together -->
   <infraFuncP>
         <infraAccPortGrp name="vCenter1_Domain_Connectivity">
            <infraRsAttEntP tDn="uni/infra/attentp-Entity_vCenter1_Domain" />
         </infraAccPortGrp>
   </infraFuncP>
   <infraAccPortP name=" Leaf101esxports ">
      <infraHPortS name="line1" type="range">
         <infraPortBlk name="block0" fromPort="3" toPort="3" />
         <infraRsAccBaseGrp tDn="uni/infra/funcprof/accportgrp-vCenter1_Domain_
   Connectivity" />
      </infraHPortS>
   </infraAccPortP>
   <infraNodeP name="Leaf101">
      <infraLeafS name="line1" type="range">
         <infraNodeBlk name="block0" from_="101" to_="101" />
      </infraLeafS>
      <infraRsAccPortP tDn="uni/infra/accportprof-Leaf101esxports " />
   </infraNodeP>
</infraInfra>
```

Using the AEP, if you simply need to add ports to the configuration, edit the interface profile infraAccPortP and add lines such as **<infraHPortS name="line2" type="range">** with new interface ranges.

Concept of Attach Entity Profile

The ACI fabric provides multiple attachment points that connect through leaf ports to various external entities such as bare-metal servers, hypervisors, Layer 2 switches such as the Cisco UCS Fabric Interconnect, and Layer 3 routers such as Cisco Nexus 7000 Series switches. These attachment points can be physical ports, port channels, or a vPC on the leaf switches.

An AEP represents a group of external entities with similar infrastructure policy requirements. The infrastructure policies consist of physical interface policies such as:

■ Cisco Discovery Protocol (CDP)

■ Link Layer Discovery Protocol (LLDP)

■ Maximum transmission unit (MTU)

■ Link Aggregation Control Protocol (LACP)

An AEP is required to deploy any VLAN pools on the leaf switches. It is possible to reuse the encapsulation pools such as VLAN pools across different leaf switches. An AEP implicitly provides the scope of the VLAN pool (associated to the VMM domain) to the physical infrastructure.

An AEP provisions the VLAN pool (and associated VLANs) on the leaf. The VLANs are not actually enabled on the port. No traffic flows unless an EPG is deployed on the port.

Without VLAN pool deployment using an AEP, a VLAN is not enabled on the leaf port even if an EPG is provisioned. A particular VLAN is provisioned or enabled on the leaf port based on EPG events either statically binding on a leaf port or based on VM events from external controllers such as VMware vCenter.

Multi-tenancy Considerations

The Cisco ACI fabric has been designed for multi-tenancy. To create a tenant, you use a REST call as shown in Example 7-2.

Example 7-2 *Tenant Creation*

```
http://10.51.66.236/api/mo/uni.xml
<polUni>
    <!-- Tenant Customer1 -->
    <fvTenant dn="uni/tn-Customer1" name="Customer1">
        <fvCtx name="customer1-router"/>
        <!-- bridge domain -->
        <fvBD name="BD1">
            <fvRsCtx tnFvCtxName="customer1-router" />
            <fvSubnet ip="10.0.0.1/24" scope="public"/>
            <fvSubnet ip="20.0.0.1/24" scope="private"/>
            <fvSubnet ip="30.0.0.1/24" scope="private"/>
        </fvBD>
        <!-- Security -->
        <aaaDomainRef dn="uni/tn-Customer1/domain-customer1" name="customer1"/>
    </fvTenant>
</polUni>
```

Example 7-2 shows a REST call used to create a tenant named Customer1, to associate a VRF instance named customer1-router and a bridge domain named BD1, and to create three subnets: 10.0.0.0/24, 20.0.0.0/24, and 30.0.0.0/24. These subnets contain the default gateways for the tenant located on the leaf switches with respective IP addresses 10.0.0.1, 20.0.0.1, and 30.0.0.1

The tenant administrator cannot see the full fabric. This administrator can use some resources, such as physical ports and VLANs, to exit the fabric or connect to the outside world and can extend the definition of EPGs to virtualized servers.

The infrastructure administrator manages the entire fabric and can control and scope the domains of VLAN and VXLAN namespaces that a given tenant can use.

Resources in the fabric may be dedicated to a given tenant, and other resources may be shared. An example of a dedicated resource is a nonvirtualized server. Examples of shared resources are virtualized servers and ports to connect outside the fabric.

To simplify the task of associating these resources with tenants, Cisco suggests the following:

■ **Create one physical domain per tenant for nonvirtualized servers:** A physical domain is a VLAN namespace. The VLAN namespace is used to further divide servers into EPGs. The physical domain is then associated with a set of ports that a tenant is eligible to use.

■ **Create one physical domain per tenant for external connectivity:** This approach defines a set of VLANs that can be used to stitch the virtual data center with an MPLS VPN cloud or across data centers. Multiple physical domains are then grouped into a single AEP because the ports used to connect to the outside are shared across multiple tenants.

Creation of one single VMM domain per tenant is theoretically possible, but this approach is not feasible because administrators will want to share the VMM across multiple tenants. In this case, the best way to aggregate VMM domains is to associate the same VMM domain with all the leaf ports that can be connected to virtualized servers in the same mobility domain.

Initial Configuration Steps

The infrastructure administrator manages the initial configuration of Cisco ACI. The fabric is self-discovered when the Cisco APIC is attached to a leaf, and the administrator validates the legitimate nodes from the GUI or with scripts.

Before configuring the infrastructure, verify that you have the following in place:

■ Clock synchronization/NTP server. If the clocks on the nodes and the controller are configured with times and dates that are too far apart, discovery may not occur.

- Out-of-band management, to connect to the Cisco APIC and potentially to the mgmt0 ports of the leaf and spine switches (at the time of this writing, Gigabit Ethernet is required for out-of-band management).

Note   Cisco APIC does not require out-of-band management; in-band can be used.

- A Dynamic Host Configuration Protocol (DHCP) server for servers and potentially for network equipment

- A Preboot Execution Environment (PXE) server for servers and potentially for network equipment

Zero-Touch Provisioning

When using Cisco ACI, you don't need to do the following:

- Configure addressing and subnetting to establish communication

- Configure the routing for the infrastructure

- Specify the subnets to advertise in an Interior Gateway Protocol (IGP) area unless routing is needed

- Specify loopback addresses for IGP announcements

- Specify the interfaces on which to peer

- Tune the routing timers

- Verify cabling and neighbors

- Remove VLANs from trunks

All of these configurations are set automatically when you connect leaf and spine nodes together.

The Cisco ACI fabric is designed to provide a zero-touch operation experience with

- A logically central but physically distributed controller for policy, bootstrap, and image management

- Easy startup with topology auto-discovery, automated configuration, and infrastructure addressing using industry-standard protocols: Intermediate System-to-Intermediate System (IS-IS), LLDP, and DHCP

- A simple and automated policy-based upgrade process and automated image management

The Cisco APIC is a physically distributed but logically centralized controller that provides DHCP, bootstrap configuration, and image management to the fabric for automated startup and upgrades. After LLDP discovery, the Cisco APIC learns all neighboring connections dynamically. These connections are validated against a loose specification rule that the user provides through REST calls or through the GUI. If a rule mismatch occurs, a fault occurs, and the connection is blocked. In addition, an alarm is created indicating that the connection needs attention.

The Cisco ACI fabric operator has the option of importing the names and serial numbers of all the fabric nodes from a simple text file into the Cisco APIC, or discovering the serial numbers automatically and assigning names from the Cisco APIC GUI, CLI, or API. The fabric activation is automatic, but the administrator needs to give an ID to each node as the controller discovers it. The spine switches should be given a number in the top range of the IDs or in the very lowest range (101 to 109), so that all leaf switches are numbered with a continuous range, to make range configurations more readable.

When the switches boot up, they send LLDP packets and a DHCP request. The Cisco APIC operates as the TFTP and DHCP server for the switches and provides the switches with a TEP address, switch image, and global configuration. The infrastructure administrator sees the leaf and spine switches as they are discovered, validates their serial numbers, and decides whether to accept them into the fabric.

Network Management

The Cisco APIC automatically configures an Infrastructure VRF instance that is used for in-band communication between the Cisco APIC and the switch node communication, and it is nonroutable outside the fabric.

The Cisco APIC serves as DHCP and TFTP server for the fabric. The Cisco APIC assigns the TEP addresses for each switch. Core links are unnumbered.

The Cisco APIC allocates three types of IP addresses from private address space:

- **Switch TEP IP address:** Switches inside a pod share a common prefix.

- **Cisco APIC IP address:** The management IP address of the Cisco APIC appliance.

- **VXLAN tunnel endpoint (VTEP) IP address:** VTEPs behind a leaf share a common prefix.

In addition, you can attach to the Cisco ACI fabric a management station that can talk to the fabric nodes or to the Cisco APIC in-band on the tenant called "mgmt."

The in-band management configuration lets you define the IP addresses for APIC controllers, leaves, and spines so that they can share a bridge domain for management purposes. The configuration includes the definition of a VLAN, which is used to enable communication between the controller and the fabric. This VLAN must be configured on the mgmt tenant and also enabled on the port that connects to the controller from the infrastructure configuration. The configuration of the mgmt tenant is shown in Example 7-3.

Example 7-3   *Tenant mgmt Configuration for In-band Management*

```
POST http://192.168.10.1/api/policymgr/mo/.xml
<!-- api/policymgr/mo/.xml -->
<polUni>
   <fvTenant name="mgmt">
     <!-- Addresses for APIC in-band management network -->
     <fvnsAddrInst name="apic1Inb" addr="192.168.1.254/24">
       <fvnsUcastAddrBlk from="192.168.1.1" to="192.168.1.1"/>
     </fvnsAddrInst>
     <!-- Addresses for switch in-band management network -->
     <fvnsAddrInst name="leaf101Inb" addr="192.168.1.254/24">
       <fvnsUcastAddrBlk from="192.168.1.101" to="192.168.1.101"/>
     </fvnsAddrInst>
   </fvTenant>
 </polUni>
[...]
<!-- Management node group for APICs -->
    <mgmtNodeGrp name="apic1">
      <infraNodeBlk name="line1" from_="1" to_="1"/>
      <mgmtRsGrp tDn="uni/infra/funcprof/grp-apic1"/>
    </mgmtNodeGrp>
    <!-- Management node group for switches-->
    <mgmtNodeGrp name="leaf101">
      <infraNodeBlk name="line1" from_="101" to_="101"/>
      <mgmtRsGrp tDn="uni/infra/funcprof/grp-leaf101"/>
    </mgmtNodeGrp>
[...]
<infraFuncP>
      <!-- Management group for APICs -->
      <mgmtGrp name="apic1">
        <!-- In-band management zone -->
        <mgmtInBZone name="apic1">
          <mgmtRsInbEpg tDn="uni/tn-mgmt/mgmtp-default/inb-default"/>
          <mgmtRsAddrInst tDn="uni/tn-mgmt/addrinst-apic1Inb"/>
        </mgmtInBZone>
      </mgmtGrp>
[...]
<!-- Management group for switches -->
      <mgmtGrp name="leaf101">
        <!-- In-band management zone -->
        <mgmtInBZone name="leaf101">
          <mgmtRsInbEpg tDn="uni/tn-mgmt/mgmtp-default/inb-default"/>
          <mgmtRsAddrInst tDn="uni/tn-mgmt/addrinst-leaf101Inb"/>
        </mgmtInBZone>
```

```
          </mgmtGrp>
        </infraFuncP>
      </infraInfra>
    </polUni>
    [...]
    <!-- api/policymgr/mo/.xml -->
    <polUni>
      <fvTenant name="mgmt">
        <fvBD name="inb">
          <fvRsCtx tnFvCtxName="inb"/>
          <fvSubnet ip="192.168.111.254/24"/>
        </fvBD>
        <mgmtMgmtP name="default">
          <!-- Configure the encap on which APICs will communicate on the in-band
    network -->
          <mgmtInB name="default" encap="vlan-10">
            <fvRsProv tnVzBrCPName="default"/>
          </mgmtInB>
        </mgmtMgmtP>
      </fvTenant>
    </polUni>
```

The configuration of the infrastructure requires the following steps:

Step 1.   Choose a VLAN pool (for example VLAN 10)

Step 2.   Define the physical domain (pointing to the VLAN pool)

Step 3.   Define a policy group with AEP

Step 4.   Configure the AEP pointing to the physical domain

Step 5.   Map the node selector and port selectors selecting the port that the APIC is associated with

Policy-based Configuration of Access Ports

The infrastructure administrator configures ports in the fabric for speed, LACP mode, LLDP, CDP, and so forth. In Cisco ACI, the configuration of physical ports is designed to be extremely simple for both small- and large-scale data centers. The infrastructure administrator prepares a template of configurations for servers based on their connectivity characteristics. For instance, the administrator categorizes servers connected with active-standby teaming, PortChannels, and vPCs and bundles all the settings for the ports into a policy group. The administrator then creates objects that select interfaces of the fabric in ranges that share the same policy-group configuration. Figure 7-17 defines the connection of servers to the fabric.

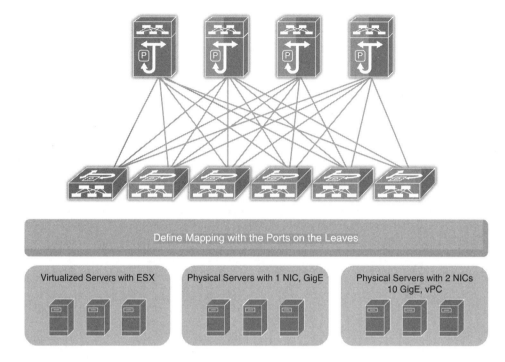

Figure 7-17 *Defining the Connection of Servers to the Fabric*

The logic is better understood by following an example of configuration. In the fabric access policy, under the switch profiles, you define one profile per switch: leaf101, leaf102, and so on, as shown in Figure 7-18.

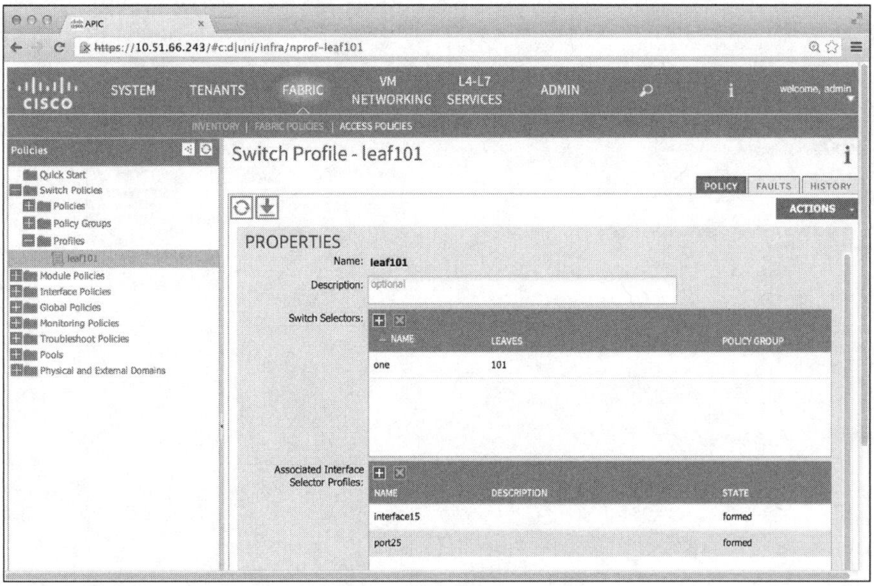

Figure 7-18 *Defining One Profile per Switch*

You have now created objects that represent each leaf device. You can also create an object that represents two leaf devices, and then create profiles that categorize ports into different groups and later add these to the switch.

If you highlight the object that represents the leaf of interest, you can then add interface profiles to it by adding entries to the field Associated Interface Selector Profiles.

The interface profile consists of a range of interfaces with similar configurations. For example, the range **kvmportsonleaf101** may select ports 1 through 10.

The configuration of the ports is based on the policy group, as shown in Figure 7-19. The policy group is a template of configurations such as speed, CDP, LLDP, Spanning Tree Protocol, LACP, and so on.

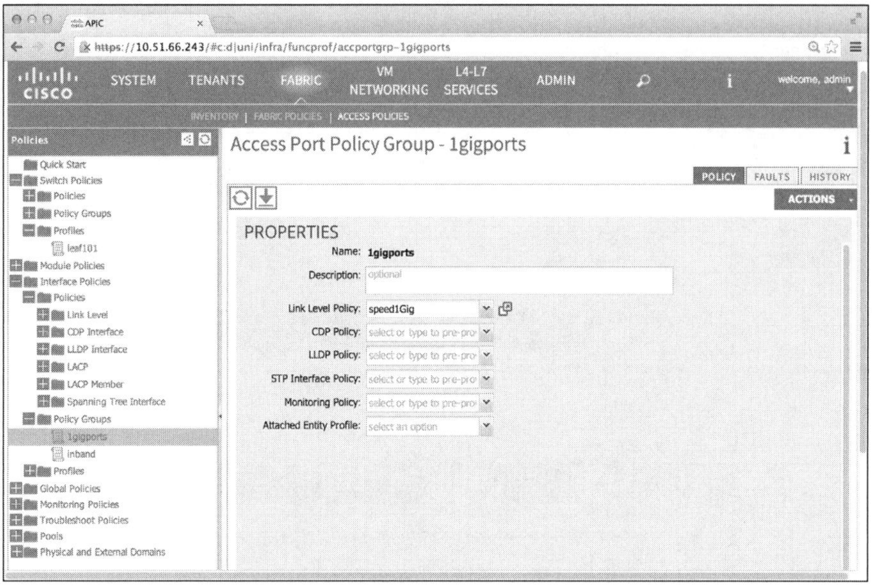

Figure 7-19   *Policy Groups*

To associate the configuration with interfaces on the leaf switches, create an interface profile. For instance, assume that port 1/15 on leaf 101 is attached to a physical server. You can create an interface profile object called **physicalserversonleaf101** and add port 1/15 to it. You can add more ports later to apply the same configuration to all ports connected to the physical servers, as shown in Figure 7-20.

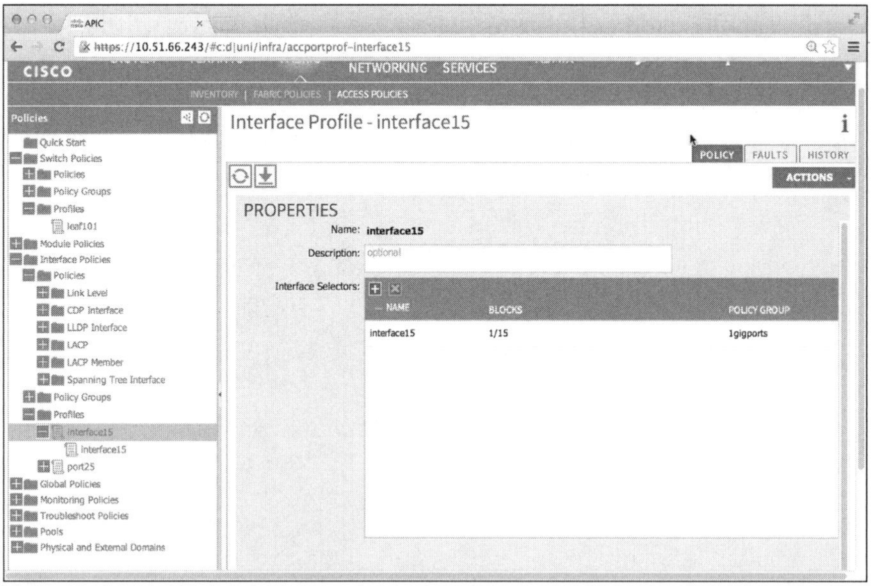

Figure 7-20   *Creating an Interface Profile*

For this selection of ports to be carved out of leaf 101, add it to the switch profile that identifies leaf 101.

Figure 7-21 shows the relationship between leaf switches, ports, AEP, domains, and VLAN pools. It illustrates the following points:

■ The infrastructure administrator can create a range of VLANs.

■ The VLAN range is associated with a physical domain.

■ The association is encapsulated in an AEP (which is configured in the Global Policy area of the GUI).

■ The left portion of the figure shows how the AEP is associated with an interface.

■ The interface profile selects an interface number.

■ The switch profile selects a switch number.

■ The policy group is basically the interface configuration, which may include an AEP (and, as a result of the various links, also includes the set of VLANs).

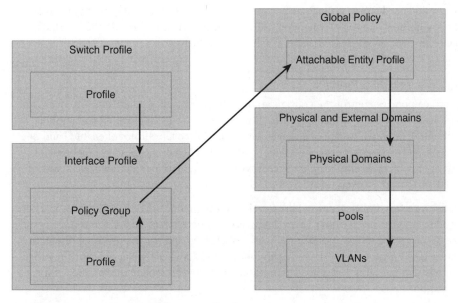

Figure 7-21   *Relationships Between Leaf Switches, Ports, AEP, Domains, and VLAN Pools*

This configuration is achieved with a single REST call.

The advantage of this approach is that you effectively apply configurations in a more logical manner. For instance, if you want to add one port to the set of physical servers, you just need to add an interface to the interface profile. If you want to change the physical port settings, you can make that change in the policy group. If you want to add a VLAN to the range, you just modify the physical domain.

Furthermore, you can create policies that apply not to just one switch at a time but to multiple switches, which is very useful for the configuration of vPCs.

Configuring Switch Profiles for Each Leaf

After bringing up the fabric, the administrator can create switch profiles. As an example, the administrator may want to create two types of switch profiles, one for single-homed server ports or active-standby ports, and another one for devices that connect with vPCs as follows:

- **One switch profile per leaf switch:** For example, switch101, switch102, and switch103 have switch profiles that select leaf 101, leaf 102, and leaf 103.

- **One switch profile per pair of leaf switches:** For example, leaf 101 and leaf 102 are selected by switch profile switch101and102, and leaf 103 and leaf 104 are selected by switch profile switch103and104.

When you need to add a range of ports to a leaf, add it to the profile that you have already defined. Similarly, when you need to add to a vPC, simply add the interface profile to the pair of leaf switches that you have predefined.

Configuring Interface Policies

Interface policies control the configuration of features such as LLDP and Cisco Discovery Protocol. For example, create one object with LLDP enabled and another with LLDP disabled. Create one object with Cisco Discovery Protocol enabled and one with Cisco Discovery Protocol disabled, and so on. The advantage of this approach is that later, when you configure interfaces, you can simply select a predefined status of LLDP or Cisco Discovery Protocol and so on.

Under Interface Policies, under Link Level, you can preconfigure Fast Ethernet links or Gigabit Ethernet links. Under Cisco Discovery Protocol Interface (CDP Interface), you can specify the configuration for the protocol enabled and for the protocol disabled. Under LACP, you can specify the configuration for LACP active (and define the other options that you want for this configuration: maximum and minimum number of links and so on).

Interface Policy Groups and PortChannels

PortChannels and virtual PortChannels are configured via policy groups.

Interface Policy Groups

Policy groups can be used as the following:

- Templates of configurations for the interfaces: the collection of features that should be applied to a given interface; these features are a list of pointers to the interface profiles that you defined in the previous section

- Templates of channel groups (when using PortChannel or vPC policy groups)

The most meaningful way to define policy groups is to consider the server types you are planning to connect and then create categories. For instance, you might create categories such as the following:

- Linux Kernel-based Virtual Machine (KVM) servers connected at 1-Gigabit Ethernet without teaming

- Linux KVM servers connected at 1-Gigabit Ethernet with PortChannels

- Microsoft Hyper-V servers connected at 10-Gigabit Ethernet

- Microsoft Hyper-V servers connected at 10-Gigabit Ethernet with PortChannels

For each category of devices, define the policy group.

Policy groups also include references to the AEP (you don't have to add the AEP right away; you can add it or change it later). Policy groups can be associated with interfaces and with switches by using the interface profiles and the switch profiles.

PortChannels

You can create PortChannels in Cisco ACI more quickly and easily than on a regular switch. The reason is that with the policy model, you just need to create a selection of interfaces and associate that with the same policy group. Each policy group of type PortChannel is a different channel group.

The LACP active or passive configuration is managed through the interface policy configuration (which is referenced by the policy group).

Figure 7-22 shows how to create the PortChannel group.

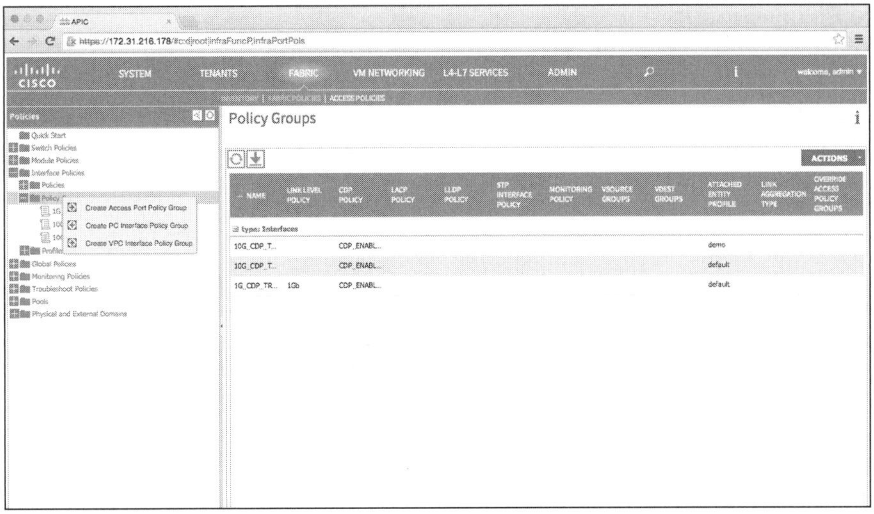

Figure 7-22 *Creating the LACP Configuration*

Configure everything in a single REST call as shown in Example 7-4.

Example 7-4 *Configuration of a PortChannel*

```
http://10.51.66.236/api/mo/uni.xml
<infraInfra>

<infraNodeP name="leafs101">
   <infraLeafS name="leafsforpc" type="range">
     <infraNodeBlk name="line1" from_="101" to_="101" />
   </infraLeafS>
   <infraRsAccPortP tDn="uni/infra/accportprof-ports22and23" />
</infraNodeP>

<infraAccPortP name="ports22and23">
 <infraHPortS name="line1" type="range">
    <infraPortBlk name="blk"fromCard="1" toCard="1" fromPort="22" toPort="23" />
    <infraRsAccBaseGrp tDn="uni/infra/funcprof/accbundle-channel-group-1"/>
 </infraHPortS>
</infraAccPortP>

<infraFuncP>
  <infraAccBndlGrp name="channel-group-1" lagT="link">
  </infraAccBndlGrp>
</infraFuncP>

</infraInfra>
```

> **Note** A bundle group defined with the setting **lagT="link"** indicates that this configuration is for a PortChannel. If the setting instead were **lagT="node"**, it would be a configuration for a vPC.

Virtual PortChannels

Creating vPCs in Cisco ACI is also simpler than creating them in regular Cisco standalone configurations because there are fewer possibilities for mistakes and you can use switch selectors to configure ports on multiple switches simultaneously.

Configuring vPCs with Cisco ACI is different than configuring them in other Cisco standalone NX-OS platforms because of the following:

- There is no need for a vPC peer link.

- There is no need for a vPC peer keepalive.

In order to create a vPC with a pair of leaf switches, one needs to create a vPC protection policy, then pair the leaf switches in the same way as you paired them in the switch profiles: that is, create vpcdomain1, vpcdomain2, etc., where vpcdomain1 selects leaf switches 101 and 102, vpcdomain2 selects leaf switches 103 and 104, and so on.

With this policy in place, create one policy group of type vPC per channel group and reference it from the interface profile.

You also may want to create a switch profile that encompasses the two leaf switches that form the vPC domain, to add all the interface configurations under the same switch profile object.

All of this configuration is accomplished with multiple REST calls or with a single REST call with all the pieces together. The configuration in Example 7-5 creates the vPC domain.

Example 7-5 *Configuration of the vPC Protection Group*

```
POST to api/mo/uni/fabric.xml
<polUni>
  <fabricInst>
    <fabricProtPol name="FabricPolicy">
    <fabricExplicitGEp name="VpcGrpPT" id="101">
      <fabricNodePEp id="103"/>
      <fabricNodePEp id="105/>
    </fabricExplicitGEp>
    </fabricProtPol>
  </fabricInst>
</polUni>
```

The configuration in Example 7-6 creates the vPC channel group; the keyword **lagT="node"** indicates that this is a vPC.

Example 7-6   *Configuration of a vPC Channel Group*

```
POST to api/mo/uni.xml
 <polUni>
   <infraInfra dn="uni/infra">
     <infraFuncP>
       <infraAccBndlGrp name="vpcgroup1" lagT="node">
       </infraAccBndlGrp>
     </infraFuncP>
 </infraInfra>
 </polUni>
```

The configuration in Example 7-7 associates ports and switches with the policy.

Example 7-7   *Association of Ports with the vPC Channel Group*

```
POST to api/mo/uni.xml
<polUni>
  <infraInfra dn="uni/infra">
   <infraAccPortP name="interface7">
      <infraHPortS name="ports-selection" type="range">
        <infraPortBlk name="line1"
 fromCard="1" toCard="1" fromPort="7" toPort="7">
        </infraPortBlk>
        <infraRsAccBaseGrp tDn="uni/infra/funcprof/accbundle-vpcgroup1" />
      </infraHPortS>
    </infraAccPortP>
<infraNodeP name="leaf103andleaf105">
        <infraLeafS name="leafs103and105" type="range">
          <infraNodeBlk name="line1" from_="103" to_="103"/>
          <infraNodeBlk name="line2" from_="105" to_="105"/>
        </infraLeafS>
        <infraRsAccPortP tDn="uni/infra/accportprof-interface7" />
    </infraNodeP>
  </infraInfra>
</polUni>
```

Virtual Machine Manager (VMM) Domains

Cisco APIC is designed to provide full visibility into virtualized servers and connectivity for virtual machines.

Multiple tenants share virtual machines on the same set of virtualized servers. The VLAN allocation to segment these virtual machines must be dynamic: the virtual machine managers and Cisco APIC negotiate the VLAN tagging that is used.

VMM domains are mobility domains and are not associated with a particular tenant. Instead, you may want to group VMM domains into a single AEP that identifies a common mobility domain for a set of virtual machine managers. For example, one mobility domain may span leaf101 through leaf 110, so the AEP with the VMM domain for VMware vCenter, Linux KVM, and Microsoft System Center Virtual Machine Manager (SCVMM) is applied to all the ports across these leaf switches.

The AEP for the VMM domain must then be attached to the set of interfaces at which virtualized hosts will connect. This attachment is achieved by defining a policy group, an interface profile, and a switch profile.

VMM Domain

A VMM domain is defined as a virtual machine manager and the pool of VLANs and VXLANs that this virtual machine manager is going to use for the purpose of sending traffic to the leaf switches. The VMM domain is associated with an AEP and a policy group and the interfaces at which it is attached to define where virtual machines can move.

In the virtual machine networking view, you can create multiple virtual machine provider domains, which define the virtual machine manager and the data center with which the Cisco APIC interfaces, and the VLAN pool that this VMM domain is entitled to use.

The VLAN pool should be dynamic, to allow the virtual machine manager and Cisco APIC to allocate VLANs as needed for the port groups that are going to be used.

For each VMM domain, Cisco APIC creates a virtual switch in the hypervisor. For example, in VMware vCenter, if the user configures two VMM domains, which in the example are associated with the same VMware vCenter but with different data centers, the Cisco APIC creates two Virtual Distributed Switches (VDS) in the hypervisor, as depicted in Figure 7-23.

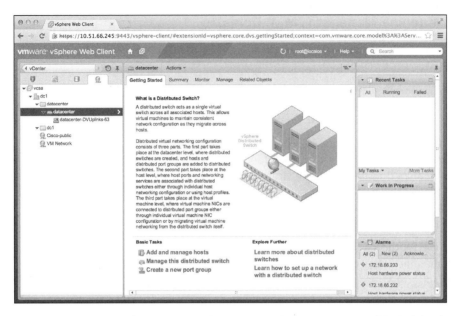

Figure 7-23   *For Each VMM Domain, Cisco APIC Creates a Virtual Switch in the Hypervisor*

AEP for Virtualized Servers Connectivity

For practical reasons, you may want to bundle multiple VMM domains of different types in the same AEP. For instance, your application will likely consist of a mix of workloads: Linux KVM, Microsoft Hyper-V, and VMware vCenter. Each defines a VMM domain, but together these domains are present on the same leaf. Therefore, you may want to create an AEP named VMM1, which includes:

- VMM domain vCenter Datacenter1

- VMM domain Hyper-V

- VMM domain KVM

Their VLAN ranges are nonoverlapping.

Then, you might organize your VLAN pools as follows:

- vlan-pool-HyperV1

- vlan-pool-KVM1

- vlan-pool-vCenter1

- vlan-pool-HyperV2

- vlan-pool-KVM2

- vlan-pool-vCenter2

Again, vlan-pool-HyperV1, vlan-pool-KVM1, vlan-pool-vCenter1, etc. are nonoverlapping.

You now have three different VMM domains for the respective virtual machine managers:

- VMM domain HyperV1

- VMM domain vCenter1

- VMM domain KVM1

Then bundle the three hypervisor types for an application into the same AEP, so you end with a configuration with these AEPs:

- VMMdomain1 (which consists of VMM domain HyperV1, vCenter1, and KVM1)

- VMMdomain2 (which consists of VMM domain HyperV2, vCenter2, and KVM2)

The AEP provides the domain–to–physical infrastructure connectivity information. It provides the span of the VLAN pool (which is associated with the VMM and physical domains) on the leaf switches and ports. The AEP just deploys the VLAN namespace (and associated VLANs) on the leaf. The VLANs are not actually provisioned or enabled on the port, so no traffic will flow without EPG provisioning. A particular VLAN is provisioned and enabled on the leaf port based on EPG events: either static EPG binding on a leaf port or LLDP discovery in the case of the VMM domain.

Besides enabling the VLAN namespace, the AEP provides the following functions: a VMM domain automatically derives all the policies for the physical interfaces, such as the MTU, LLDP, CDP, and LACP, from the interface policy groups associated with the AEP.

Configuring a Virtual Topology

Figure 7-24 shows a simple network topology.

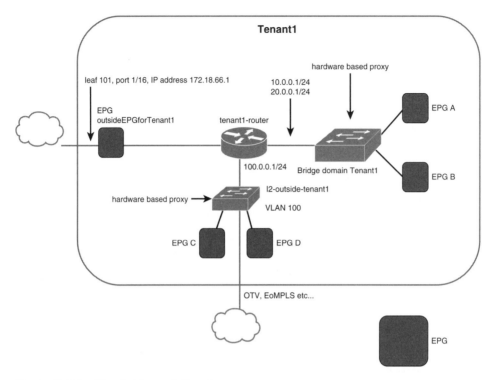

Figure 7-24   *Simple Network Topology*

The topology consists of an inside network with one bridge domain divided into EPGs: EPG A and EPG B. It also includes an extended Layer 2 network that includes local and remote workloads, further divided in EPGs—EPG C and EPG D—and connectivity to the outside through multiple Layer 3 hops with a Layer 3 interface.

Figure 7-25 illustrates an example of a relationship between the network switching and routing functionalities and how they map to the network, bridge domain, EPG, and application network profiles that can span across the EPGs. The bridge domain and EPG are explained in the following two sections.

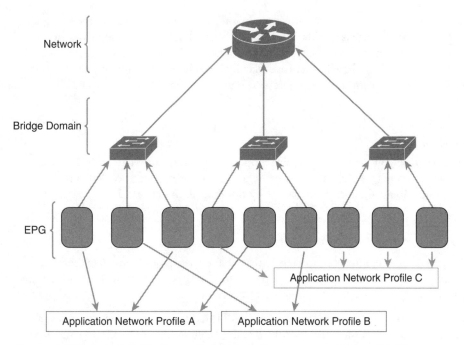

Network

Bridge Domain

EPG

Application Network Profile C

Application Network Profile A

Application Network Profile B

Figure 7-25 *Relationship Between Network Components and the ACI Fabric Terminologies*

Bridge Domain

The bridge domain can be compared to a giant distributed switch. Cisco ACI preserves the Layer 2 forwarding semantics even if the traffic is routed on the fabric. The TTL is not decremented for Layer 2 traffic, and the MAC addresses of the source and destination endpoints are preserved.

The XML configuration to create the bridge domain is **<fvBD name="Tenant1-BD"/>.**

Hardware Proxy

By default, Layer 2 unknown unicast traffic is sent to the spine proxy. This behavior is controlled by the hardware proxy option associated with a bridge domain. If the destination is not known, send the packet to the spine proxy. If the spine proxy also does not know the address, discard the packet (default mode). The implicit configuration is as follows:

```
<fvBD arpFlood="no" name="tenant1-BD" unicastRoute="yes" unkMacUcastAct="proxy"
unkMcastFlood="yes"/>
```

The advantage of the hardware proxy mode is that no flooding occurs in the fabric. The potential disadvantage is that the fabric has to learn all the endpoint addresses. With Cisco ACI, however, this is not a concern for virtual and physical servers that are part of the fabric: the database is built for scalability to millions of endpoints. However, if the fabric had to learn all the IP addresses coming from the Internet, it would clearly not scale.

Flooding Mode

Alternatively, you can enable flooding mode: if the destination MAC address is not known, flood in the bridge domain. By default, ARP traffic is not flooded but sent to the destination endpoint. By enabling ARP flooding, ARP traffic is also flooded:

```
<fvBD arpFlood="yes" name="VLAN100" unicastRoute="no" unkMacUcastAct="flood"
unkMcastFlood="yes"/>
```

This mode of operation is equivalent to that of a regular Layer 2 switch, except that in Cisco ACI this traffic is transported in the fabric as a Layer 3 frame with all the benefits of Layer 2 multipathing, fast convergence, and so on.

Hardware proxy and unknown unicast and ARP flooding are two opposite modes of operation. With hardware proxy disabled and without unicast and ARP flooding, Layer 2 switching does not work.

The advantage of disabling hardware-based proxy and using flooding for unknown hosts and ARP is that the fabric does not need to learn millions of source IP addresses coming from a given port.

fvCtx

In addition to the bridge domain, a tenant normally also is configured with a VRF instance for routing. ACI calls this VRF a *private network*. You need to configure more router instances if more overlapping IP addresses are required:

```
<fvCtx name="Tenant1-router"/>
```

Endpoint Connectivity

Endpoint connectivity in the virtual network is defined by carving the bridge domain into EPGs and associating these EPGs with either a virtual machine manager or a physical server (static binding).

For the EPG configuration to work—that is, for endpoints to be discovered and EPG to be propagated to the virtual machine manager—remember to do the following:

- Associate the EPG with the bridge domain.
- Create a router in the tenant.

- Associate the bridge domain with the router.

- Enable unicast routing (if you want traffic to be routed; that is, if you want a pervasive gateway).

Connecting a Physical Server

As noted previously, the **<fvCtx name="Tenant1-router"/>** configuration defines connectivity for a physical server to an EPG. EPGs are always part of an application network profile **<fvAp>**, which in Example 7-8 is called **"test"**. Here, **fvRsPathAtt** indicates that the physical server connected to port 1/33 on leaf101 can send traffic untagged (**mode="native"**), and on leaf 101 the traffic from this server is tagged as **vlan-10** (which has local significance). All the traffic from this server is associated with the bridge domain **"Tenant1-BD"**.

Example 7-8   *Configuration of Connectivity to a Physical Server*

```
Method: POST
http://10.51.66.243/api/mo/uni.xml
<polUni>
  <fvTenant dn="uni/tn-Tenant1" name="Tenant1">
    <fvAp name="test">
      <fvAEPg name="EPG-A">
        <fvRsBd tnFvBDName="Tenant1-BD" />
        <fvRsPathAtt tDn="topology/pod-1/paths-101/pathep-[eth1/33]"
  encap="vlan-10"  mode="native"/>
      </fvAEPg>
    </fvAp>
  </fvTenant>
</polUni>
```

If hardware proxy is enabled for the bridge domain, as it is by default, the endpoints are discovered when they send the first frame, and they appear in the operational view under Client Endpoints.

Connecting a Virtual Server

Example 7-9 shows the configuration that provides connectivity for a virtual server to an EPG. EPGs are always part of an application network profile **<fvAp>**, which in this case is called **"test"**. The EPG called **"EPG-A"** appears on the virtualized server as a port group named **Tenant1|test|EPG-A**. The virtual server administrator then associates the virtual machine with the port group.

Example 7-9 *Configuration of Connectivity to a Virtualized Server*

```
Method: POST
http://10.51.66.243/api/mo/uni.xml
<polUni>
  <fvTenant dn="uni/tn-Tenant1" name="Tenant1">
    <fvAp name="test">
      <fvAEPg name="EPG-A">
        <fvRsBd tnFvBDName="Tenant1-BD" />
        <fvRsDomAtt tDn="uni/vmmp-VMware/dom-vCenter1"/>
      </fvAEPg>
    </fvAp>
  </fvTenant>
</polUni>
```

The virtual machines associated with the EPG show in the Operational view under Client-Endpoints. You also find on which virtualized servers they are located.

External Connectivity

The Cisco ACI fabric distinguishes internal endpoints from external routes. Every endpoint that is internal to the fabric is known by means of discovery of the endpoint itself. The external routes are known by peering with Open Shortest Path First (OSPF) or Border Gateway Protocol (BGP) with neighboring routers or by configuring static routes.

The configuration of Layer 3 connectivity requires identification of the leaf that will be the border leaf for this specific tenant, the interfaces that will be used, the IP addresses that should be used, and the routing instance of the tenant with which the routes should be associated. An example is depicted in Example 7-10 below.

Example 7-10 *Configuration of External Connectivity*

```
<fvTenant name="Tenant1">
  <l3extOut name="Internet-access-configuration">
    <l3extInstP name="outsideEPGforTenant1">
      <fvRsCons tnVzBrCPName="ALL"/>
      <l3extSubnet ip="0.0.0.0" />
    </l3extInstP>
    <l3extLNodeP name="BorderLeafConfig">
    <l3extRsNodeL3OutAtt tDn="topology/pod-1/node-101">
        <ipRouteP ip="0.0.0.0">
          <ipNexthopP nhAddr="172.18.255.254"/>
        </ipRouteP>
    </l3extRsNodeL3OutAtt>
      <l3extLIfP name="L3If">
```

```
            <l3extRsPathL3OutAtt tDn="topology/pod-1/paths-101/pathep-[eth1/16]"
    ifInstT="l3-port" addr="172.18.66.1/16"/>
        </l3extLIfP>
        </l3extLNodeP>
        <l3extRsEctx tnFvCtxName="Tenant1-router"/>
    </l3extOut>
</fvTenant>
```

Example 7-10 shows the following:

- l3InstP is an EPG for the traffic coming from the outside.

- l3extSubnet is a filter in case the user wants to categorize external traffic into multiple EPGs.

- fvRsCons defines the contract that is consumed by this EPG, and as a result it establishes the communication path to internal EPGs.

- l3extLNodeP is the location where you put the configuration for the border leaf (for example, for static routes).

- l3extRsNodeL3OutAtt identifies a particular leaf that you select as the border leaf for the tenant.

- l3extLIfP is the location where you can configure the ports and subinterfaces of the border leaf with IP addresses and so on.

- l3extRsEctx is the location where you associate the configuration with the routing instance for the tenant.

Summary

This chapter described the topology of an ACI fabric and how to configure it as an infrastructure administrator and as tenant administrator. It covered the configuration of physical interfaces, PortChannels, virtual PortChannels, and VLAN namespaces as part of the infrastructure configurations. This chapter also explained the topics of segmentation, multitenancy, connectivity to physical and virtual servers, and external connectivity as part of the tenant configuration.

Chapter 8

Service Insertion with ACI

Cisco Application Centric Infrastructure (ACI) technology provides the capability to insert Layer 4 through Layer 7 functions using an approach called a *service graph*. The industry normally refers to the capability to add Layer 4 through Layer 7 devices in the path between endpoints as *service insertion*. The Cisco ACI service graph technology is considered a superset of service insertion. The goal of this chapter is to describe the service graph concept and how to design service insertion with the service graph.

As Figure 8-1 shows, Layer 4 through Layer 7 services can be physically located anywhere in the fabric, and the services can be running as physical or virtual appliances.

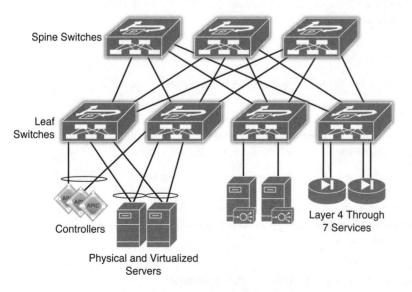

Figure 8-1 *ACI Fabric with Layer 4 Through Layer 7 Services*

Overview of ACI Design with Layer 4 Through Layer 7 Services

The main purpose of a data center fabric is to move traffic from physical and virtualized servers and forward it to its destination, and while doing so apply Layer 4 through Layer 7 services such as:

- Traffic inspection

- SSL offloading

- Application acceleration

- Load balancing

Benefits

The main benefits of using a Cisco ACI fabric to provision Layer 4 through Layer 7 services are as follows:

- Single point of provisioning through the GUI, the Representational state transfer (REST) API, or Python scripts

- Scripting and programming environment with a Python software development kit (SDK)

- Capability to provision complex topologies instantaneously

- Capability to add and remove workloads from the load balancers or configurations without human intervention

- Capability to create a logical flow of functions instead of just a sequence of Layer 4 through Layer 7 devices

- Multitenancy (network slicing) on the fabric and on the service devices

- Capability to create portable configuration templates

Cisco ACI enables you to concatenate functions offered by individual Layer 4 through Layer 7 devices instead of simply connecting discrete boxes in sequence.

Appliances don't need to be placed in any particular place in the fabric. They can run as physical appliances connected to any leaf, or as virtual appliances running on any virtualized server. They can be connected on any leaf port of the ACI fabric. Physical appliances can run with multiple virtual contexts as well. Cisco ACI models this concept in the construction of the policy.

Connecting Endpoint Groups with a Service Graph

A service graph is a variation of the contract concept. In the Cisco ACI policy model, a contract connects two endpoint groups (EPG). A contract also offers functions such as traffic filtering, traffic load balancing, and SSL offloading. Cisco ACI locates the devices that provide such functions and inserts them into the path as defined by the service graph policy. As Figure 8-2 shows, a sequence of Layer 4 through Layer 7 functions can be used to connect two EPGs.

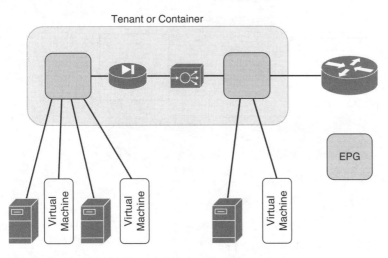

Figure 8-2   *Cisco ACI with Service Graphs*

Extension to Virtualized Servers

Virtual appliances are automatically inserted into the Cisco ACI fabric by the Cisco Application Policy Infrastructure Controller (APIC).

Cisco ACI locates the virtual network interface card (vNIC) of the virtual firewalls and virtual load balancers and automatically connects them to the correct EPG.

Management Model

The user can define configurations on the Cisco APIC in multiple ways, as shown in Figure 8-3. These configurations can include the definition of the service graph. The Cisco APIC communicates with the load balancers and firewalls to allocate the necessary network path to create the desired service graph path.

You can define the service graph configuration using the following options:

- The GUI running on the same appliance that provides the controller function

- REST calls with XML- or JSON-formatted payloads that are sent to the Cisco APIC; these can be sent in many ways, using tools such as POSTMAN or Python scripts that send REST calls

- Custom-built GUI that sends REST calls

- Command-line interface (CLI) to navigate the object model from the Cisco APIC

- Python scripts that use the associated Cisco ACI libraries

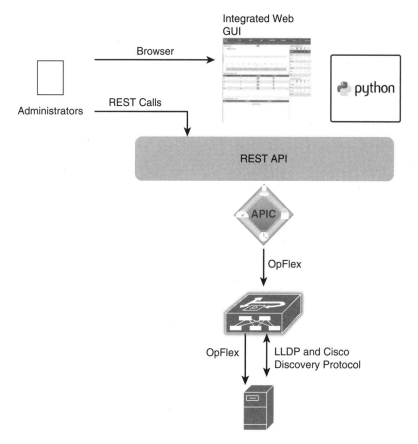

Figure 8-3 *Cisco APIC Provides the Capability to Configure Services with REST, Scripts, or a GUI*

Service Graphs, Functions, and Rendering

The concept of the service graph is different from simply doing service insertion. A service graph is a concatenation of functions (and not of network devices). The service graph specifies that the path from one EPG to another EPG must pass through certain functions. The Cisco APIC translates the definition of the service graph into a path through firewalls and load balancers, called *rendering*.

As Figure 8-4 shows, the Cisco APIC is aware of the pool of load balancers and firewalls (concrete devices) and translates the user intentions expressed in the service graph by using the available pool of resources.

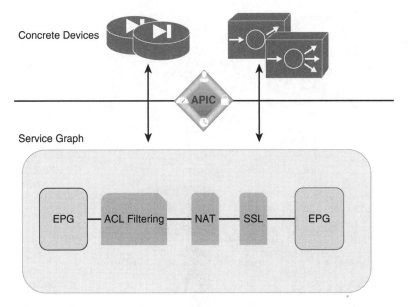

Figure 8-4 *Concept of a Service Graph*

Therefore, the service graph is more like a template, which can be ported to different data centers and rendered with locally available resources. The rendering involves the following:

- Allocation of the necessary bridge domains

- Configuration of IP addresses on the firewall and load balancer interfaces

- Creation of the VLAN on these devices to create the path for the functions

- Performance of all the work necessary to make sure that the path between EPGs is the path defined in the service graph

Hardware and Software Support

The Cisco APIC communicates with the firewalls or load balancers to render the graph defined by the user. For Cisco ACI to be able to talk to firewalls or load balancers, it needs to speak to their APIs. The administrator must install plug-ins on the Cisco APIC that enable this communication. A plug-in is referred to as a *device package*, and the vendor of a firewall and load balancer must provide the plug-in so that the Cisco APIC can communicate with it.

As shown in Figure 8-5, the device package includes a description of the device and lists the parameters it is exposing for Cisco APIC configuration and the scripts that allow Cisco ACI to talk to this device.

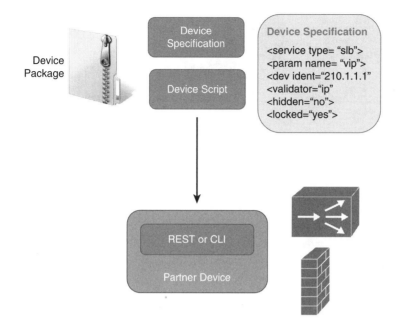

Figure 8-5 *Device Package*

Before you perform any configuration based on service graphs, install the plug-in on the Cisco APIC to enable communication between the Cisco APIC and the device.

Figure 8-6 illustrates how to import the device package in Cisco APIC.

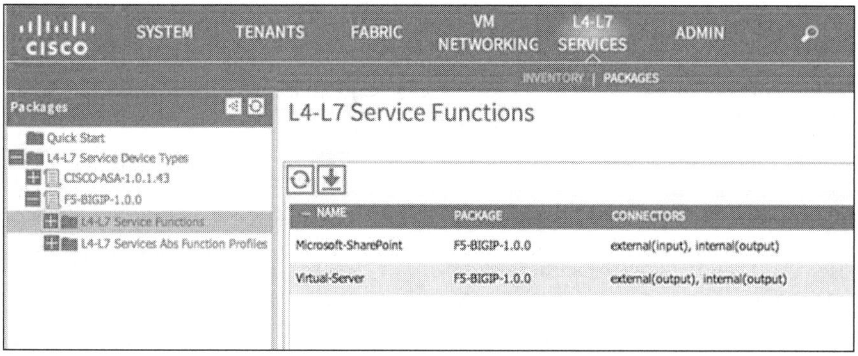

Figure 8-6 *Using the GUI to Import the Device Package*

Cisco ACI Modeling of Service Insertion

This section describes how to define workload connectivity with services in Cisco ACI. To understand the concept of the service graph, you must be familiar with the overall goal of Cisco ACI. ACI intends to create portable configuration templates—abstracted configurations that can be applied in multiple fabrics (data centers). The goal of ACI is to enable the network administrator to define connectivity a single time and copy the template multiple times. The template of configuration is then adapted to the IP addressing scheme, VLANs, and so forth of the fabric where it is applied. The service graph concept is part of this goal.

Instead of specifying which exact firewall or load balancer needs to be concatenated, the service graph defines a sequence of functions from metadevices. For instance, the service graph doesn't say that firewall ASA with IP address a.b.c.d must be connected to load balancer Citrix with IP address. a.b.c.e. Instead, the service graph says that traffic filtering from a Cisco Adaptive Security Appliance (ASA) device of a given software version must be concatenated with traffic load balancing from a load balancer of type Citrix, with a certain version. The service graph definition must then be translated into a sequence of "concrete devices" (or, in other words, the devices connected to the fabric) and the bridge domains and VLANs that connect them. This translation is the rendering of the service graph with the networking devices that are configured and known by the APIC controller in a particular fabric.

Service Graph Definition

The service graph is a sequence of functions. You can define these functions either using XML format or using the GUI. The GUI allows you to choose the functions exported with the device package and to concatenate them.

You can pick functions individually and stitch them together through the GUI, as shown in Figure 8-7. Note that the function or device that is inserted is a metadevice; that is, it is not a specific load balancer or firewall, but instead is simply a load balancer or firewall of a certain type. The association of the metadevice (such as a function from a load balancer of type Citrix or F5 or from a firewall of type Cisco ASA) with an actual device connected to the fabric is performed in the rendering stage.

Figure 8-7 *Using Load Balancer Functions to Create a Service Graph*

The service graph also defines the virtual services and server pools that you want Cisco ACI to program on the load balancer or firewall when the graph is instantiated. Figure 8-8 shows the optional parameters that you can add to the load balancer used in this example.

CONFIG PARAMETERS								
FOLDER/PARAM	NAME	VALUE	MANDATORY	LOCKED	APPLY TO SPECIFIC DEVICE	APPLY TO SPECIFIC CONNECTOR	OVERRIDE NAME/VALUE TO	
LocalTraffic				false			epg	
Network				false			epg	
Function Config	Function							
ClientSSL				false			epg	
FastL4				false			epg	
HTTP				false			epg	
HTTPRedirect				false			epg	
Listener				false			epg	
NetworkRelation				false			epg	
Pool				false			epg	

Figure 8-8 *Parameters to Be Configured on the Service Devices Upon Rendering*

Not all parameters need to be hard-coded IP addresses. You can also define parameters that are populated by the appearance of a new endpoint in a particular EPG in the fabric. The graph is rendered when it is associated with a contract. When the graph is rendered, configurations appear in the device that is part of the graph. For instance, in the case of an F5 BIG-IP load balancer, you may see Self IP appear in the interface and a server pool being programmed.

Concrete Devices and Logical Devices

Service graphs are composed of abstract nodes, which are metadevices. The Cisco APIC translates the intention expressed by the user in the abstract graph into a sequence of concrete devices that are actually connected in the fabric.

Firewalls and load balancers are never deployed as single devices. Instead, they normally are deployed as clusters of active-standby pairs. Cisco ACI provides an abstraction to represent these clusters. Cisco ACI calls this abstraction a *device cluster* or a *logical device*. You must help Cisco ACI perform the mapping between the service graph and the clusters of firewalls and load balancers. It is necessary to inform Cisco ACI as to which pairs of concrete devices constitute a cluster.

The GUI also asks you to configure logical interfaces. A logical interface defines a naming convention for the building block of the cluster and its mapping to the concrete device and to the metadevice. For instance, the metadevice of an F5 load balancer defines an external and an internal interface. The cluster model in Cisco ACI defines two interfaces and lets you choose the name (logical interface [LIf]). Each interface maps to a metadevice interface and also to a physical (concrete) device interface. This process allows Cisco ACI to correctly render the graph.

The interface naming process may seem complicated at first. Cisco ACI allows you to model concrete devices into clusters of devices and then to select these clusters of devices to render the service graph policy.

Logical Device Selector (or Context)

To help Cisco ACI render the service graph, you need to indicate which cluster of devices (logical devices) can be used for which purposes. This configuration is called the *logical device context* or *cluster device selector*. The device cluster selector lets you indicate which interface should be associated with which bridge domain and the mapping of the connector in the graph with the logical interface.

Splitting Bridge Domains

For traffic to flow through service devices correctly, you need to make sure that bridge domains and Virtual Routing and Forwarding (VRF) instances are correctly provisioned.

Cisco ACI categorizes service devices into two types:

- **GoThrough devices:** Devices operating in bridge mode; also called transparent devices

- **GoTo devices:** Devices operating in routed mode

If the service node is a GoThrough device (Layer 2 device), these configurations are required:

- Split the bridge domain (and create an EPG shadow).

- Disable IP-based forwarding on the bridge domain.

- Enable MAC address–based forwarding.

- Enable flood-and-learn semantics.

If there is a routed hop (routed fabric, GoTo service, GoTo IP, and Layer 3 external connectivity domain router) between the two ends of the service chain, then the following configurations are required:

- Create a VRF split and a bridge domain split.

- Create shadow EPGs.

- IP-based forwarding is OK, unless the next bridge domain leads to a GoThrough service.

Cisco ACI adds the static routes on the service device and on the VRF instances in the Cisco ACI fabric.

Configuration Steps

Configuring service insertion equates to configuring a service graph and providing the configurations for ACI to render it with the devices that are connected to the fabric.

The following steps are necessary to provision the service devices so that they can be used to render a graph:

Step 1.   Configure the management IP address for the pair of load balancers or firewalls.

Step 2.   Connect the management interface to a management EPG that you configure, or use out-of-band connectivity.

Step 3.   Configure the service devices in active-standby or active-active mode.

Step 4.   Connect the devices to a leaf node

Step 5.   Alternatively, install the virtual appliance on a virtualized server and make sure that the management vNIC is connected to a network that can be reached by the Cisco APIC.

Step 6.   Make sure the device package is installed on the Cisco APIC.

Then model the devices using the ACI policy model as shown in the following steps:

Step 1.   Configure the logical device **vnsLDevVip**. This is the representation of the cluster of active and standby devices.

Step 2.   Configure the concrete device **vnsCDev** under **vnsLDevVip**. This is the information about the individual devices that constitute the cluster of devices.

Step 3.   Create the logical interface **vnsLIf vnsLDevVip**.

If a service device is dedicated to a tenant, perform the configuration steps within the tenant context. If a service device is shared across multiple tenants, configure it in the management (mgmt) tenant and then export it to the desired tenant.

If the concrete devices are virtual appliances, provide the name of the virtual machine, the vNIC name (with the exact spelling and capitalization of the network adapter, with spaces: for instance, **Network adapter 2**), and the name of the VMware vCenter configuration (as defined in the Cisco APIC).

Depending on whether the devices are GoTo or GoThrough, split the bridge domain as needed and associate subnets with it to help ensure that the forwarding path is ready for the deployment.

Within a tenant context, you should then perform the following steps:

Step 1.   Create a service graph (**vnsAbsGraph**).

Step 2.   Create selection criteria (logical device context, **vnsLDevCtx**) to render the service graph.

Step 3.   Associate the service graph with a contract.

You can also achieve the previous configurations by using REST calls following the XML model.

Definition of a Service Graph

The key to understanding how to configure the graph consists of understanding which interface is called what and how different interfaces are pointing to each other.

Defining the Boundaries of the Service Graph

The following is a sample configuration of a service graph in XML format:

- The service graph is contained within an abstract container.

- The service graph container starts with **AbsTermNodeProv-<name-of-your-choice>/AbsTConn.**

- The service graph container ends with **AbsTermNodeCon-<name-of-your-choice>/ AbsTConn.**

Example 8-1 shows the elements that give a name to the boundaries of the abstract container.

Example 8-1 *Definition of the Boundary of the Service Graph*

```
<vnsAbsGraph name = "WebGraph">
[...]
<vnsAbsTermNodeCon name = "Consumer">
  <vnsAbsTermConn name = "consumerside">
  </vnsAbsTermConn>
</vnsAbsTermNodeCon>

<vnsAbsTermNodeProv name = "Provider">
  <vnsAbsTermConn name = "providerside" >
  </vnsAbsTermConn>
</vnsAbsTermNodeProv>
[...]
</vnsAbsGraph>
```

These names are necessary to define how the sequence of functions (such as firewall and load balancing) is connected to each other and specifically to the abstract container. The direction of the graph-to-EPG attachment depends on which EPG is a provider of the contract and which is the consumer of the contract. This determines which EPG connects to the **vnsAbsTermNodeProv** and which EPG connects to the **vnsAbsTermNodeCon.**

Example 8-2 illustrates how the service graph is associated with a contract, and Figure 8-9 illustrates the data path between two EPGs with the service graph in between.

Example 8-2   *Contract that Connects Two EPGs Has a Reference to a Graph*

```
<polUni>
<fvTenant name="Customer1">
   <vzBrCP name="webCtrct">
    <vzSubj name="http">
     <vzRsSubjGraphAtt graphName="WebGraph"/>
    </vzSubj>
  </vzBrCP>
</fvTenant>
</polUni>
```

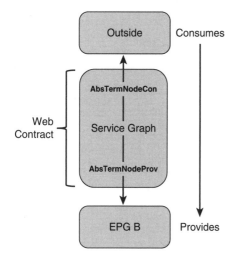

Figure 8-9   *Association of Service Graph with Contract*

The Metadevice

Metadevices are functions or devices defined by the device packages. When you install a device package, you can find via the GUI which interfaces are defined on this service appliance. Figure 8-10 shows a metadevice that provides a load-balancing function. For the purpose of building the service graph, you need to know which label this metadevice uses to connect. In this example, the two labels are "external" and "internal".

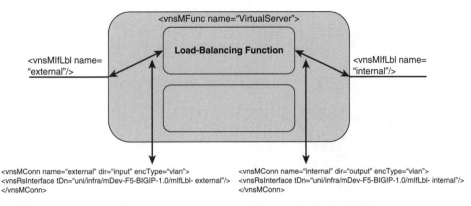

<vnsMConn name="external" dir="input" encType="vlan">
<vnsRsInterface tDn="uni/infra/mDev-F5-BIGIP-1.0/mIfLbl- external"/>
</vnsMConn>

<vnsMConn name="internal" dir="output" encType="vlan">
<vnsRsInterface tDn="uni/infra/mDev-F5-BIGIP-1.0/mIfLbl- internal"/>
</vnsMConn>

Figure 8-10   *Metadevice*

You could have a metadevice that provides firewalling function as a Cisco ASA of a certain version, or a metadevice that provides load balancing as a Citrix appliance of a certain version or as an F5 of a certain version.

Defining an Abstract Node's Functions

A service graph is a sequence of abstract nodes (**vnsAbsNode**). The abstract node provides functions defined in a metadevice. For instance, if the node is a firewall, the abstract node capabilities are defined by a metadevice of type ASA of a given version.

Each abstract node is a device of type GoTo or GoThrough depending on whether it is operating in routed mode or bridged mode. Each node provides a specific abstract function, such as a virtual server or firewalling. This is specified by a relations configuration such as **<vnsRsNodeToMFunc tDn="uni/infra/mDev-ABC-1.0/mFunc-Firewall"/>**, which indicates that this particular abstract node is providing the firewall function as defined by the ABC metadevice. A visual example is provided in Figure 8-11.

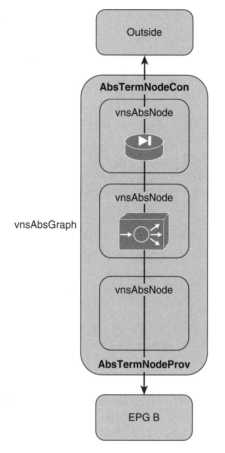

Figure 8-11   *Service Graph Is a Sequence of Abstract Nodes*

Each abstract node provides the functions defined by the relation that was previously indicated and it provides configurations to be rendered on the device. These configurations are delimited by the XML tags: **<vnsAbsDevCfg>** and **<vnsAbsFuncCfg>**. Within these XML boundaries you find things like the IP addresses to give to the firewall or load balancer interfaces, the load balancing configurations, access control lists and so on.

Example 8-3 illustrates a load-balancing configuration that is defined in the context of a graph.

Example 8-3   *Example of Load-Balancing Configuration*

```
<vnsAbsFuncCfg>
  <vnsAbsFolder key="Listener" name="webListener">
    <vnsAbsParam key="DestinationIPAddress" name="destIP1"
                     value="10.0.0.10"/>
      <vnsAbsParam key="DestinationPort" name="port1"
                     value="80"/>
```

```
        <vnsAbsParam key="DestinationNetmask" name="Netmask1"
                        value="255.255.255.255"/>
        <vnsAbsParam key="Protocol" name="protoTCP"
                        value="TCP"/>
    </vnsAbsFolder>
</vnsAbsFuncCfg>
```

Defining an Abstract Node's Connectors

Each node in the graph has connectors, as shown in Figure 8-12.

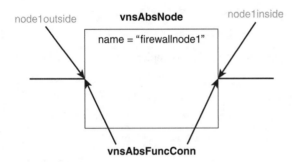

Figure 8-12 *Abstract Node Connectors*

Example 8-4 shows how to name the connectors.

Example 8-4 *Definition of the Connectors of the Abstract Node*

```
<vnsAbsNode name = "firewallnode1" funcType="GoThrough" >
   <vnsAbsFuncConn name = "node1outside">
   </vnsAbsFuncConn>
   <vnsAbsFuncConn name = "node1outside">
   </vnsAbsFuncConn>
</vnsAbsNode >
```

These connectors must be mapped to something more precise that is related to the device that they are going to be rendered onto. The metadevice has interfaces that are defined in the device package. Example 8-5 shows that the connector node1inside is mapped to the "internal" interface of the metadevice, and node1outside is mapped to the "external" interface of the metadevice.

Example 8-5 *Another Definition of the Connectors of the Abstract Node*

```
<vnsAbsFuncConn name = "node1inside">
   <vnsRsMConnAtt
     tDn="uni/infra/mDev-ABC-1.0/mFunc-Firewall/mConn-internal" />
```

```
</vnsAbsFuncConn>

<vnsAbsFuncConn name = "node1outside">
   <vnsRsMConnAtt
      tDn="uni/infra/mDev-ABC-1.0/mFunc-Firewall/mConn-external" />
</vnsAbsFuncConn>
```

Abstract Node Elements Summary

In summary, within the abstract node you have the following elements:

- The arbitrary name that you give to the abstract node

- Whether the abstract node is a GoTo or GoThrough device (**funcType**)

- Which abstract function the abstract node is going to implement (**vnsRsNodeToMFunc**)

- The configurations to be installed on the service device (**vnsAbsDevCfg** and **vnsAbsDevCfg**)

- The name of the abstract function connector (**vnsAbsFuncConn**)

- Which interface the **vnsAbsFuncConn** maps to with reference (**Rs**) to the meta-device interface definition (**vnsRsMConnAtt**)

Connecting Abstract Nodes to Create the Graph

The goal of the service graph is to define a sequence of functions within abstract nodes that are connected to each other to form a sequence of firewall, load balancing, SSL offloading, and so on. Figure 8-13 illustrates how to create the graph.

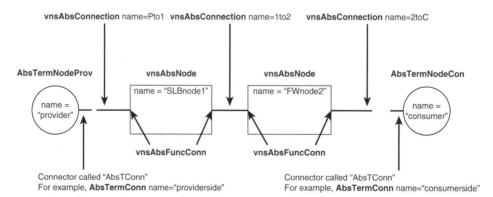

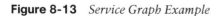

Figure 8-13 *Service Graph Example*

For each **vnsAbsNode**, you defined two **vnsAbsFuncConn** elements in Examples 8-4 and 8-5 with a name. The glue between the **vnsAbsFuncConn** from each **vnsAbsNode** is called a *vnsAbsConnection*.

The **vnsAbsConnection** configuration creates an object with an arbitrary name chosen by the user. This object has the two entities that need to be stitched together to create a connection, as shown in Example 8-6.

Example 8-6 *Connecting Two* **vnsAbsNodes** *Together*

```
<vnsAbsConnection name = "1to2" adjType="L3">
   <vnsRsAbsConnectionConns tDn="uni/tn-<name-of-tenant>/AbsGraph-<name-of-
graph>/AbsNode-<name-of-node>/AbsFConn-<name-of-connector>" />
   <vnsRsAbsConnectionConns tDn="uni/tn-<name-of-tenant>/AbsGraph-<name-of-
graph>/AbsNode-<name-of-node>/AbsFConn-<name-of-connector>" />
</vnsAbsConnection>
```

A specific case of connection is the linking of the abstract node to the provider or consumer end of the graph, as shown in Example 8-7.

Example 8-7 *Connecting the Node to the Boundary of the Graph*

```
<vnsAbsConnection name = "Pto1"
<vnsRsAbsConnectionConns tDn="uni/tn-<name-of-tenant>/AbsGraph-<name-of-
graph>/AbsTermNodeProv-<name-of-boundary>/AbsTConn" />
<vnsRsAbsConnectionConns tDn="uni/tn-<name-of-tenant>/AbsGraph-<name-of-
graph>/AbsNode-<name-of-node>/AbsFConn-<name-of-connector>" />
 </vnsAbsConnection>
```

Example 8-8 illustrates a complete graph with a single node.

Example 8-8 *Example of Service Graph*

```
<polUni>
   <fvTenant name="Sales">
   <vnsAbsGraph name = "WebGraph">

   <vnsAbsTermNodeCon name = "Consumer">
      <vnsAbsTermConn name = "consumerside">
      </vnsAbsTermConn>
   </vnsAbsTermNodeCon>

     <!-- Node1 Provides Virtual-Server functionality -->
     <vnsAbsNode name = "firewallnode1" funcType="GoTo">
       <vnsAbsFuncConn name = "node1inside">
```

```
                    <vnsRsMConnAtt tDn="uni/infra/mDev-ABC-1.0/mFunc-Firewall/mConn-internal" />
                 </vnsAbsFuncConn>


                 <vnsAbsFuncConn name = "node1outside">
                    <vnsRsMConnAtt tDn="uni/infra/mDev-ABC-1.0/mFunc-Firewall/mConn-external" />
                 </vnsAbsFuncConn>


                 <vnsRsNodeToMFunc tDn="uni/infra/mDev-ABC-1.0/mFunc-Firewall "/>
                 <vnsAbsDevCfg>

      </vnsAbsNode>


         <vnsAbsTermNodeProv name = "Provider">
             <vnsAbsTermConn name = "providerside" >
             </vnsAbsTermConn>
         </vnsAbsTermNodeProv>


         <vnsAbsConnection name = "Cto1" adjType="L3">
             <vnsRsAbsConnectionConns tDn="uni/tn-Sales/AbsGraph-WebGraph/AbsTermNodeCon-
      Consumer/AbsTConn" />
             <vnsRsAbsConnectionConns tDn="uni/tn-Sales/AbsGraph-WebGraph/AbsNode-firewall-
      node1/AbsFConn-node1outside" />
          </vnsAbsConnection>


         <vnsAbsConnection name = "1toP">
             <vnsRsAbsConnectionConns tDn="uni/tn-Sales/AbsGraph-WebGraph/AbsNode-firewall-
      node1/AbsFConn-node1inside" />
             <vnsRsAbsConnectionConns tDn="uni/tn-Sales/AbsGraph-WebGraph/AbsTermNodeProv-
      Provider/AbsTConn" />
          </vnsAbsConnection>


          </vnsAbsGraph>
       </fvTenant>
   </polUni>
```

Definition of Concrete Devices and Cluster of Concrete Devices

The previous section described how to define the sequence of firewalling, load-balancing functions, and so on. The abstract graph is a model that needs to be rendered based on the resources that are connected to the fabric. This section shows how to model the virtual appliances or physical appliances that are connected to the fabric so that ACI can render an abstract graph when it is associated with a contract.

Figure 8-14 illustrates the service insertion configuration. The top shows the service graph definition, while the bottom shows the available elements that can be used to render the graph.

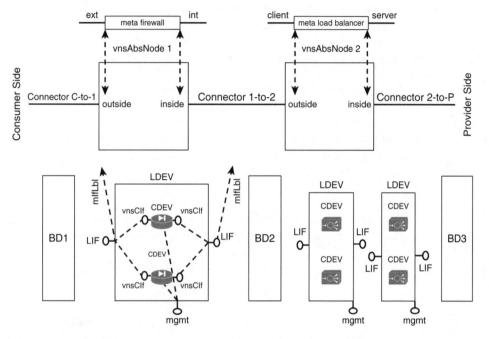

Figure 8-14 *Service Graph Mapping to the Fabric Service Devices*

At the top of Figure 8-14, notice the sequence of vnsAbsNodes: vnsAbsNode1 and vnsAbsNode2. Each one has a reference to a metadevice: vnsAbsNode1 points to a meta firewall, while vnsAbsNode2 points to a meta load balancer.

The bottom of Figure 8-14 shows what is available on the fabric. The fabric has bridge domains, BD1, BD2, and BD3, and a collection of logical devices (LDev), which are clusters of active/standby service devices. One logical device is a cluster of firewalls; the other two logical devices are clusters of load balancers. This means that for the rendering of vnsAbsNode2, ACI can choose from two options.

Figure 8-14 illustrates what is inside an LDev: two concrete devices (**Cdevs**) whose interfaces (**vnsCIf**) are mapped to the LDev interfaces (**LIf**). Each LIf also points to the definition of the interface according to the metadevice definition (**mIfLbl**).

Configuration of the Logical Device and Concrete Device

Example 8-9 assumes a cluster of two firewalls: Firewall 1 is active and Firewall 2 is standby. It shows a logical device within the context of a tenant called *Sales*. The logical device has the name *firewallcluster1* and is a cluster of virtual appliances.

Example 8-9 *Definition of a Logical Device*

```
<polUni>
  <fvTenant dn="uni/tn-Sales" name="Sales">
      <vnsLDevVip name="firewallcluster1" devtype="VIRTUAL">
          <vnsRsMDevAtt tDn="uni/infra/mDev-ABC-1.0"/>
          <vnsRsALDevToDomP tDn="uni/vmmp-VMware/dom-datacenter"/>
          <vnsCMgmt name="devMgmt" host="172.18.66.149" port="443"/>
          <vnsCCred name="username" value="admin"/>
          <vnsCCredSecret name="password" value="password"/>

          <vnsLIf name="fwclstr1inside">
            <vnsRsMetaIf tDn="uni/infra/mDev-ABC-1.0/mIfLbl-internal"/>
            <vnsRsCIfAtt tDn="uni/tn-Sales/lDevVip-F5Virtual/cDev-FW-1/cIf-1_2"/>
          </vnsLIf>

         <vnsLIf name="fwclstr1outside">
            <vnsRsMetaIf tDn="uni/infra/mDev-ABC-1.0/mIfLbl-external"/>
            <vnsRsCIfAtt tDn="uni/tn-Sales/lDevVip-firewallcluster1/cDev-FW-1/cIf-
  1_1"/>
         </vnsLIf>

    </vnsLDevVip>
  </fvTenant>
</polUni>
```

The IP address for management (vnsCMgmt) indicates how to connect to the logical device. This is the floating IP of an active/standby pair of firewalls; in other words, the management IP for the device that is active.

The **vnsLIf** configuration under **LDevVip** defines the association of the cluster interface with the interface of each concrete device. It also specifies the type of interface according to the package. The logical interface definition (vnsLIf) defines two interfaces that Example 8-9 calls *fwclstr1inside* and *fwclstr1outside*. They map to the concrete device interfaces called *1_1* and *1_2*, regardless of which firewall is currently active or standby.

This means that both concrete devices that define the currently active firewall and the currently standby firewall must call the interfaces with the same name *1_1* and *1_2* so that no matter which device is active or standby, the logical device mapping still holds true.

Notice that there is no direct mapping from the definition of the logical device to the interfaces defined in the graph. Instead, there is a relation to the metadevice definition of the interface.

The definition of the concrete device looks like Example 8-10 (virtual appliance) and Example 8-11 (physical appliance). In both examples, two vnsCDev devices make the logical device. For each vnsCDev, the configuration specifies the management IP address and credential.

The configuration also indicates which interface is which. The **vnsRsCIfPathAtt** configuration points to a specific port on the fabric or to the name of the vNIC. For instance, vnsCIf 1_1 is mapped to a particular vNIC in the case of the virtual appliance definition, and it is mapped to a particular physical port on the fabric for the physical appliance. This way, when the logical device is being rendered, it knows how to render the interface 1_1 by looking at the definition in the concrete device.

Example 8-10 *Configuration of Concrete Device that Is a Virtual Appliance*

```
<polUni>
  <fvTenant dn="uni/tn-Sales" name="Sales">
    <<vnsLDevVip name="firewallcluster1" devtype="VIRTUAL">

      <vnsCDev name="ASA-1" vcenterName="vcsa" vmName="vASA-1">
            <vnsCIf name="1_1" vnicName="Network adapter 2"/>
            <vnsCIf name="1_2" vnicName="Network adapter 3"/>

        <vnsCMgmt name="devMgmt" host=<mgmtIP> port="443"/>
        [...]

      <vnsCDev name="ASA-2" vcenterName="vcsa" vmName="vASA-1">
            <vnsCIf name="1_1" vnicName="Network adapter 2"/>
            <vnsCIf name="1_2" vnicName="Network adapter 3"/>

        <vnsCMgmt name="FW-2" host=<mgmt. IP> port="443"/>
        [...]

    </vnsCDev>

    </vnsLDevVip>
  </fvTenant>
</polUni>
```

Example 8-11 *Configuration of Concrete Device that Is a Physical Appliance*

```
<polUni>
  <fvTenant dn="uni/tn-Sales" name="Sales">
    <<vnsLDevVip name="firewallcluster1" devtype="PHYSICAL">

      <vnsCDev name="ASA-1">
        <vnsCIf name="1_1">
          <vnsRsCIfPathAtt tDn="topology/pod-1/paths-103/pathep-[eth1/19]"/>
        </vnsCIf>
```

```
        <vnsCIf name="1_2">
          <vnsRsCIfPathAtt tDn="topology/pod-1/paths-103/pathep-[eth1/20]"/>
        </vnsCIf>

        <vnsCMgmt name="devMgmt" host=<mgmtIP> port="443"/>
        [...]

      <vnsCDev name="ASA-2">
        <vnsCIf name="1_1">
          <vnsRsCIfPathAtt tDn="topology/pod-1/paths-103/pathep-[eth1/21]"/>
        </vnsCIf>
        <vnsCIf name="1_2">
          <vnsRsCIfPathAtt tDn="topology/pod-1/paths-103/pathep-[eth1/22]"/>
        </vnsCIf>
        <vnsCMgmt name="FW-2" host=<mgmt. IP> port="443"/>
        [...]

  </vnsCDev>

  </vnsLDevVip>
  </fvTenant>
</polUni>
```

Configuration of the Logical Device Context (Cluster Device Selector)

The selection of which logical device renders which vnsAbsNode from the graph is based on the definition of a context, which is a set of metatags used to create a mapping between the logical definition of the graph and the concrete rendering of the graph. The metatags are contract name, graph name, and node label. The logical device context not only defines which logical device to use to render a particular graph, but also defines which bridge domains should be used for which interface. Example 8-12 illustrates how to configure this mapping.

Example 8-12 *Logical Device Context Base Configuration*

```
<vnsLDevCtx
ctrctNameOrLbl=<name of the contract>
 graphNameOrLbl=<name of the graph>
 nodeNameOrLbl=<name of the node in the graph, e.g. N1>
/>
```

The configuration in Example 8-13 specifies that the cluster of firewalls called **firewallcluster1** can render the node **firewallnode1** in the service graph **WebGraph** when it is used by the contract **webCtrct**. This configuration also specifies that the connector that has a label of **1toP** in the graph can be rendered by the **firewallcluster1** interface called **fwclstr1inside**.

Example 8-13 *Example Configuration of Logical Device Context*

```
<vnsLDevCtx ctrctNameOrLbl="webCtrct" graphNameOrLbl="WebGraph"
  nodeNameOrLbl="firewallnode1">
  <vnsRsLDevCtxToLDev tDn="uni/tn-Sales/lDevVip-firewallcluster1"/>
  <vnsLIfCtx connNameOrLbl="1toP">
   <vnsRsLIfCtxToLIf tDn="uni/tn-Sales/lDevVip-firewallcluster1/lIf-fwclstr1in-
   side"/>
   <vnsRsLIfCtxToBD tDn="uni/tn-Sales/BD-SalesBDApp"/>
  </vnsLIfCtx>
  <vnsLIfCtx connNameOrLbl="Cto1">
      <vnsRsLIfCtxToLIf tDn="uni/tn-Sales/lDevVip-firewallcluster1/lIf-fwclstr1out-
   side "/>
      <vnsRsLIfCtxToBD tDn="uni/tn-Sales/BD-SalesBDWeb"/>
  </vnsLIfCtx>
</vnsLDevCtx>
```

Naming Summary

This section summarizes the key terms that you must be familiar with to configure a service graph successfully.

Figure 8-15 shows the name of the XML tags that define each configuration object. The name value assigned by the administrator is displayed with quotes.

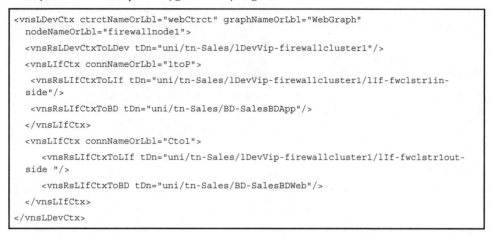

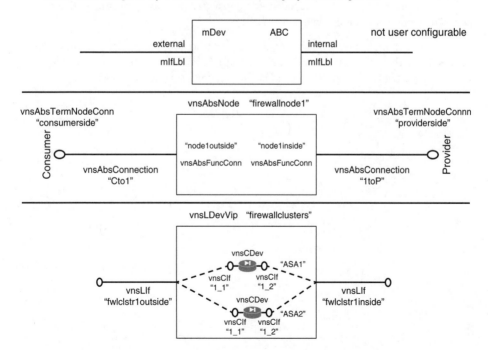

Figure 8-15 *Naming of the Building Blocks of a Service Graph*

For mapping assistance, refer to Table 8-1.

Table 8-1   *Naming Conventions for Interface Used in the Service Graph Building Blocks*

Metadevice	Concrete Device	Cluster of Devices: LDev	Abstract Node	Logical Device Context
mIfLbl for the device **mConn** for an mFunc	**vnsCIf** to be mapped to vNIC or to physical interface path	**vnsLIf** includes reference to the mIfLbl of an mDev and to vnsCIf	**vnsAbsFuncConn**	**connNameOrLbl**

Summary

Cisco ACI provides an advanced data center networking methodology that abstracts networking constructs from application deployments. In addition, it offers a set of network telemetry, security, and Layer 4 through Layer 7 automation functions.

The service graph is a concept that allows the definition of a sequence of functions such as load balancing, traffic filtering, and so forth in a way that can be abstracted from the concrete implementation in a given data center.

Cisco APIC communicates with the service devices to render the service graph by using the resources that are available in the fabric. These functions are implemented using the GUI or programmatically in Python and are automated using the REST API.

Chapter 9

Advanced Telemetry

The growth of network devices in a fabric increases the difficulty of troubleshooting and correlating events. Additionally, the workload being distributed and mobile within the network fabric adds another degree of complexity. Finally, the desire for service-level agreement (SLA) monitoring in a shared environment is increasing. ACI offers several new technologies to address these requirements:

- Atomic counters

- Latency metrics

- Health scores and health monitoring

The new telemetry tools provide a comprehensive troubleshooting methodology that enables the network administrator to quickly identify, isolate, and remediate a network issue on the network fabric.

Atomic Counters

This section explains the principle of atomic counters and provides an example of how they integrate with the Cisco APIC.

The Principle

The ACI fabric atomic counters are packet and byte counters that are read atomically across the entire ACI fabric. *Atomic* means that the values in the counters are consistent regardless of where they are in the fabric or the amount of latency or distance that exists between them.

For instance, suppose a set of atomic counters is configured to count the number of FTP packets sent from a given host, and that host sends 10,005 FTP packets across the fabric from leaf switch L1 through the spine switches to leaf switch L2. When the counters are read, the counter at L1 has the exact same value as the counter at switch L2, assuming that there are no packet drops between the two switches. Furthermore, the values are identical no matter when they are read. For example. they may be read while the FTP traffic is in transit and some value between 0 and 10,005 is read. But no matter when it is read, the same value is found at both the ingress leaf and the egress leaf. It is as if the counters were read simultaneously and all packets traverse the network in zero time. This is accomplished not by attempting to read the counters atomically, but rather by updating them (incrementing the packet count and adding packet length to byte count) atomically with respect to the packet, not with respect to time. In other words, all of the counters across the network that a given packet updates are revised before the counters are read. Once all of the counters have been updated, the fabric stops revising them until they have all been read.

To avoid missing some counts (updates), two sets of counters are kept. While one set is being read, the other set is being updated, and vice versa. These sets are called the *even* set and the *odd* set. The two sets make a counter pair. There is a marker bit set in the packet header that distinguishes the counters that need to be updated for each packet. When the bit is clear, the even counters are updated, and when the bit is set, the odd counters are updated. To make the feature much more useful, there is a filter applied to each packet to determine which of N counters are updated. The header fields from the packet are applied to a TCAM (**Ternary content-addressable memory** is a specialized type of high-speed memory that searches its entire contents in a single clock cycle), and the result of the TCAM tells the hardware which counter pair to update. The marker bit in the packet header then informs the hardware which of the two counters in the pair to update. This allows the system to be configured to count multiple kinds of traffic simultaneously. For example, you can count FTP traffic and web traffic simultaneously. To make it all work seamlessly across an entire ACI fabric, the following must occur:

- Global coordination of setting the marker bit at each leaf switch

- Waiting for in-flight packets to propagate out of the fabric

- Reading all of the counters before repeating

Further Explanation and Example

The implementation occurs in the VXLAN header, by adding a tag on the M bit. This bit indicates which bank of atomic counters the fabric should use for this packet: 0 for the odd set and 1 for the even set, as shown in Figure 9-1.

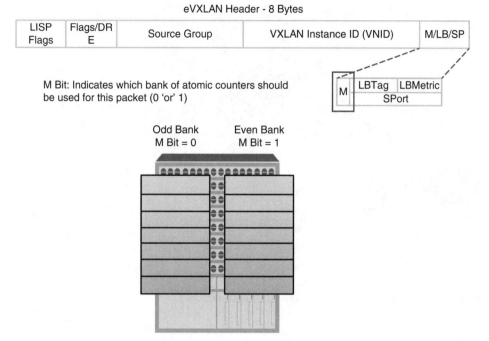

Figure 9-1 *Atomic Counters in the VXLAN Header*

As mentioned in the previous section, by the laws of physics, it is not feasible to check counters at exactly the same time on multiple nodes as packets are moving, and some can be dropped. The leverage of the odd and even bank of counters with the choice of marking a packet odd or even ensures the consistency in the counting. The counters are atomic to the packet and not the time.

In the example depicted by Figure 9-2, traffic is sent between two workloads; one workload is attached on Leaf 2 and the other on Leaf 5. The packets are able to take four different paths because there are four spine switches and Leaf 2 and Leaf 5 are connected to all of them. Notice that for path 1, Leaf 5 received fewer packets (two) from Leaf 2 than Leaf 2 sent to Leaf 5. This means that there are still two packets in flight. With the atomic counters, it's possible to quickly identify any packet issue in the fabric—whether it be dropped packets or replicated packets—and where in the fabric this occurs.

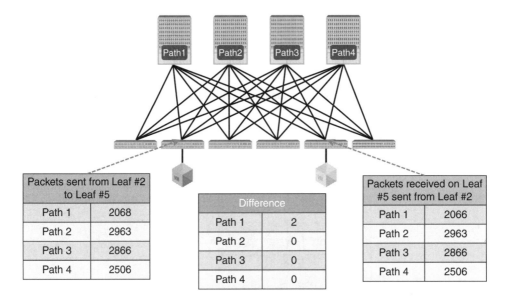

Packets sent from Leaf #2 to Leaf #5	
Path 1	2068
Path 2	2963
Path 3	2866
Path 4	2506

Difference	
Path 1	2
Path 2	0
Path 3	0
Path 4	0

Packets received on Leaf #5 sent from Leaf #2	
Path 1	2066
Path 2	2963
Path 3	2866
Path 4	2506

Figure 9-2 *Example of Atomic Counter Implementation*

Atomic Counters and the APIC

The atomic counters come together when mapped and correlated by the APIC. There is a second bank of counters that is used for on-demand type of monitoring; this is useful for troubleshooting purposes. The counters are incremented if a programmed TCAM entry is matched and at the same time the odd or even bit is set. The TCAM matching criteria is programmed on the switches via a policy that resides on the APIC. This allows the policy to be distributed to all the nodes. The matching criteria is applied against an EPG, an IP address, a TCP/UDP port number, a tenant VRF, or a bridge domain. Then the APIC extracts and correlates the observed counters. This is illustrated in Figure 9-3.

The end user has complete flexibility in terms of deciding what to monitor. For example, the user could choose to monitor the counters between two endpoints; or between an endpoint and a whole subset of devices in a given application network profile, or between an EP in an EPG and a tenant. This provides the proper tools for a high-level visibility or a drill down to the host level.

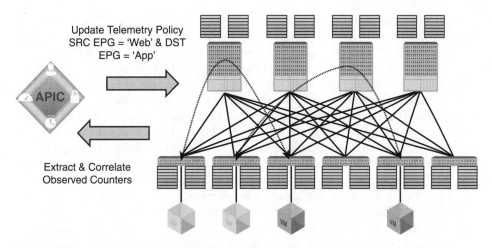

Figure 9-3 *APIC Role in Correlating Counters to Bridge Domain, Tenant, EPG, and Hosts*

Latency Metrics

The ACI fabric offers sub-microsecond type of latency for forwarding and for trouble-shooting per leaf or per spine.The ACI fabric switches are equipped with a pulse per second (PPS) hardware input port. This allows the switch to be connected to an external clock source that has nanosecond type of accuracy and to use the source clock to set its own time. The PPS port is displayed in Figure 9-4.

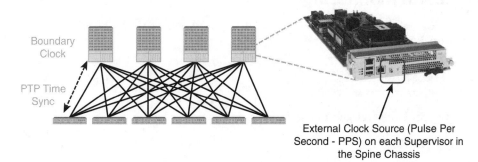

Figure 9-4 *PTP Capabilities in ACI Fabric*

The PPS port synchronization is not mandatory for the Precision Time Protocol (PTP) feature. However, it provides better accuracy to the fabric time synchronization because it avoids the multiple hops of the IEEE 1588 protocol to be transmitted. After the switches have the time synchronized, via the support of PTP as defined in IEEE 1588, they serve as a boundary PTP clock source to the remaining switches in the ACI fabric. Note that the leaf switches can also serve as a PTP time source for the server and application; however, this is not specifically related to the latency feature of the ACI fabric. With PTP, the time synchronizes across switches, and packets are tagged with a PTP timestamp. With PTP, the timestamp is enforced on all fabric switches. This monitors hardware-level latency performance of the ACI fabric, where each switch reads and tags with a PTP timestamp the traffic traversing it. It provides an end-to-end hardware latency real-time knowledge of the traffic going through the ACI fabric. The data is useful for understanding the baseline end-to-end latency performance. It also helps to identify where there could be delays of latency introduced in the fabric due to such things as buffering. With the ACI API model, it is possible to build real-time tools to monitor the latency at any given place of the ACI fabric.

Three types of latency measurements are tracked in the ACI fabric:

- Average, Maximum, Accumulated latency and jitter per port, up to 576 nodes

- 99% of all packets have recorded latency per port, up to 576 nodes

- Bucket histogram, showing the latency dispersion with a 48-bucket-capable histogram, for up to 576 nodes

ACI Health Monitoring

Cisco ACI health monitoring has four main activities to observe the ACI fabric, as shown in Figure 9-5:

- Collecting statistics

- Collecting faults and events

- Collecting logs, diagnostics, and forensics

- Computing health score results

The ACI health monitoring capabilities apply to the whole fabric. This includes all switches and controllers. ACI is also able to receive input about the health of end systems using the fabric with services such as load balancers and firewalls, but also end nodes such as hypervisors and virtual machines.

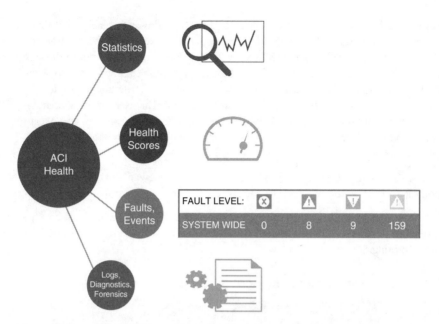

Figure 9-5 *ACI Health Monitoring Capabilities*

Statistics

The ACI health monitoring agent monitors various statistics, such as:

- **Physical port information:** Packet counters, interface counters, bandwidth utilization, drops, errors

- **Control plane resources:** Memory available, CPU usage, latency, disk size, etc.

- **Environmental information:** Temperature, fan speed, power

- **Network resources:** Table usage

- **EPG monitoring:** Packet counters for endpoints for unicast and multicast for ingress and egress, security group violations, etc.

The agent organizes the statistics into three functional categories:

- **Infrastructure statistics:** Selects a target group for the physical statistics, such as a switch number, line card number, or all the way down to the port number, and collects the statistics for them.

- **Tenant statistics:** Collects information about the data in each tenant. This includes the application network profile, the EPG, and the endpoint.

- **Path statistics:** Provides information about a specific EGP, including the selection of spine and leaf switches for source and destination.

This multidimensional statistics approach enables the ACI end user to receive real-time information for a multitude of systems and isolate specific talkers or nodes of interest, instead of having to manually collect statistics with dedicated tools or compute the values to make sense of what is happening in the fabric. This statistical approach allows narrowing of information about the application and the fabric infrastructure very quickly. The statistics are archived continuously for the whole fabric. The user can find information by searching for hours, days, weeks before the event he is interested in, and because the information is collected for the whole fabric, it is possible to correlate the data and faster isolate a root cause.

All the processes described in the following sections can be viewed and also acknowledged on the GUI or on the API level of the APIC.

There are four levels of fabric troubleshooting. The first two levels are ongoing, and the next two, more detailed levels are on demand. Figure 9-6 depicts the four levels of fabric troubleshooting.

Fabric Troubleshooting Levels

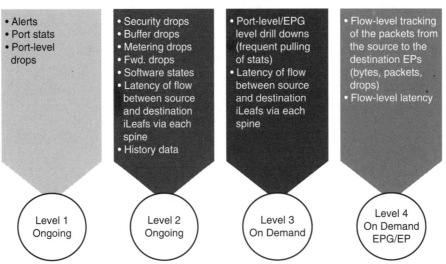

Figure 9-6 *ACI Fabric Troubleshooting Levels*

Faults

Faults that occur in the ACI fabric are monitored by the fault agent. They have explicit representation as managed objects such as policies, ports, etc. Faults have properties such as severity, ID, and description. They are stateful and mutable and their lifecycle is controlled by the system. Finally, faults, like any other ACI health category, are queried using standard APIs.

Faults are originally detected by the switch operating system (NX-OS). The NX-OS process notifies the fault manager on the switch. The fault manager then processes the notification according to the fault rules configured. The fault manager creates a fault instance in the ACI object information model and manages the lifecycle according to the fault policy. Finally, the fault manager notifies the controller of state transitions and can also trigger further actions such as a syslog message, SNMP trap, call home, and so forth. Figure 9-7 depicts faults and events.

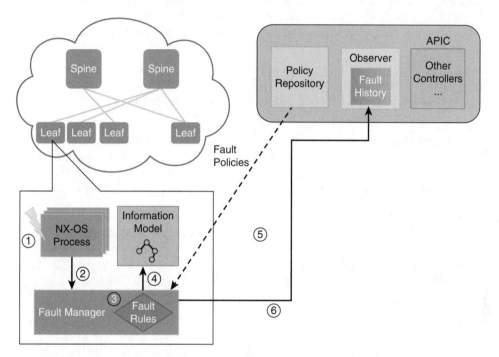

Figure 9-7 *Fault Management Flow*

The APIC maintains a comprehensive, up-to-date, run-time representation of the administrative and operational state of the ACI fabric system in a collection of managed objects (MO). In this model, a fault is represented as a mutable, stateful, and persistent MO. When a specific condition occurs, such as a component failure or an alarm, the system creates a fault MO as a child object to the MO that is primarily associated with the fault.

For a fault object class, the fault conditions are defined by the fault rules of the parent object class. In most cases, a fault MO is automatically created, escalated, de-escalated, and deleted by the system as specific conditions are detected. If the same condition is detected multiple times while the corresponding fault MO is active, no additional instances of the fault MO are created. A fault MO remains in the system until the fault condition is cleared. The fault MO is deleted according to the settings in the fault collection and fault retention policies. A fault MO is read-only unless it is in the cleared and retained state, when it can be deleted by the user by acknowledging it. The creation of a fault MO is triggered by internal processes such as finite state machine (FSM) transitions, detected component failures, or conditions specified by various fault policies, some of which are user configurable. For instance, you can set fault thresholds on statistical measurements such as health scores, data traffic, or temperatures.

Packages in the Management Information Model are a collection of related classes and objects. In the *Cisco APIC Management Information Model Reference*, the fault package contains the fault-related object classes. There are fault objects, fault records, and fault logs.

A fault object is represented by one of the following two classes:

- **fault:Inst:** When a fault occurs in an MO, a fault instance MO is created under the MO that experienced the fault condition.

- **fault:Delegate:** To improve the visibility of a fault that might otherwise go unnoticed, some faults generate a corresponding fault delegate MO in a more visible logical MO in the APIC. The identity of the MO that experienced the fault condition is stored in the fault:Delegate:affected property of the fault delegate MO.

For instance, if the system attempts to deploy the configuration for an endpoint group to multiple nodes and encounters issues on one of the nodes, the system raises a fault on the node object affected by the issue. It also raises a corresponding fault delegate on the object that represents the EGP. The fault delegate allows the user to see all the faults related to the EGP in a single place, regardless of where they were triggered.

For every fault, a fault record object (fault:Record) is created in the fault log. A fault record is an immutable object that records a state transition for a fault instance object. Record creation is triggered by fault instance MO creation or deletion or by modification of key properties such as severity, lifecycle, or acknowledgment of the fault instance object. Although a fault instance object is mutable, the fault record object is not. All properties of the record are set at the time the record object is created.

A record object contains a complete snapshot of the fault instance object and is logically organized as a flat list under a single container. The record object contains properties from the corresponding instance object (fault:Inst) such as severity (original, highest, and previous), acknowledgment, occurrence, and lifecycle, as well as inherited properties that provide a snapshot of the fault instance and the nature and time of its change. The record is meant to be queried using time-based filters or property filters for severity, affected DN, or other criteria.

When a fault record object is created, it is added to the fault log. The object creation can also trigger the export of record details to an external destination by syslog, SNMP trap, or other methods.

Finally, the fault log collects and retains fault records. Records are purged only when the maximum capacity of the log is reached and space is needed for new fault records. Depending on the log space availability, a fault record can be retained in the fault log long after the fault object itself has been deleted. The retention and purge behavior is specified in the fault record retention policy (fault:ARetP) object.

Table 9-1 displays the list of fault types along with their respective descriptions.

Table 9-1 *Fault Types*

Type	Description
Generic	Generic issue detected
Equipment	System has detected that a physical component is inoperable or has another functional issue
Configuration	System is not able to configure a component
Connectivity	Connectivity issue such as unreachable adapter
Environmental	Power issue, thermal issue, voltage issue, or a loss of CMOS
Management	Critical services could not be started Components in the instance include incompatible firmware version
Network	Network issue such as link down
Operational	System has detected an operational issue, such as a log capacity limit or a failed component discovery

The fault monitoring has a lifecycle. APIC fault MOs are stateful. They are faults raised by the APIC when there are transitions through more than one state during its lifecycle. In addition, the severity of a fault might change due to its persistence over time, so modification in the state may also cause a change in severity. Each change of state causes the creation of a fault record and, if external reporting is configured, can generate a syslog or other external report. Only one instance of a given fault MO can exist on each parent MO. If the same fault occurs again while the fault MO is active, the APIC increments the number of occurrences. The lifecycle is shown in Figure 9-8.

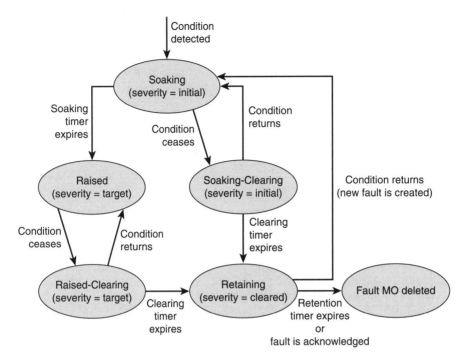

Figure 9-8   *Fault Lifecycle*

The characteristics of each state are as follows:

■ **Soaking:** A fault MO is created when a fault condition is detected. The initial state is *Soaking*, and the initial severity is specified by the fault policy for the fault class. Because some faults are important only if they persist over a period of time, a soaking interval begins, as specified by the fault policy. During the soaking interval, the system observes whether the fault condition persists or whether it is alleviated and reoccurs one or more times. When the soaking interval expires, the next state depends on whether the fault condition remains.

■ **Soaking-Clearing:** If the fault condition is alleviated during the soaking interval, the fault MO enters the Soaking-Clearing state, retaining its initial severity. A clearing interval begins. If the fault condition returns during the clearing interval, the fault MO returns to the Soaking state. If the fault condition does not return during the clearing interval, the fault MO enters the Retaining state.

■ **Raised:** If the fault condition persists when the soaking interval expires, the fault MO enters the Raised state. Because a persistent fault might be more serious than a transient fault, the fault is assigned a new severity, the target severity. The target severity is specified by the fault policy for the fault class. The fault remains in the Raised state at the target severity until the fault condition is alleviated.

- **Raised-Clearing:** When the fault condition of a raised fault is alleviated, the fault MO enters the Raised-Clearing state. The severity remains at the target severity, and a clearing interval begins. If the fault condition returns during the clearing interval, the fault MO returns to the Raised state.

- **Retaining:** When the fault condition is absent for the duration of the clearing interval in either the Raised-Clearing or Soaking-Clearing state, the fault MO enters the Retaining state with the severity level cleared. A retention interval begins, during which the fault MO is retained for the length of time that is specified in the fault policy. This interval ensures that the fault reaches the attention of an administrator even if the condition that caused the fault has been alleviated, and that the fault is not deleted prematurely. If the fault condition reoccurs during the retention interval, a new fault MO is created in the Soaking state. If the fault condition has not returned before the retention interval expires, or if the fault is acknowledged by the user, the fault MO is deleted.

The soaking, clearing, and retention intervals are specified in the fault lifecycle profile (fault:LcP) object.

Events, Logs, Diagnostics

Events occurring in the ACI fabric are monitored by this agent. The faults have explicit representation as managed objects such as policies, ports, and so forth. They have properties such as severity, ID, and description. They are stateful and mutable, and their lifecycle is controlled by the system. Finally, the faults, just as any other ACI health category, can be queried using standard APIs.

The APIC maintains a comprehensive, up-to-date, run-time representation of the administrative and operational state of the ACI fabric system in a collection of MOs. Any configuration or state change in any MO is considered an event. Most events are part of the normal workflow and there is no need to record their occurrence or to bring them to the attention of the user unless they meet one of the following criteria:

- The event is defined in the model as requiring notification.

- The event follows a user action that is required to be auditable.

In the *Cisco APIC Management Information Model Reference*, the event package contains general event-related object classes, although some event types are found in other packages.

A loggable event is represented by an event record object, which is an immutable, stateless, and persistent MO created by the system to record the occurrence of a specific set of conditions at a given point in time. Although an event record MO is usually triggered by situations in another MO, it is not contained by that MO but is contained in an event log.

Each new event record MO is added to one of three separate event logs, depending on the cause of the event:

■ **Audit log:** Holds objects that are records of user-initiated events such as logins and logouts (aaa:SessionLR) or configuration changes (aaa:ModLR) that are required to be auditable

■ **Health score log:** Holds records of changes in the health score (health:Record) of the system or components

■ **Event log:** Holds records of other system-generated events (event:Record) such as link state transitions

Each log collects and retains event records. An event MO remains in the log until it is purged when the log reaches capacity and space is needed for new event records. The retention and purge behavior for each log is specified in a record retention policy (event:ARetP) object associated with each log.

The creation of an event record object can also trigger the export of record details to an external destination by syslog, SNMP trap, or other methods.

APIC event MOs are stateless. An event MO created by the APIC is never modified or cleared; it is deleted by the rotation of the event log as newer events are added and log space is needed.

Health Score

The health score is a number between 0 and 100. It reflects the following:

■ Weighted information from the state of the system

■ Drops

■ Remaining capacity

■ Latency

■ Remaining objects that depend on the ACI fabric health statistics

The health score is a number that is displayed for the whole fabric, for each individual node, and also for EPGs or even endpoints or services integrated into the ACI fabric such as load balancers, firewalls, and so on. This capability provides the end user the benefit of monitoring globally the health score of the fabric and then drilling down specifically to the identified problematic issue to be diagnosed. It is important to note that for the services integrated into the ACI fabric, the health score is provided directly by the service appliance's software to the ACI fabric; the fabric does not compute the services health score. The concept of health score is depicted in Figure 9-9.

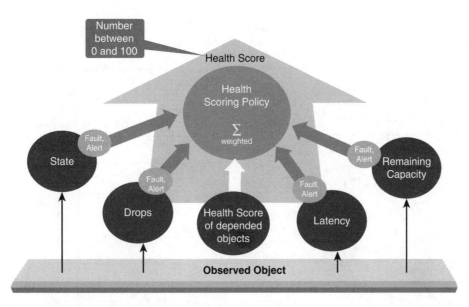

Figure 9-9 *Health Score Concept*

There is a hierarchical relationship used in the health score and this is naturally used
to compute the health score value. For example, the health score of the whole fabric
depends on the tenants, which depends on the EPGs in each tenant. Furthermore, for
a given EPG health score, the number depends on the number of switches in the EPG,
the number of switch ports associated to the EPG, and the EPG's health score on the
individual system. The hierarchical relationship enables the end user to quickly visualize
a health issue in the fabric and drill down to the specific problem(s). Finally, the health
score takes into consideration the acknowledged faults provided. For example, if there
is a fan failure and the user acknowledges the fan failure, the health number improves.
However, naturally it will not go back to full health unless the fan is replaced.

The Centralized show tech-support ACI Approach

The ACI fabric provides a centralized approach to capture comprehensive show-tech
information for all the fabric. The show-tech output contains the majority of information used for troubleshooting purposes by Cisco TAC. The implementation of the show-
tech is centralized with a process that consists of a periodic collection of all switches'
show-tech output and also the correlation of the information model data points, fault
manager, health scores, and data from all the APICs. This information is consolidated by
the APIC and can be stored on external storage, as displayed in Figure 9-10. ACI simplifies the troubleshooting steps and data collection, which allows for a faster time to isolate and root cause a network issue.

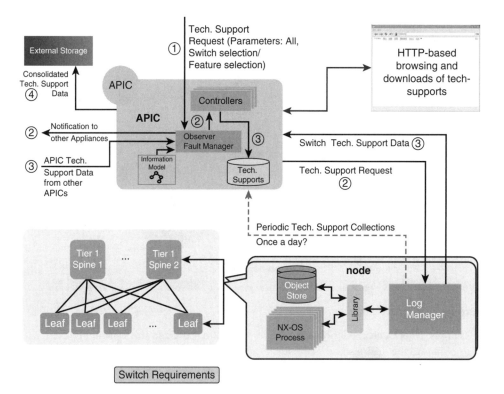

Figure 9-10   *Show Tech Centralized Process*

Summary

Cisco ACI and the policy model bring a centralized approach for diagnostics and provide aggregated metrics for the health of the system by leveraging monitoring technology on each node such as atomic counters, latency monitoring, and fault and diagnostic information. To troubleshoot the ACI fabric, take a fabric-wide approach: examine the global fabric statistics, faults, and diagnostics provided for all elements of the fabric. When thresholds are reached, the health score and faults reflect the changes and globally alert the administrator. At that point, drilling down on particular nodes, looking at the atomic counters or on-demand diagnostics such as show tech-support, provide the relevant information to the administrator, as illustrated in Figure 9-11.

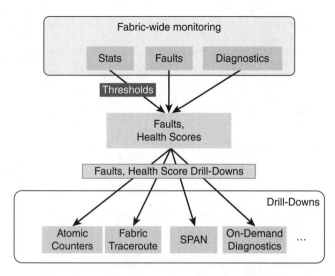

Figure 9-11   *Approach to ACI Fabric Troubleshooting*

Chapter 10

Data Center Switch Architecture

The goal of this chapter is to provide explanations of architectural characteristics of switches used in data centers. It is divided into three sections:

- The hardware switch architecture, explaining the separation of the forwarding plane with the management and control plane, allowing nondisruptive operation of a production data center even during software upgrades.

- The fundamental principles of switching based on the switch hardware architecture.

- Quality of Service within the data center. This section places in context the switching architecture and the reasoning behind the implementation of switching functionalities.

Data, Control, and Management Planes

This section explains how data, control, and management planes interact with each other while still maintaining the separation of roles. The isolation among these elements is necessary in order to support functions such as Cisco In-Service Software Upgrade (ISSU). The isolation enables the system to shut down altogether in case of failure of the data plane or control plane, avoiding traffic black holing. The control plane is protected from attacks or high activity from protocols competing for CPU resource utilization by Cisco Control Plane Policing (CoPP).

Separation Between Data, Control, and Management Planes

You can imagine the operations that a network device performs as the combination of three different elements: data, control, and management planes.

The control plane is the component to a switch that focuses on how this individual device interacts with its neighbors. It is related to the device itself and not the switched data, allowing the switch to decide what to do when a packet arrives; for instance, providing and receiving spanning-tree messages (bridge protocol data units), participating in routing protocols, and so on. Certain control plane protocol activities can be offloaded on the data plane to provide better performance, such as, for example, Link Aggregation Control Protocol (LACP) activities or Bidirectional Forwarding Detection (BFD).

The management plane of a network device includes all the activities related to the management of the device itself, such as Secure Shell (SSH), Telnet, Simple Network Management Protocol (SNMP), syslog, and so forth. A dedicated CPU module called a *supervisor module* hosts the control and management plane activities. Although both control and management planes exist simultaneously on the supervisor, they are distinct and separate entities.

The data plane of a networking device represents the packet forwarding activity (switching, routing, security, NAT, and so on) or, more simply put, where a packet is moved from the entry port of the device to the exit port. The data plane capabilities are hardware based, enabled by purpose-built silicon called application-specific integrated circuits (ASIC).

The decoupling of the three planes has these benefits, as shown in Figure 10-1:

■ Protection between data, control, and management plane activities.

■ Line-rate data forwarding capabilities regardless of control plane or management activity (high CPU due to SNMP, for example).

■ Capability to upgrade the switch software in a nondisruptive fashion so that the CPU can reload while the data plane continues forwarding packets. Then the CPU can start with the upgraded software and firmware, from the same previous machine level state, which was backed up prior to the upgrade. This capability is also known as In-Service Software Upgrade (ISSU).

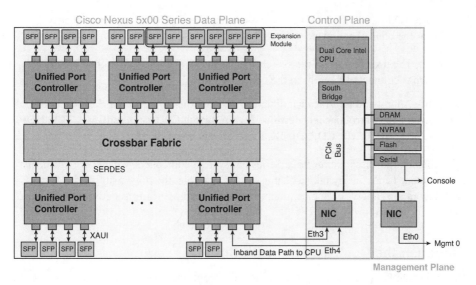

Figure 10-1 *Example of Switch Architecture for Nexus 5000 Switch*

Interaction Between Control, Data, and Management Planes

This section details the control and management interfaces and functions. The control plane interacts with the data plane and is connected by one or multiple interfaces to the ASIC(s), depending on the model of Cisco Nexus switch series that is used.

The Cisco Nexus 9000, 6000, 5000, and 3000 series switches have three types of Ethernet interfaces servicing the functionalities of control and management planes:

- **Eth0:** The mgmt0 port of the switch. This is the out-of-band management network, which is connected directly to the control plane.

- **Eth3:** An in-band interface on the control plane, handling traffic from the data ports of the switch. It handles low-priority control packets destined for the switch CPU, such as Internet Group Management Protocol (IGMP), TCP, User Datagram Protocol (UDP), IP, and Address Resolution Protocol (ARP) traffic. It is defined as inbound-low, processing data traffic of lower priority.

- **Eth4:** Also an in-band interface on the control plane, handing traffic from the data ports of the switch. It handles high-priority control packets destined for the switch CPU, such as Spanning Tree Protocol (STP), LACP, Cisco Discovery Protocol (CDP), Data Center Bridging Exchange (DCBX), Fibre Channel, and Fibre Channel over Ethernet (FCoE) traffic. It is also defined as inbound-hi, processing data traffic of highest priority.

The Cisco Nexus 7000 Series has two types of internal Ethernet interfaces to carry traffic for the control and management planes:

- **Eth1:** The mgmt0 port of the switch. This is the out-of-band management network, which is connected directly to the control plane.

- **Eth0:** An in-band interface handling traffic from the data ports of the switch. It manages all control packets destined for the switch CPU, such as IGMP, TCP, UDP, IP, ARP, STP, LACP, CDP, DCBX, Fibre Channel, and FCoE.

Additionally, the Cisco Nexus 9500 Series has system controllers, which offload further control plane functions by taking charge of, for example, the power supply/fan tray access from the supervisor engine, the intra-system communications between line cards and fabric, and so forth.

Protection of the Control Plane with CoPP

Control Plane Policing (CoPP) protects the CPU from one type of traffic monopolizing the CPU cycles, restricting other traffic. For example, during a broadcast storm attack, CoPP limits the number of ARP packets per second that are able to reach the CPU, allowing the other types of packets to still reach the CPU module without being dropped. This concept is not data center specific; it applies to any Cisco networking device. It is an important part of the control plane. The data center–specific implementation is explained later in this section.

CoPP applies to the in-band interface (or inbound-hi and inbound-low on some platforms). It is used specifically for all the control plane traffic.

Note CoPP does not apply to the management traffic on the out-of-band management interface connected to the control plane. To limit the packets for that specific management interface, access-control lists (ACLs) can be applied to the interface directly.

Control Plane Packet Types

The packets traveling in the control plane can be categorized into four types:

- **Receive packets:** Packets that have the destination address of a router. The destination address can be a Layer 2 address (such as a router MAC address) or a Layer 3 address (such as the IP address of a router interface). These packets include router updates and keepalive messages. This category also includes multicast packets, which are packets that are sent to multicast addresses used by a router; for example, multicast addresses in the reserved 224.0.0.x range.

- **Exception packets:** Packets that need special handling by the supervisor module. For example, if a destination address is not present in the Forwarding Information

Base (FIB) and results in a forwarding lookup miss, then the supervisor module sends an ICMP unreachable packet back to the sender. Another example is a packet with IP options set.

■ **Redirected packets:** Packets that are redirected to the supervisor module. Features such as Dynamic Host Configuration Protocol (DHCP) snooping or dynamic ARP inspection redirect some packets to the supervisor module.

■ **Glean packets:** If a Layer 2 MAC address for a destination IP address is not present in the adjacency table, the supervisor module receives the packet and sends an ARP request to the host.

All of these different packets could be maliciously used to attack the control plane and overwhelm the Cisco NX-OS device. CoPP process assigns these packets to different classes and provides a mechanism to individually control the rate at which the supervisor module receives these packets.

The CPU has both the management plane and control plane and is critical to the operation of the network. Any disruption or attacks to the CPU module result in serious network outages. For example, excessive traffic to the CPU module could overload and slow down the performance of the entire Cisco NX-OS device. There are various types of attacks on the supervisor module, such as denial of service (DoS) that generate IP traffic streams to the control plane at a very high rate. These attacks force the control plane to spend a large amount of time handling these packets and prevent the processing of genuine traffic.

Examples of DoS attacks are as follows:

■ Internet Control Message Protocol (ICMP) echo requests

■ IP fragments

■ TCP SYN flooding

■ Time To Live (TTL) expiry behavior attack

These attacks can impact the device performance and have the following negative effects:

■ Reduced service quality (such as poor voice, video, or critical applications traffic)

■ High CPU processor utilization

■ Route flaps due to loss of routing protocol updates or keepalives

■ Unstable Layer 2 topology

■ Slow or unresponsive interactive sessions with the CLI

■ Processor resource exhaustion, such as the memory and buffers

■ Indiscriminate drops of incoming packets

For example, a TTL attack occurs when packets with a TTL=0 are sent to the switch. The switch, per RFC 5082, needs to drop the TTL=0 messages. A TTL attack sends a high volume of TTL=0 messages to the switch, usually causing high CPU processor utilization. Two behaviors are implemented with CoPP to prevent this from happening. First, up to 20 ICMP response messages per second are sent back when a TTL=0 is received, as this is useful for troubleshooting purposes. Second, when the number of messages received is above 20, and usually in the million count, with CoPP, the switch drops silently in hardware packets, protecting the CPU from rising.

CoPP Classification

For effective protection, the Cisco NX-OS devices classify packets that reach supervisor modules, allowing administrators to apply different rate-controlling policies based on the type of the packet. For example, restrictions might be lower for a protocol packet such as Hello messages but stricter with a packet that is sent to the supervisor module because the IP option is set. Modular QoS CLI (MQC) is used with class maps and policy maps to configure the packet classification and rate-controlling policies for CoPP.

CoPP Rate-Controlling Mechanisms

After the packets are classified, the Cisco NX-OS device has two different mechanisms to control the rate at which packets arrive at the supervisor module. One is called *policing* and the other is called *rate limiting* or *shaping*.

You can use hardware policers to define separate actions for traffic that conforms to or violates certain conditions. The actions include transmitting the packet, marking down the packet, or dropping the packet. Policing is implemented on the Cisco Nexus switches with either of the following approaches:

- **Packets per second (PPS):** Number of packets per second allowed to the CPU for a specific type of packets
- **CIR and BC:**
    - **Committed information rate (CIR):** Desired bandwidth, specified as a bit rate
    - **Committed burst (BC):** The size of a traffic burst that can exceed the CIR within a given unit of time and not impact scheduling

Depending on the data center switches, CoPP is defined by using either PPS or a combination of CIR and BC.

For instance, the Cisco Nexus 7000, 6000, and 5000 series switches use the CIR and BC configuration mechanism for CoPP, whereas the Cisco Nexus 3000 series switches use the PPS concept. Using either implementation provides the same result. The configuration with PPS is easier to perform.

Recommended practice is to leave the default CoPP settings and follow the proper setup prompt when configuring the switch for the first time. CoPP settings are automatically applied depending on the switch use: Layer 2 only, Layer 3 only, or Layer 2 and Layer 3.

Monitoring CoPP continuously is also recommended. If drops occur, determine if CoPP dropped traffic unintentionally or in response to a malfunction or attack. In either event, analyze the situation and evaluate the need to use a different CoPP policy or modify the customized CoPP policy.

Data Center Switch Architecture

This section explains the key switch architecture concepts used in data center switching: cut-through, crossbar, and SoC switch architectures. It examines their specific enhancements, such as superframing, overspeed, and queuing models, along with the important concepts of head-of-line blocking (HOLB) and virtual output queuing (VoQ). It covers switching architecture and the various Cisco data center products.

To understand the switching architecture decisions, it is important to specify the key requirements for a data center switch fabric, such as:

- Provide a no-drop fabric infrastructure that allows flow control of the input port that is causing the congestion

- Achieve 100 percent throughput at high speed

- Provide low to ultra-low latency

- Prevent head-of-line blocking

The typical switch architectures are bus, mesh, two-tier, crossbar, and centralized shared memory often called *SoC*. The switch ASIC(s) called *SoC*, or *System on Chip* or *Switch on Chip* refers to the all-in-one, feature-rich characteristics of the ASIC. In the data center, the two main switch architectures used are the crossbar and the SoC. The data center switch can be a mix of these two types; for example, SoC with crossbar, SoC with SoC fabric, and so on. The queuing mechanism for crossbar can be input or output, whereas for the SoC it is a shared memory, as depicted in Figure 10-2.

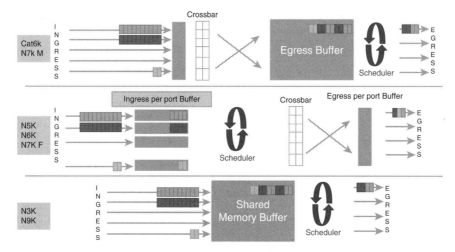

Figure 10-2   *Summary of the Switch Architectures*

Cut-through Switching: Performance for the Data Center

A switch makes time-critical forwarding decisions based on the destination address present in each received frame. In Ethernet, the first field following the start-of-frame delimiter is the destination address entry. Therefore, at the beginning of the lookup information, the switch knows which egress port the frame needs to be sent to. There is no need to wait for the entire frame to arrive before making this forwarding decision to the egress port. This allows the switch to start forwarding the frame immediately, before the rest of the frame has been received. This mechanism is called *cut-through switching*. It is different from store-and-forward switching, where the entire frame is stored first before a lookup-and-forwarding decision is made. Consequently, the cut-through mechanism reduces the latency of the lookup-and-forwarding decision operation and is a major performance improvement for switches. Figure 10-3 shows the constant ultra-low latency (ULL) of a cut-through switch compared to a store-and-forward switch, where the latency increases with packet size. Cut-through switches process frames with a first bit in, first bit out method.

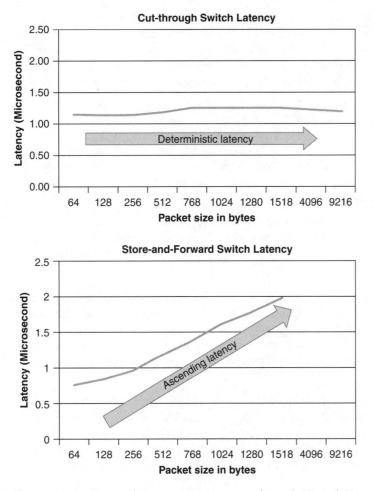

Figure 10-3 *Network Latency Consequence from the Switch Type*

The first Ethernet switch on the market was a cut-through switch developed by Kalpana Corporation and acquired by Cisco. Grand Junction Systems, a Kalpana competitor and also acquired by Cisco, provided store-and-forward switching. A major motivation for store-and-forward switches is the capability to inspect the whole frame first, before forwarding. This ensures the following:

- **Collision detection:** The packet is stored in its entirety, making it possible to determine if it is a frame resulting from a collision.

- **No packets with errors are propagated:** The CRC checksum is checked prior to forwarding.

Store-and-forward switches are the most popular type of switches on the market. Yet, in the past five years, cut-through switches have made a comeback in data center environments, lead by Cisco and followed by other silicon switch manufacturers. This is primarily due to the latency performance gains, optimization of the fabric utilization, and the benefit of the improved physical layer products, creating less CRC errors on the wire.

The store-and-forward benefit mechanisms have been implemented in cut-through switches to include

- A mechanism to signal a malformed packet that fails the CRC checksum by adding a CRC stomp at the end of the packet. This is the only possible mechanism, because the beginning of the packet is already sent on the wire and there is no time machine to revert this action.

- A fragment-free mechanism. To ensure that collision fragments are not forwarded, switching is delayed until the end of the first 64 bytes of the packet. Cut-through switching therefore starts at 64 bytes' packet size. Usually, this delay is needed anyway to perform the table lookup.

Cut-through type switching is principally used in data center networks. There are key benefits to this switch method such as ultra-low and predictable latency, which results in smaller buffer requirements as well as optimized fabric replication for multicast traffic. This switching type also provides an architectural advantage in an environment where sending the data as fast as possible is key to providing a better application and storage performance.

A cut-through or store-and-forward switch can use any of the following: a crossbar fabric, a multistage crossbar fabric, an SoC, or a multistage SoC with either, respectively, a crossbar or SoC fabric. These capabilities are explained in the following sections about the data center switch architecture. Table 10-1 shows the forwarding mode the various models are capable of: cut-through or store-and-forward across the data center switch products.

Table 10-1   *Forwarding Type per Switch Model*

Switch Model	Forwarding Type
Cisco Nexus 9000 Series	Cut-through
Cisco Nexus 7700 Series	Store-and-forward
Cisco Nexus 7000 Series	Store-and-forward
Cisco Nexus 6000 Series	Cut-through
Cisco Nexus 5500 Series	Cut-through
Cisco Nexus 5000 Series	Cut-through

Switch Model	Forwarding Type
Cisco Nexus 3500 Series	Cut-through
Cisco Nexus 3100 Series	Cut-through
Cisco Nexus 3000 Series	Cut-through
Cisco Nexus 2000 Series	Cut-through
Cisco Catalyst Series	Store-and-forward

The outlier that represents a cut-through switch mechanism is only possible when the speed of the receiving port is higher or equal to the speed of the egress port and the fabric in between, in case of a fabric in the architecture. For example, Table 10-2 shows the cut-through behavior for the Cisco Nexus 6000 and 5000 series switches. One outlier in the table is the 1 GE to 1 GE speed, which is also store-and-forward. This is the result of a crossbar fabric operating at 10 or 40 GE, introducing a speed mismatch from 1 GE to a higher fabric speed.

Table 10-2   *Cut-through Nexus 6000 and 5000 Series Switches Forwarding Mode*

Source Speed	Destination Speed	Switching Mode
40 GE	40 GE	Cut-through
40 GE	10 GE	Cut-through
10 GE	40 GE	Store-and-forward
10 GE	10 GE	Cut-through
10 GE	1 GE	Cut-through
1 GE	10 GE	Store-and-forward

Crossbar Switch Fabric Architecture

Crossbar switches are the building blocks for the switching fabrics. Crossbar switch fabric architecture provides multiple conflict-free paths, higher bandwidth capacity, a non-blocking architecture, and larger port counts.

In a crossbar switch, every input is uniquely connected to every output through what is called a *crosspoint*. A crosspoint is the smallest unit of the switching function, which can be built using a variety of electronic components such as transistors, AND gates, and photodiodes. Figure 10-4 shows a visual of a crossbar grid structure mechanism.

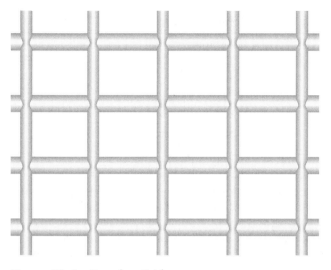

Figure 10-4 *Crossbar Grid*

Because a crosspoint exists for every connection, the crossbar fabric of the switch is considered strictly nonblocking. Blocking occurs only when multiple packets are sent to the same output at the same time. The complexity of a crossbar switch lies in the high number of crosspoints. For example, for an *n* by *n* crossbar (*n* input, *n* output ports), the complexity of the number of crosspoints needed is n^2. Arbitration and scheduling are used to avoid the blocking scenario in the crossbar fabric. Figure 10-5 illustrates the crossbar grid with the crosspoints concept at each input-output crossing.

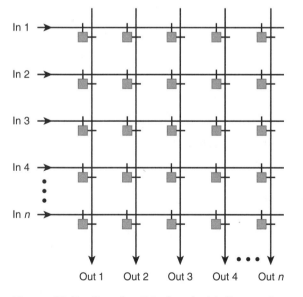

Figure 10-5 *Crossbar Displayed with Crosspoints*

The advantages of crossbar architectures are as follows:

- Highly scalability, allowing high port density and port speed in one physical device

- Nonblocking architecture, allowing network designs with predictable behavior

- Ability to provide lossless transport and therefore carry loss-sensitive traffic such as Fibre Channel frames. This ability is provided by a flow control model mechanism. This flow control mechanism is easier to implement, as the congestion is created at ingress.

Unicast Switching over Crossbar Fabrics

The traffic is balanced in the crossbar fabric: each port has access to all the output ports. When there is a unicast traffic stream, traffic arriving at a given ingress port takes the crossbar fabric on the crosspoint path connecting to the specific egress port where the unicast traffic is to be sent. Multiple traffic streams can be sent simultaneously in the same fabric. Figure 10-6 shows the parallel forwarding of unicast packets between different pairs of source and receiving ports.

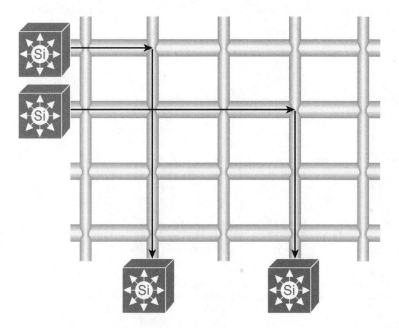

Figure 10-6 *Unicast Switching Across Crossbar*

Multicast Switching over Crossbar Fabrics

When multicast traffic is sent to the crossbar fabric, replication occurs at the fabric. This results in creating numerous multicast streams at the crosspoint in which the multicast frames arrive. An advantage is that the source line card or port ASIC does not have to replicate for packets going to another line card or port ASIC destination.

Overspeed in Crossbar Fabrics

The crossbar fabric is clocked several times faster than the physical port interface to the fabric speed. This is called *overspeed*. Overspeed is needed to achieve 100 percent throughput capacity for each port, also called *line rate*. When there is a contention for an outgoing port that has to receive traffic from multiple ingress ports, the scheduler arbitrates the order in which the packets can be sent to that outgoing port. This takes time and slows down the packets that have to wait, incurring an idle time and interpacket gap. This idle time is where the packet waits until a grant is given from the scheduler for the packets to cross the fabric. Therefore, it's not possible to achieve line rate, because the arbitration process creates a natural idle-time delay. To remediate this slowdown effect, or latency added by the scheduler, the crossbar fabric functions with overspeed. Figure 10-7 shows the overspeed concept in a crossbar fabric, and Figure 10-8 shows the overspeed for the crossbar switches.

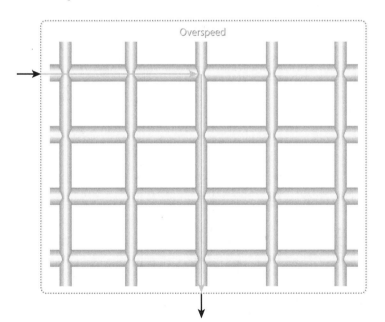

Figure 10-7   *Overspeed Concept in the Crossbar*

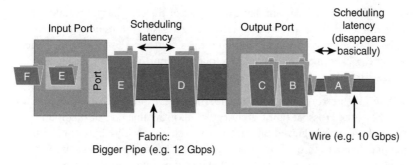

Figure 10-8   *Overspeed in the Cut-through Crossbar Switch*

Superframing in the Crossbar Fabric

Superframing refers to bundling packets in a larger-sized frame when they are sent to the crossbar fabric. This occurs per transaction, or *grant*. A superframe is used only during the transit of frames in the crossbar. It is removed when the packets leave the crossbar to reach the outgoing interface. Therefore, it is transparent to the traffic going through the switch.

When frames are sent to the crossbar fabric, there is a delay added by two factors: an interpacket gap due to scheduling activity, and an extra overhead header being added during the transit in the fabric for signalization purposes. This overhead has a fixed size. Therefore, when it's added to small packets along with the interpacket gap, it represents a significant addition to the packet size. This reduces the overall possible throughput of data traffic at a given smaller packet size. Superframing allows throughput rate to remain unaffected by the packet size by bundling the packets together when needed. Figure 10-9 displays the superframing concept.

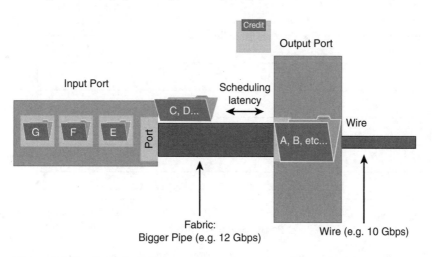

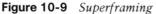

Figure 10-9   *Superframing*

Superframing is an inherent mechanism that can be part of the crossbar fabric and is typically not configurable. There is no fixed superframe size. Also, it does not add latency to the switch, because there is no waiting to fill up the superframe. For example, if there is only one 64-byte packet in the queue, and the outgoing port is free, the scheduler grants fabric access to this packet immediately.

Figure 10-10 shows the performance without superframing. It proves that superframing is a building block of the crossbar fabric architecture allowing line rate throughout. Line rate without superframing is achieved only from a packet size of 4096 bytes or greater. With superframing, line rate throughout is attained from the smallest packet size possible to send on the wire: 64 bytes. Figure 10-11 shows the same throughput test on the Cisco Nexus 5000 series with superframing enabled.

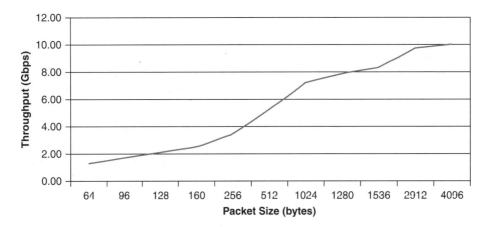

Figure 10-10   *Example of Throughput Without Superframing Enabled on a Cut-through Switch*

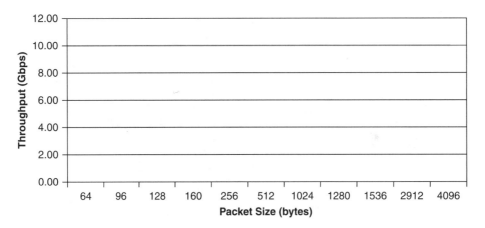

Figure 10-11   *Example of Throughput with Superframing Enabled on a Cut-through Switch*

Note The Cisco switches do not allow a user to disable the superframing capability. Figures 10-10 and 10-11 are meant to illustrate the efficiency of superframing.

The Scheduler

The role of the scheduler, also called *arbiter*, is to service frames across the fabric. The scheduler is a key building block of a switch fabric. It not only has to prevent head-of-line blocking and provide efficient buffer utilization, but must also have the capability to isolate congested sources or congested output ports. The scheduler also has a weighting mechanism to ensure priority traffic and lossless capability is serviced before bulk traffic. During load, the scheduler must be able to maximize the throughput.

Two models are used in the Cisco Nexus series switches to schedule communication between the fabric and the ports:

- **Credit model:** Based on a token credit exchange, where the scheduler provides credits to traffic desiring to cross the switch. The credit is returned to the scheduler after it is used by the superframe. Frames may have to wait in the queue until credit is received. The location of the wait depends on the queuing mechanism: input, output, or centralized. This is the most common scheduling model found in the Cisco Nexus 9000, 7000, 5000, 3000, and 2000 series switches.

- **Collision model:** Two messages are exchanged between the ports and the fabric scheduler: ACK/NACK. In this model, there is no need to wait for a credit. One or multiple input ports compete for an output. The input ports that receive an ACK from the scheduler proceed to send traffic to the crossbar fabric. Other input ports can receive a NACK, which is a denial of fabric utilization. Then they retry another fabric path until an ACK is received. This model has been implemented on the Cisco Nexus 6000 series switches, and provides in this architecture latency reduction to cross the fabric, versus the Nexus 5000 credit-based scheduler.

To achieve line rate throughput, a combination of fabric overspeed, superframing, and an efficient scheduler is used. A good scheduler ensures line rate under most traffic flow conditions, providing a very low latency hit at line rate versus very small traffic load. Typically, the latency added by a scheduler servicing frames at line rate will increase up to 10 percent from the total switch latency.

Crossbar Cut-through Architecture Summary

Crossbar switch architecture combined with cut-through switching permits line rate switching with a constant low to ultra-low latency regardless of packet size. This allows for possible storage networking with lossless Ethernet and ULL and big data/supercompute environments with a predictable latency. The fabric has more crosspoints than the minimum needed, virtual output queues, overspeed, and superframing. Cut-through switching provides the best and predictable performance across packet sizes, and this technique is used with the Cisco Nexus 9000, 6000, 5000, 3000, and 2000 series switches. The Nexus 6000 and 5000 series are cut-through with a crossbar, and the Cisco Nexus 9000 and 3000 series are centralized memory based. The Cisco Nexus 7000 series has a store-and-forward crossbar switching mechanism incorporating the crossbar benefits of overspeed, superframing, and so forth. The following sections describe each of the queuing models for crossbar. Centralized memory (applicable to SoC) is covered in the section "Centralized Shared Memory (SoC)," later in this chapter.

Output Queuing (Classic Crossbar)

When designing a high-bandwidth switch, one of the central concerns is the limited memory bandwidth. The memory is a building block of the queuing mechanism the switch has; therefore, a limiting factor for the switch speed is how fast this memory can operate. A switch that uses the memory bandwidth efficiently can run faster than other switches. Depending on the switch architecture, the queuing can take place at the input, at the output, at both input and output, or at a centralized location. There are three queuing techniques: output queuing, input queuing, and centralized shared memory. Output and or input queuing are used in a crossbar switch architecture. This section explains the output queuing model, as shown in Figure 10-12.

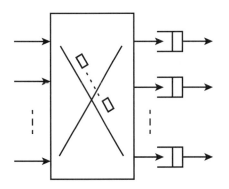

Figure 10-12 *Output Queuing*

In output queuing switches, all queues are placed at the output part of the switch. An output queuing switch has the capability to provide high throughput and guaranteed quality of service (QoS). The lack of queues at the ingress means all arriving frames must immediately be delivered to their outputs. From a QoS and throughput standpoint, this is an advantage, because the frames appear immediately at the output and QoS is guaranteed. A disadvantage is when too many frames arrive simultaneously; the output then is required to have a lot more internal bandwidth and memory bandwidth. For example, to be able to receive X frames at the same time, the output queuing memory needs to support X write accesses for each frame, as the frames arrive to the memory. The switch then needs to support a memory speedup of $X+1$ times the speed to accommodate this scenario.

Two categories of switch family use output queuing in the Cisco data center portfolio: Catalyst 6500–based modular switches (not discussed in this book, just used as a comparison) and the Cisco Nexus 7000 series modular switches with M-series line cards. These switches have a large output queuing memory or egress buffer. They are store-and-forward crossbar architectures. Because they offer large memory, they provide large table size space for MAC learning, routing, access lists, and so on. However, the density of ports and speed is less in the other category of switches.

Input Queuing (Ingress Crossbar)

Input queuing, unlike output queuing, has no speedup requirement for the memory. Queues are at the input and don't have to send or receive more than one frame at the same time. Therefore, the memory is required to operate at only twice the line rate, making input queuing a key to building high-bandwidth switches. However, input queuing does have an issue with the head-of-line blocking (HOLB). This can be eliminated by simply using virtual output queuing (VoQ). HOLB is discussed in the next section. Figure 10-13 illustrates input queuing.

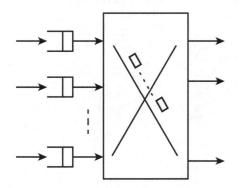

Figure 10-13   *Input Queuing Model*

This input queuing model, also referred to as *ingress queuing* or *ingress buffering*, is used in Cisco Nexus 7000 F-series line card switches and Nexus 5500 and Nexus 5000 switches. These switches benefit from the following enhancements:

- A tightly coupled scheduler and crosspoints, providing 20 percent speedup

- Dedicated unicast and multicast schedulers

- VoQ to prevent HOLB

- Three times fabric overspeed

- Three times more crosspoints than needed to better handle many-to-one congestion scenarios and superframing

The combination of all these features enables the switch to provide the same latency and performance for any load up to line rate, for any packet size, and with any feature turned on (ACL and so on).

Understanding HOLB

When frames for different output ports arrive on the same ingress port, a frame destined to a free output port can be blocked by the frame just in front of it, which is destined to a congested output port. Therefore, the frame destined to a free output port has to wait in queue to be processed until the other output port is no longer congested. This creates backpressure called *HOLB* and unnecessarily penalizes other traffic, which should remain unaffected. This backpressure creates out-of-order frames and degrades the communication. Also, the throughput is affected by HOLB. Research has shown that, under certain conditions, throughput in presence of HOLB can be limited to 58.6 percent. Figure 10-14 illustrates HOLB.

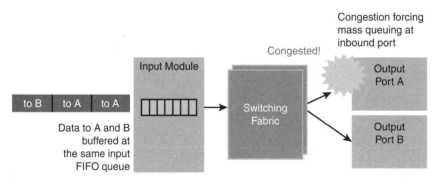

Figure 10-14   *Switch HOLB Phenomenon*

Overcoming HOLB with VoQ

Input queuing has been avoided in the switch industry for a long time due to the HOLB issue it creates. Recently this problem has been overcome with VoQ. In a VoQ switch, all input maintains a simple queue structure consisting of multiple first-in, first-out (FIFO) queues, one for each output. With this mechanism, all the frames in each FIFO queue are destined to the same output queue. Therefore, frames cannot be blocked by a frame in front that is destined to a different output port: with VoQ there is no longer HOLB. Although VoQ can appear complicated, the memory bandwidth implementation for a VoQ ingress queuing is the same as a single FIFO ingress queuing structure because at most one frame can arrive and depart from each input at a time. With pointers, all queues at an input can share the same physical memory. With VoQ, the scheduler is more advanced, as it needs to be able to service a lot more queues than a single FIFO input queuing structure. Please note that VoQ and buffering functions are performed at the input switch ASIC where the scheduler resides, not on the crossbar fabric module itself. Figure10-15 illustrates VoQ.

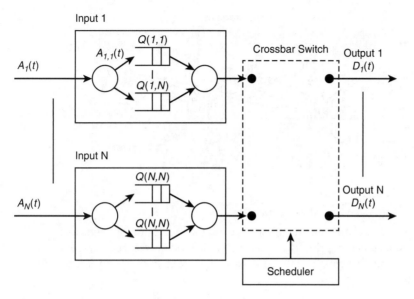

Figure 10-15   *VoQ Illustration*

Multistage Crossbar

Certain architectures implement a multiple-stage crossbar fabric approach to achieve even higher fabric capacity scale. For example, the Nexus 7000 has a three-stage fabric crossbar. The first and last stages of the fabric are implemented on the I/O modules, whereas the second stage is implemented on the fabric module cards. This approach enables the end user to control the fabric oversubscription ratio to provide up to line rate forwarding on the Nexus 7000 chassis, for example. This is achieved by deciding on the number of stage 2 fabrics the switch will have, from one fabric module up to five fabric modules. All the crossbar concepts previously explained continue to apply to a multistage crossbar fabric. The multistage crossbar achieves the same principle of scaling out as a data center spine-and-leaf fabric network architecture (covered earlier in the book), allowing it to support more bandwidth than with a single switch. The techniques are different with spine-leaf, which is usually flow based; crossbar is packet based. Figure 10-16 illustrates an example of multistage crossbar fabric.

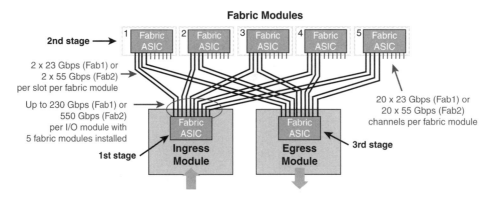

Figure 10-16   *Multistage Crossbar Fabric*

In crossbar switch architecture, the fabric executes the replication of multicast traffic. The scheduling occurs prior to or after the fabric module, respectively, for input or output queuing. The crossbar fabric can have multiple stages in the example of the Nexus 7000.

Centralized Shared Memory (SoC)

Centralized shared memory is another data center switch architecture, typically used in lower-bandwidth switches. The memory is shared by all inputs and all outputs. Each input and output port can access the switch memory one at a time. The memory is portioned into multiple queues, one for each output. The memory portioning can be static or dynamic. This queuing technique provides the same behavior for the frames as output queuing: logically a shared memory scheme can be viewed as an output queuing mechanism with all queues moved to a central memory location. Another benefit is lower frame loss or drop probability: because the memory is shared, unused buffers can be given to ports under load. One of the challenges of shared memory architectures is the internal speedup requirement for the memory, and the output queuing model, needing to function 2xN times faster than the line rate, N being the number of ports. Figure 10-17 shows the SoC queuing model.

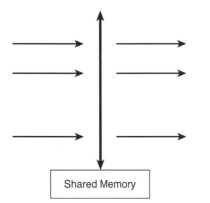

Figure 10-17   *Centralized Memory: SoC*

SoC has become more popular in the past few years with the evolution of nanotechnology and clocking speed that has the ability to place a large number of transistors (over 1 billion) in a compact form factor that directly maps all the switching Ethernet ports to this SoC. This removes the need to have a crossbar solution for the port density supported by an SoC: typically from 48 to 128 10-GE ports at the time of writing. It is still quite less than the scale achieved by crossbar fabrics, which allow for a much higher scale.

SoC includes the switch-on-chip single ASIC switches, such as the top-of-rack Nexus 3000, 3100, 3500, and 9000 series family switches. Cisco Nexus SoCs used in these top-of-racks are cut-through, providing the same latency across packet size, throughput, and features.

Recently Cisco has developed a hybrid approach of the three queuing methods: the Nexus 6000 product line. This product has ingress queuing for unicast traffic and output queuing for multicast traffic (reducing the amount of fabric replication), with the ingress and egress sharing a common centralized memory for each three physical 40-GE ports. This hybrid approach enables the Nexus 6000 cut-through crossbar switch to provide ULL with the same 1-microsecond latency across all ports, packet sizes, any load and any L2/L3 features turned on with a large queuing memory capacity (buffering) up to 25 MB for each three 40-GE ports.

Multistage SoC

With the SoC type of switch architecture, it is possible to combine multiple SoCs to achieve larger scale. There are two approaches: crossbar fabric with SoC, and SoC fabric with SoC.

Crossbar Fabric with SoC

This type of architecture consists of using the SoC to perform all the switching and queueing operations and using a fabric to interconnect the various SoC. For the SoC models that can be programmed for different operations when located ingress or egress of the crossbar fabric, this architecture is then similar to the input or output queuing crossbar architecture.

For example, the Nexus 7000 series line card uses an SoC and a crossbar fabric to interconnect all the SoCs. This model is an input queuing crossbar model, where the SoC at ingress has a forwarding engine, ingress queuing with VoQ, and then sends the traffic to the crossbar fabric, as depicted in Figures 10-18 and 10-19. Notice the presence of output queuing (egress buffer). This is used to accommodate statically frames that have already passed the input queuing stage and, while in flight in the crossbar fabric, have encountered congestion at the destination egress port they are going to. Because the fabric is a non-drop element, the frames must be buffered on the egress for this specific scenario. Figure 10-18 and Figure 10-19 show the crossbar and SoC architecture of the Cisco Nexus F series line card and the functionalities inside the SoC of this same line card.

N7K-F248XP-25

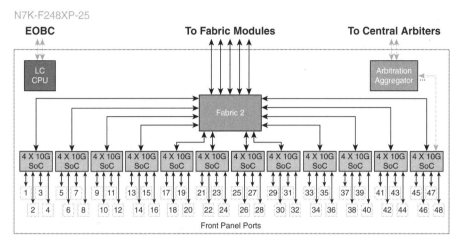

Figure 10-18   *SoC and Crossbar Architecture on the Cisco Nexus F2 Series Line Card*

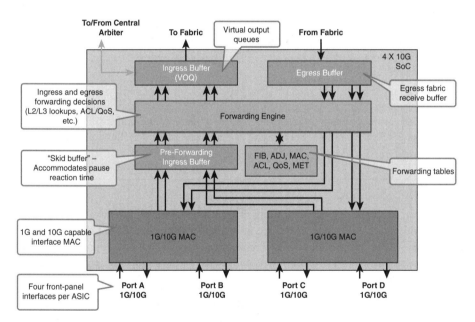

Figure 10-19   *View of the SoC Functionalities of the Cisco Nexus F2 Series Line Card*

SoC Fabric

This architecture consists of building a nonblocking switching architecture with the same type of SoC, avoiding the need to use a different ASIC type for the crossbar fabric to interconnect the SoC. However, this can potentially introduce more complexity for the communication between SoCs and an overall much higher density of SoCs needed to build the end product. For example, a mechanism to synchronize all the switching and routing entry tables across all SoCs needs to be implemented; otherwise, issues such as flooding or lack of MAC learning can occur. Newer SoCs provide dedicated, faster inter-SoC communication links, sometimes called a *high-gig port*. This model has a control and communication mechanism between SoCs, which avoids the concerns illustrated in Figure 10-20. From a port-count perspective, with an SoC of 64 nonblocking ports, to build a switch with 128 nonblocking ports, a total of six 64-port SoCs are needed, as Figure 10-20 illustrates. Four are used for the port side and two for the nonblocking fabric. This concept allows a very high scale in terms of port density, comparable to a crossbar, and is capable of scaling higher than certain crossbars. The Cisco Nexus 9000 switch family uses this SoC fabric concept and provides, at the time of writing, the densest modular switch platform available on the market.

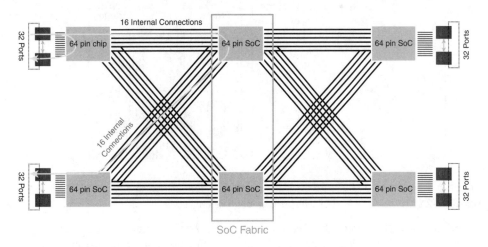

Figure 10-20   *Fabric SoC Architecture*

QoS Fundamentals

Quality of Service requirements in the data center are different than the ones in the campus. The use of Quality of Service in the data center is important to prioritize correct latency-sensitive applications over elephant flows, to make storage traffic work correctly and other specific requirements described in this section.

Data Center QoS Requirements

The starting point is to look at QoS requirements from a traffic, application, and SLA perspective—for example, voice and video. Today, Voice over IP (VoIP) and video are mainstream technologies. Building network equipment to provide reliable and high-quality VoIP and video streaming over the network is well documented and well understood. It is critical to understand the per-hop, end-to-end behavior of voice and video over digital media For example, with voice traffic, a codec takes an analog stream and generates binary data with a 20-ms sample, as shown in Figure10-21. To ensure that the voice traffic is not interrupted, the latency cannot exceed the human ear perception gap of 150 ms after decoding the signal between the sender and the receiver. To meet this requirement, the network equipment has a priority queue. Therefore, when the traffic arrives at the end of the networks, it looks the same as when it left. Video adds a different set of requirements: the data rate is not as consistent. For example, if the video is streaming, the data can be buffered, but it should not be buffered if the video is live. Compared to voice, video is less resilient to loss, has a higher volume of data, and the codec samples every 33 ms.

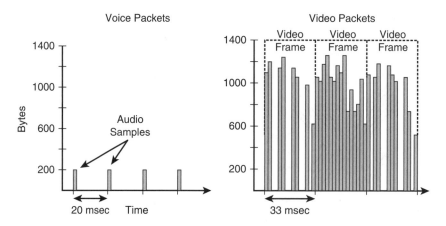

Figure 10-21   *Voice and Video Sampling at the Packet Level*

The enterprise and campus specialization for voice- and video-embedded QoS in the hardware network equipment has created a set of RFCs providing guidance and best practice on how to map the applications to a QoS model. This is the case with medianet: RFC 4594 is shown in Table 10-3: Understanding QoS resulted into building Cisco network equipment that answered specific requirements.

Table 10-3   *Medianet RFC 4594*

Application Class	Per-hop Behavior	Admission Control	Queuing and Dropping	Application Examples
VoIP Telephony	EF	Required	Priority Queue (PQ)	Cisco IP Phones (G.711, G.729)
Broadcast Video	CS5	Required	(Optional) PQ	Cisco IP Video Surveillance/Cisco Enterprise TV

Application Class	Per-hop Behavior	Admission Control	Queuing and Dropping	Application Examples
Real-time Interactive	CS4	Required	(Optional) PQ	Cisco TelePresence
Multimedia Conferencing	AF4	Required	BW Queue + DSCP WRED	Cisco Unified Personal Communicator, WebEx
Multimedia Streaming	AF3	Recommended	BW Queue + DSCP WRED	Cisco Digital Media System (VoDs)
Network Control	CS6		BW Queue	EIGRP, OSPF, BGP, HRSP, IKE
Call Signaling	CS3		BW Queue	SCCP, SIP, H.323
Ops/Admin/Mgmt (OAM)	CS2		BW Queue	SNMP, SSH, Syslog
Transactional Data	AF2		BW Queue + DSCP WRED	ERP Apps, CRM Apps, Database Apps
Bulk Data	AF1		BW Queue + DSCP WRED	Email, FTP, Backup Apps, Content Distribution
Best Effort	DF		Default Queue + RED	Default Class
Scavenger	CS1		Min BW Queue (Differential)	YouTube, iTunes, BitTorrent, Xbox Live

Data Center Requirements

Similar to the traditional campus specializations, there is an emerging data center specialization in activities such as compute storage, virtualization, cloud computing, and more. Specialization in this area requires understanding how to handle protocol convergence in the fabric, including storage protocols such as FCoE, iSCSI, NFS, and how to facilitate interprocess and computer communication (such as vMotion). These requirements are different from voice and video QoS and campus-based QoS. The goal of a data center design is to optimize the balance of end-to-end fabric latency with the ability to absorb traffic peaks and prevent any associated traffic loss. A balanced fabric is a function of maximum throughput and minimal loss (also known as *goodput*), as illustrated in Figure 10-22. There are also different protocols and mechanisms to consider, such as 802.1Qbb, 802.1az, and ECN, all of which are covered in the following sections.

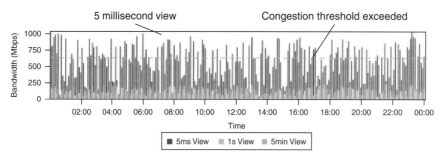

Figure 10-22 *Goodput*

Type of QoS Used in Different Data Center Use Cases

The data center designs have to account for many different traffic types such as:

- No-drop storage traffic

- High-performance compute workload

- Storage

- vMotion

The different trends from a QoS requirement perspective are as follows:

- **Ultra-low latency networking:** The design is network QoS free, where queuing is performed as little as possible to avoid creating delay in the network for the applications.

- **High-performance compute and big data workloads:** The traffic is bursty, with an east-west direction, soliciting throughput and buffering from incast (many-to-one conversations) and speed mismatch.

- **Massively scalable data centers:** A requirement is to optimize the throughput of TCP by avoiding to drop traffic. This is described by the use of ECN and DCTP.

- **Virtualized data center:** QoS can be useful to prioritize various traffic types that are common in non-virtualized data centers as well as traffic types that are specific to virtualized servers, such as vMotion traffic.

Trust, Classification, and Marking Boundaries

A key consideration for QoS is to understand where to classify and mark traffic. In the campus environment the trust boundary starts at the first cable going to the access network device. By default, the assumption is to not trust what is outside of the network, as depicted in Figure 10-23. In the data center, it is common to trust by default. Therefore, the default QoS settings are different.

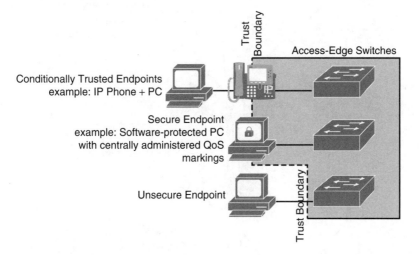

Figure 10-23   *Trust Boundary*

In the data center, the QoS trust boundary is where the virtual machine connects to a virtual switch. The access boundary is moved within the server and is trusted by default. Layer 2 QoS (COS based) is performed on any network equipment up from the host until the Layer 3 boundary. Layer 3 QoS (DSCP based) is performed on the network equipment going to the outside.

Figure 10-24 depicts the trust boundary and where to classify and mark. With the default behavior of trust, the data center Nexus switches trust by default any marking arriving onto the switches: COS or DSCP. It is possible to change this default behavior to untrusted, if needed. The traffic leaving a VM usually is not marked. Therefore, the virtual switch needs to be configured to mark with CoS values traffic for different VMs.

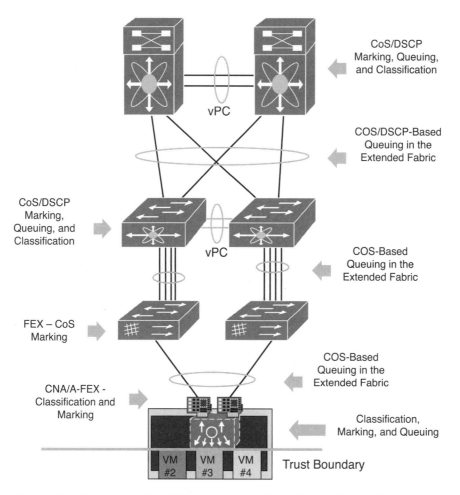

CoS/DSCP
Marking, Queuing,
and Classification

COS/DSCP-Based
Queuing in the
Extended Fabric

CoS/DSCP
Marking,
Queuing, and
Classification

COS-Based
Queuing in the
Extended Fabric

FEX – CoS
Marking

COS-Based
Queuing in the
Extended Fabric

CNA/A-FEX -
Classification and
Marking

Classification,
Marking, and Queuing

Trust Boundary

Figure 10-24 *CoS and DSCP Boundaries in a Data Center Network Topology*

The data center QoS model is a four-, six-, or eight-class model. The number of classes available depends on the hardware used and also on the place in the data center fabric the hardware is deployed. There is a strong requirement for Layer 2 QoS or COS-based QoS for the data center because there is IP and non-IP traffic to be considered (FCoE). Therefore, the common denominator is to use COS-based QoS.

In a multi-tenant network, as shown in Table 10-4, FCoE uses a CoS of 3 and, in Table 10-3 voice bearer control traffic uses CoS 3. There is a potential for overlap and conflict. In this scenario, a case-per-case approach is used for the overall design and the choice of what CoS values to use to remark one of these traffics classes. Typically voice and FCoE do not exist at the same place, and they can coexist, each one using a value of CoS 3. In that case, a remapping is performed on the switches where type of traffic merge together.

Table 10-4 *CoS Suggestions for Traffic Type*

Traffic Type	Network Class	CoS	Class, Property, BW
Infrastructure	Control	6	Platinum, 10%
	vMotion	4	Silver, 20%
Tenant	Gold, Transactional	5	Gold, 30%
	Silver, Transactional	2	Bronze, 15%
	Bronze, Transactional	1	Best effort, 10%
Storage	FCoE	3	No drop, 15%
	NFS data store	5	Silver
Nonclassified	Data	1	Best effort

Data Center QoS Capabilities

This section's coverage of QoS capabilities starts by explaining the fundamental switching concepts of buffering and the buffer bloat. They apply to any platform, and are not data center specific. Next, the data center–specific capabilities implemented in the Cisco Nexus product portfolio are detailed, including the handling of storage traffic and priority traffic, and new emerging concepts such as data center TCP and flowlet switching.

Understanding Buffer Utilization

Understanding buffering is key to understanding the QoS capabilities, switch architecture, and more generally how to design a data center fabric. This section explains when buffering is used and the consequences on a spine-leaf data center design in terms of making buffering size choices for spine switches and leaf switches.

Buffers on data center switches are used under the following four conditions:

- **Oversubscription caused by many-to-one conversations:** This is also called *incast* or *many-to-one* conversations and is shown in Figure 10-25. In this scenario, multiple input ports are sending traffic going out of a specific output port. While the scheduler services a frame for a given virtual output queue, other frames that arrived while the scheduler was busy have to wait for their turn. The waiting delay is a factor of the scheduler latency, which for Nexus switches is in the order of magnitude of nanoseconds. During this wait time, the frames are buffered ingress until they are serviced. A common scenario for this in the data center is servers sending traffic to the Internet via the switch uplinks or writing to a remote storage device.

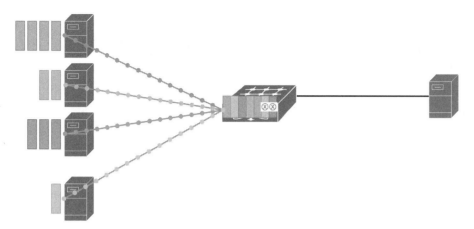

Figure 10-25 *Incast*

■ **Speed mismatch:** This is also called *uplink speed mismatch* and is shown in Figure 10-26. When the speed of the receiving port is different from the speed of the outgoing port, buffering occurs. There are two scenarios: lower to faster speed, and faster to lower speed. In the lower to faster speed scenario, the value of the serialization delay of the outgoing port being lower compared to the other port makes that enough frames need to be stored in order to be sent faster on the outgoing port, incurring in buffering memory. In the other scenario, faster to slower, frames can arrive faster than the serialization delay of the output port, and buffering occurs as well.

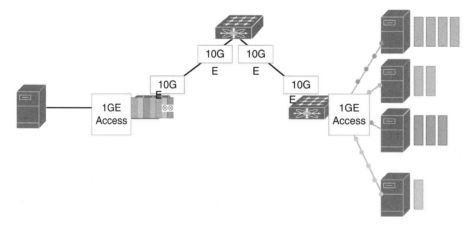

Figure 10-26 *Speed Mismatch*

■ **Burst:** This occurs when a burst of packets is sent on the wire and it constitutes a value above the number of packets per second the switch can treat for line rate. For example, above 10 GE on a 10-GE interface, the switch buffers packets from the burst. This is observed in high-frequency trading (HFT) environments, where there is a multicast burst of packets for a very short duration. This is also called *microburst*. It is also observed in data center benchmarking, when a switch is tested for through-put. If the tester sends 100 percent of throughput on a port, it can actually be faster than what the switch treats as 100 percent of throughput on the same port speed. To avoid this scenario, it is recommended to send 99.98 percent of throughput traf-fic to the switch under test to compensate for the standard deviation rules.

■ **Storage:** Buffer-to-buffer credit, in order to provide lossless storage transport across the Ethernet network, is translated in a statically carved buffer on the data center switches. The buffer allocated is a function of the speed for the Fibre Channel traf-fic and the distance between two switches or a switch and the target or the initiator.

It is important to understand which data center switch to use for spine buffering and for leaf buffering. Buffer pressure at a leaf switch uplink port and the spine switch ports is about the same, so the buffer size between the leaf and the spine needs to be in the same order of magnitude. The congestion and buffering due to oversubscription is more important at the leaf than at the spine switch. Increasing leaf buffering is more effective at the leaf layer, where there is a speed mismatch along with the incast, versus the spine layer, where there is no speed mismatch.

The Buffer Bloat

Hardware switching provides performance, scalability, and reliability. Only so much logic can be embedded on a switch ASIC, however. It is bound to the size of the ASIC, the frequency of the ASIC, and the number of gates the ASIC can hold. The larger the ASIC, the larger the possible failure rate of the silicon.

In the hardware, the following categories are bound to the logic space available:

■ The buffer size

■ The table size (Layer 2, Layer 3, unicast, and multicast)

■ The number of hardware features (forwarding, ACLs, NAT, etc.)

The Cisco Nexus switches are designed to be deployed in specific places in the data center design, and the buffer size is optimized to that purpose. There is mainly a need to have more buffering capability usually at the leaf layer than at the spine layer, and the order of magnitude of spine and leaf need to be in proportion. With the switches capable of handling faster and faster speeds (10 GE, 40 GE, and 100 GE), the amount of buffering for the same amount of traffic to transit the switch is obviously less.

Figure 10-27 shows the network view for a Hadoop terasort job of 1 TB of data trans-ferred in an east-west network. The buffer utilization is measured for two scenarios for the same job and loaded on the network. The first case consists of 1-GE NICs and switch ports, and the second is with 10-GE speed. Because the job completes faster with the 10-GE NICs, the main difference observed is the buffer utilization. There are fewer buffers used on the switches when the speed is 10 GE versus when it's 1 GE. The faster the speed, the lower the buffer used for the exact same application job. Figure 10-27 displays the results from the tests.

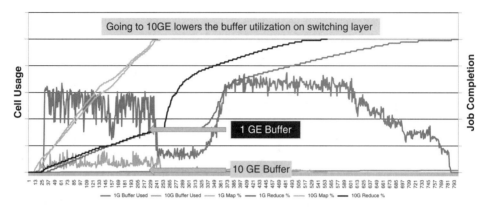

Figure 10-27   *Buffer Utilization on an SoC Switch Used at 10 GE or 1 GE During the Same Test*

Priority Flow Control

Priority flow control (PFC) is a QoS technique used to provide a lossless transport media capability for storage types of traffic. PFC is defined in the IEEE 802.1Qbb documentation. The idea behind this technology is to use a PAUSE frame signal messaging methodology: the switch and the other node, whether it is another switch, a target, an initiator, etc., sends PAUSE with a specific COS field used for this class of traffic as defined in IEEE 802.1p. This CoS field is the one assigned to the non-drop class of traffic; in general, FCoE uses CoS 3. The remaining traffic in other classes assigned with other CoS values continues to transmit and, on upper-layer protocols, retransmit. Although this non-drop class for PFC is not intended only for FCoE, currently it is mainly used for FCoE. Figure 10-28 illustrates PFC.

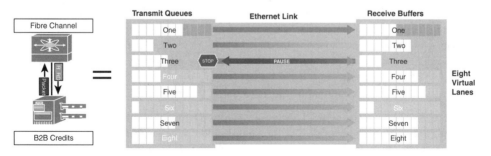

Figure 10-28   *Priority Flow Control*

For example, an uplink is congested on a switch. When the switch buffering starts to fill up to a certain threshold, the switch creates a PAUSE and relays it downstream to ask the sender of the traffic to pause. Vice versa, the Nexus switch is also compliant and PAUSEs its traffic when requested; then, as its buffer fills up, it creates a PAUSE and relays it. The other traffic assigned to other CoS values continues to transmit and relies on upper-layer protocols for retransmission.

Note Be very careful with iSCSI traffic. Do not use the non-drop queue for iSCSI, because it can create HOLB when used in a multi-hop topology. Only a very specific design scenario benefits from iSCSI being in a non-drop class: when the target and initiator are on the same switch and there is no multi-hop. Therefore, the recommendation is not to allocate iSCSI to the non-drop queue in general.

Enhanced Transmission Selection

Enhanced Transmission Selection (ETS) is a QoS technique used for bandwidth management. It is defined in IEEE 802.1Qaz. ETS is used to prevent a single class of traffic from utilizing all the bandwidth and starving other classes. ETS is implemented on all Nexus switches.

When a given class of traffic or queue does not fully employ its allocated bandwidth percentage, it becomes available to other classes. This helps accommodate bursty classes of traffic. Another way to describe ETS is from a scheduler point of view. With ETS, which is the "bandwidth percentage" allocation to classes of traffic, it provides a corresponding weight to the scheduler. When frames from different classes are scheduled to go through the crossbar fabric or SoC, they have a weight corresponding to their class, and the scheduler services frame volume according to this weight. Figure 10-29 shows ETS configured for three classes of traffic: HPC, storage, and LAN.

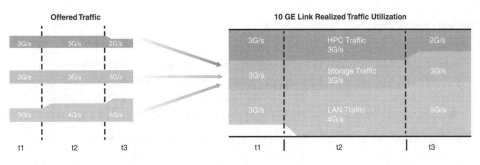

Figure 10-29 *ETS Implemented for Three Queues*

Data Center Bridging Exchange

Data Center Bridging Exchange (DCBX) is an extension to ETS incorporated in the IEEE standard 802.1Qaz. DCBX negotiates the Ethernet capabilities with peer DCBX potential. It includes negotiation for:

- **PFC:** The type of traffic in a particular queue

- **ETS:** The amount of bandwidth percentage allocated to each queue

- **CoS:** The CoS values used between Data Center Bridging peer devices

DCBX simplifies the management by allowing configuration and distribution of the parameters from one node to another. DCBX is responsible for logical Link Up/Link Down signaling of Ethernet and Fibre Channel. It can be seen as an equivalent of LLDP with new TLV (Type-Length-Value) fields. The original, prestandard was called *CIN* (Cisco, Intel, Nuova). DCBX added additional TLVs to CIN. When DCBX negotiation fails, it results in per priority pause to not be enabled on CoS values; the virtual Fibre Channel (vFC) interface does not come up when FCoE is used. However, this can be manually configured when there is a peer connected to Nexus that is not DCBX capable. DCBX can be summarized as a handshake taking care of the data center QoS configuration (PFC, ETS, CoS). Cisco Nexus switches are all DCBX capable and DCBX is enabled by default.

Note TLV represents optional information that can be encoded as a type-length-value or TLV element inside of the protocol. TLV is also known as *tag-length value*. The type and length are fixed in size (typically 1 to 4 bytes), and the value field is of variable size.

vFC represents the Fibre Channel portion of FCoE. vFC is configured as a virtual Fibre Channel interface.

ECN and DCTCP

Early Congestion Notification (ECN) and Data Center TCP (DCTCP) are mechanisms to help TCP increase the data center goodput. They push the congestion events out of the network and help avoid TCP dropping. When TCP drops, the window size half drops for TCP packets and the throughput slowly increases over time, which is a nonoptimal throughput. ECN and DCTCP are intended to prevent this TCP drop when possible.

ECN is an extension to TCP that provides end-to-end congestion notification to avoid dropping packets. Both the network infrastructure and the end must be capable of supporting ECN for it to function properly. ECN uses the two least significant bits in the DiffServ field in the IP header to encode four different values. During periods of congestion, a router marks the DSCP header in the packet indicating congestion (0x11) to the receiving host, who notifies the source host to reduce its transmission rate. Nexus devices support ECN, which means that when ECN is also enabled on the hosts, the Nexus devices are able to slow down when appropriate to avoid having TCP drop—or, vice versa, when a host is getting congested, it is marked with ECN.

DCTCP is an enhancement of ECN. The goal of DCTCP is to react in proportion of the extent of the congestion and not only to its presence. It reduces the variance in sending rates, lowering the queuing requirements. The DCTCP marking is based on instantaneous queue length. This allows fast feedback to better deal with burst, knowing the packet size or congestion depth.

With different ECN marks, DCTCP reduces the window size with a variable value, whereas with ECN it is a fixed value of 50 percent; Table 10-5 displays this difference.

Table 10-5 *DCTCP Benefits to TCP*

ECN Marks	TCP	DCTCP
1 0 1 1 1 1 0 1 1 1	Cut window by 50%	Cut window by 40%
0 0 0 0 0 0 0 0 0 1	Cut window by 50%	Cut window by 5%

Priority Queue

The priority queue concept on Nexus switches is different from the priority queue concept on Catalyst switches. It's important to understand the difference for data center designs.

On Nexus switches, there is only one priority queue, and no shaping or rate limiting is possible. The principle of the priority queue is that any traffic mapped to the priority queue is always serviced first by the scheduler, and there is no limit in the bandwidth this queue can take. This is irrespective of all traffic in other queues, including storage traffic. Be very cautious when deciding to use the priority queue, as it can use up all the bandwidth. Usually it is used for voice control traffic or for specific low-bandwidth type of traffic, which needs priority. Another consequence when using the priority queue is the bandwidth percentage allocated to all the remaining queues. They receive a percentage of the available bandwidth once the priority queue is serviced. The bandwidth percentages are applied only when there is congestion. If only one class of traffic is going through the switch, it can take up all the bandwidth if it needs to.

As an example, suppose three QoS queues are used: Priority, Bulk, and Scavenger. Bulk has a bandwidth percentage allocated of 60 percent and Scavenger of 40 percent. Priority has no percentage allocated in the configuration and usually displays a value of 0. Assume there are 10 GE of traffic used on a link, and Priority represents at that time 20 percent, or 2 GE. The remaining 80 percent, or 8 GE, is allocated to Bulk and Scavenger. Bulk then has 60 percent of the 8 GE, representing 4.8 GE, and Scavenger has 40 percent of the 8 GE, representing 3.2 GE.

The Nexus exception to having only one priority queue and not having shaping is the Nexus 7000 with specific line cards. Usually this is the M series line card, which provides a closer to Catalyst implementation for the enterprise core or aggregation for traffic going out of the data center. The trend of moving to F line cards encourages the adoption of this specific handling of the priority queue in the data center.

Flowlet Switching: Nexus 9000 Fabric Load Balancing

The Cisco Nexus 9000 product family implements in the hardware a new fabric load-balancing capability called *flowlet switching*. The current state of the art, equal-cost multipathing (ECMP), hashes flow with a 5-tuples-decision algorithm using different uplink paths in a Layer 3 fabric. ECMP to date is not able to send multiple bursts of the same flow on multiple paths, nor does it take into consideration the fabric utilization.

In ACI, Equal Cost Multipathing can be replaced by flowlet load balancing in order to reduce the chance of creating congestion hotspots. Flowlet load balancing does this by distributing traffic more equally depending on the bandwidth available between the originating and destination switches along all paths. Flowlet switching is based on load balancing of individual bursts of a given flow (called flowlets) and the ability to adapt the weight of the load balancing based on the congestion on the fabric.

With flowlet load balancing, the fabric tracks the congestion along the full path between ingress and egress leaf switches via data plane hardware measurements. It detects switch-to-switch port congestion or external wires and also internal SoC-to-SoC congestion or internal wires. There is a dynamic shedding of active flows from congested paths to less-congested paths. There is also no packet reordering with flowlet load balancing. There is an algorithm calculating the distance taken for each packet flow, and the interpacket gap must be higher than the time it takes each packet from the same flow to traverse the fabric. Figure 10-30 illustrates flowlet load balancing.

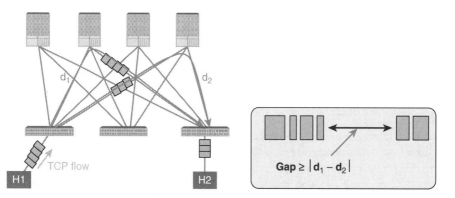

Figure 10-30   *Flowlet Load Balancing Across the Fabric*

ACI also provides the ability to prioritize smaller flows over larger flows (elephant flows) with a feature called Dynamic Flow Prioritization. In a data center there is a mix of frame sizes. Production traffic has large and small flows. Dynamic flow prioritization consists in prioritizing smaller flows rather than the larger flows and placing them in a priority queue. Priotizing a smaller flow against an elephant flow has little effect on the completion time for the transmission of the elephant flow, but it has a significant benefit to the completion of the transmission of the smaller flow. The prioritization is depicted in Figure 10-31.

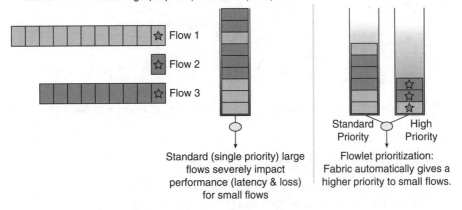

Real traffic is a mix of large (elephant) and small (mice) flows.

Figure 10-31 *Flowlet Prioritization of Smaller Flows Versus Larger Flows*

Figure 10-32 depicts the application performance improvements of the Cisco Nexus 9000 series flowlet switching compared to ECN/DCTCP. The picture shows the Flow Completion Time for different levels of traffic load in normal conditions and in the presence of link failures. Using flowlet load balancing with dynamic flow prioritization and congestion detection, compared to Datacenter TCP, has the following advantages: It doesn't require changes on the host stack; it is independent of the protocol (TCP versus UDP), and it provides faster detection time in case of congestion.

Note   More information can be found at the following reference from SIGCOMM 2014: "CONGA: Distributed Congestion-Aware Load Balancing for Datacenters" (available at http://simula.stanford.edu/~alizade/publications.html).

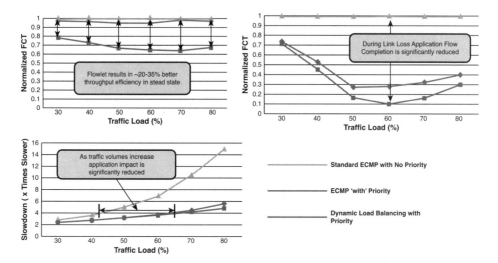

Figure 10-32 *Flowlet Switching Application Performance Improvements Versus ECN/DCTCP*

Nexus QoS Implementation: The MQC Model

The QoS configuration model in the Nexus data center switches is consistent across platforms. All models use the Modular QoS CLI (MQC) class-based model.

The Nexus switches support a set of QoS capabilities designed to provide per-system class-based traffic control for:

■ Lossless Ethernet: PFC (IEEE 802.1Qbb)

■ Traffic protection: ETS (IEEE 802.1Qbb)

■ Configuration: DCBX (IEEE 802.1Qaz)

These capabilities are added to, and managed by, the common Cisco MQC, which defines a three-step configuration model:

Step 1. Define matching criteria via a class map.

Step 2. Associate action with each defined class via a policy map.

Step 3. Apply policy to the system or an interface via a service policy.

The Nexus 1000v/3000/5000/6000/7000/9000 leverage the MQC **qos-group** capabilities to identify and define traffic in policy configuration, as displayed in detail in Table 10-6.

Table 10-6 *QoS Configuration Principles*

	(1) Type QoS	(2) Type Network QoS	(3) Type Queuing
Classification	ACL, CoS, DSCP, IP RTP, Precedence, Protocol	System class matched qos-group	System class matched by qos-group
Policy	Sets qos-group to the system class this traffic flow is mapped to Set DSCP (7k/5500/3k)	MTU Queue-Limit (5k) Set cos Mark 802.1p ECN WRED (3k)	Bandwidth management: Guaranteed scheduling deficit weighted round robin (DWRR) percentage Priority and Pause no-drop: strict priority scheduling; only one class can be configured for priority in a given queue policy

QoS is enabled by default with one default class (NX-OS Default).

A Qos policy defines how the system classifies traffic, assigned to user-defined **qos-groups**. The **qos-group** is mapped to a hardware queue with a number; for instance, **qos-group 1** refers to the first hardware queue. The Cisco Nexus 7000 family uses predefined **qos-group** names, whereas the Cisco Nexus 6000, 5000, 3000 family uses the **qos-group** number concept. The QoS policy can be applied either to an interface or globally to the system.

A Network QoS policy defines system policies, such as which CoS values all ports treat as drop versus no-drop, or MTU size for frames. It is only globally significant for the whole system and the command is **network-qos.**

An ingress queuing policy defines how ingress port buffers ingress traffic for all destinations over fabric. An egress queuing policy defines how an egress port transmits traffic on wire. Conceptually, it controls how all ingress ports schedule traffic toward the egress port over fabric (by controlling the manner in which bandwidth availability is reported to the arbiter). The queuing policy can be applied either to an interface or globally to the system.

For the type **network-qos** policies, it is important to apply policies consistently across switches, as depicted in Figure 10-33:

- Define global queuing and scheduling parameters for all interfaces in the switch. Identify the drop and no-drop classes, MTU, etc.

- One network-qos policy per system applied to all ports

- The recommendation is that in the data center network, the network-QoS policy should be applied consistently network wide, especially when no drop end-to-end consistency is mandatory

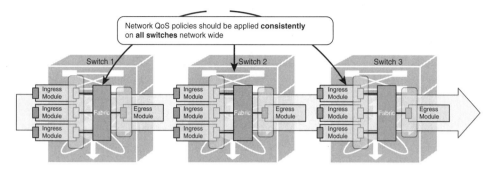

Figure 10-33 *Consistency in the Network-QoS Policy*

For example, a data center network has traffic that requires an MTU of 1500 bytes. It also has storage traffic with an MTU of 9216 bytes. If both data center network traffic and storage traffic need to cross the same spine switch, and have a common traffic pattern, the MTU on all network devices can be set to the jumbo 9216 bytes. This provides a consistent **network-qos** policy across the data center network.

Summary

This chapter described the difference between switch architectures based on crossbar and architectures based on Switch on Chip fabric. One difference from legacy general-purpose switching is the queuing mechanism. In data centers, the queuing is mainly performed ingress instead of egress, which allows better performance. The crossbar historically provides the capability to scale to larger port densities. Crossbar switch architectures combined with cut-through switching allows line rate switching with a constant low to ultra-low latency regardless of packet size. These architectures support the capability to perform storage networking with lossless Ethernet, ultra-low latency, and big data environments with a predictable latency. The optimizations that support this are the use of a cut-through switching mechanism and a crossbar fabric, where the fabric has more crosspoints than the minimum needed, virtual output queues, overspeed, and superframing. There is a newer trend with building multistage SoC architectures using an SoC fabric. Table 10-7 summarizes the architectures per switch model.

Table 10-7 *Switch Architectures per Model*

Switch Model	Switch Type	Architecture*	Queuing
Cisco Nexus 9500	Cut-through	Multistage SoC	Centralized shared output
Cisco Nexus 9300	Cut-through	SoC	Centralized shared output
Cisco Nexus 7700/7000 F	Store-and-forward	Multistage crossbar with SoC	Input queuing
Cisco Nexus 7000 M Series	Store-and-forward	Multistage crossbar with PC	Output queuing

Switch Model	Switch Type	Architecture*	Queuing
Cisco Nexus 6000	Cut-through	Crossbar with UPC	Input and output shared
Cisco Nexus 5500/5000	Cut-through	Crossbar with UPC	Input queuing
Cisco Nexus 3500	Cut-through	SoC	Centralized shared output
Cisco Nexus 3100	Cut-through	SoC	Centralized shared output
Cisco Nexus 3000	Cut-through	SoC	Centralized shared output
Cisco Nexus 2000	Cut-through	UPC	Centralized shared output

*PC is a port-controller ASIC and UPC is a Unified Port Controller ASIC capable of FC/FCoE

In the data center, the switches have the requirements to accommodate various applications along with storage. Different application patterns exist depending on the environment: ULL, HPC, big data, virtualized data center, MSDC. The storage also can be either Fibre Channel or IP based. These requirements drive the switch architecture to accommodate specific QoS functionalities developed for the data center environment: PFC, ETS, and DCBX. With the need for higher 40-GE and 100-GE port density, newer switches offer denser crossbar fabric architectures with a nonblocking multistage SoC fabric architecture such as the Cisco Nexus 9000 series—providing the capability to scale up to 1 million routes at ULL cut-through switching. This chapter also described the latest developments in terms of traffic distribution on equal cost uplinks, congestion detection, and prioritization of smaller flows. These newer techniques provide significant enhancements to goodput, reduce the chance for congestion hotspots, and improve application completion times in case of loss of links.

Conclusion

As the authors of this book, we hope to have thoroughly explained and clarified the changes happening in the data center and, more precisely, how to build a modern data center with Cisco ACI. We believe that networking is at the verge of a significant change that is driven by the need for speed of application deployment and by a more cost-effective methodology for data center operations.

Networking is adopting a model of operations that has already been proven in the realm of server management. As you can conclude from reading this book, the future of the data center is characterized by several changes, which include

- The use of policies to define connectivity of workloads instead of (or in conjunction with) the classic use of subnets, VLAN stitching, and ACLs

- The shift toward host-based routing with a mapping database for traffic routing to the endpoint

- The adoption of scripting, and in particular of Python as one of the most widely used languages

- The adoption of automation tools and self-service catalogs for developers to start and stop their own carving of the network

- The emergence of technology that helps operate small and large infrastructures more easily from a unified entry point (the controller)

- The emergence of new troubleshooting tools that make it easier to correlate potential performance issues on "applications" with networking

This book explained the following:

- The policy-driven data center concept and the operational model involved

- How to use Cisco ACI to build networks with these concepts

- The methodology to design an ACI solution

- How to integrate the network with services

- How to integrate hypervisors, and how to integrate OpenStack

Our goal in writing this book was to explain the new data center concepts and methodology and to present the Cisco ACI architecture, implementation design, and overall technology.

Index

B

C

N

O

R